The Professional Altruist

*A Publication of the Center for the Study of the
History of Liberty in America
Harvard University*

The Professional Altruist

THE EMERGENCE OF SOCIAL WORK
AS A CAREER
1880–1930

Roy Lubove

HARVARD UNIVERSITY PRESS

Cambridge, Massachusetts

Third Printing, 1971
Distributed in Great Britain by Oxford University Press

Publication of this book has been aided by a grant from
the Ford Foundation

Library of Congress Catalog Card Number: 65-12786
SBN 674-71200-5

Printed in the United States of America

The work of the Center for the Study of the History of Liberty
in America has been supported by grants from the Carnegie Corporation
of New York and the Lilly Endowment, Inc.

TO

Carole

Foreword

THE persistence of voluntary patterns of communal action has been an important element in the history of liberty in the United States; not everything that men wished to do co-operatively had to be done coercively under the aegis of the state. The availability of other modes of collaboration long extended the range of individual choice and imbued the social order with freedom.

The development of voluntarism was particularly significant in philanthropy. Although state and local bodies had assisted the poor since colonial times, government never preëmpted the entire field. Numerous charitable endeavors, animated by religious impulses, could take sectarian form only if divorced from politics; and the general fragmentation of American communal life compelled each social group to organize its own activities.

During the nineteenth century, private organizations bore much of the burden of support for dependency. Unpaid laymen, equipped with the desire to do good and with the compelling urge to shape the value system of the poor, mobilized important philanthropic resources. As urbanization and industrialization intensified problems of social control and economic deprivation, however, complaints about the inadequacy of voluntary philanthropic efforts became increasingly vocal. The magnitude of the task seemed to call for more efficient organization, more highly developed technical skills, and greater monetary support than agencies controlled by volunteers could command. Ultimately, the emergence of a professional corps of social workers, bureaucratically administered, changed the character of private charitable association and altered the status and role of the volunteer.

Dr. Lubove's careful study is not a history of social welfare, but rather an analysis of social work's development as a profession. He devotes particular attention to such influences as functional specialization, the formation of a professional subculture, and the impact of formal organization and bureaucracy. Private philanthropy did not cease, but professionalism radically altered its nature after the turn of the twentieth century.

OSCAR HANDLIN

Contents

I Charity Organization and the New Gospel of
   Benevolence   1

II From Friendly Visiting to Social Diagnosis   22

III Mind and Matter: Psychiatry in Social Work   55

IV Inner vs. Outer Need: Psychiatry and Fragmentation   85

V In-group and Out-group: The Molding of a
   Professional Subculture   118

VI Agency and Community: The Apotheosis of
   Efficiency   157

VII Federation and the Bureaucratic Imperative   183

   Conclusion   220

   Appendix. Professional Organization and
   Education since the 1930's   223

   Bibliographical Note   227

   Notes   243

   Index   281

The Professional Altruist

Chapter I

Charity Organization
and the New Gospel of Benevolence

IT seemed that philanthropy at last had emerged from the sloughs of sentimentality and alms-giving, and achieved scientific status. The charity organization movement of the 1880's had produced days "full of hope for humanity"; a great flood of light descended upon the "dreary prospect of human misery."[1] Investigation, registration, cooperation and coordination, "adequate" relief, and friendly visiting formed the basis of this youthful science of social therapeutics, which promised no less than the eradication of pauperism and the salvation of the industrial city.

No charity organization principles ranked higher in importance than coordination of the community's welfare services and the stimulation of volunteer friendly visiting, or personal contact between rich and poor as a substitute for alms. Successful coordination and recruitment of an effective corps of volunteers depended upon the establishment of neighborhood district committees composed of local residents and representatives of relief and welfare agencies. Working under the supervision of the central office, the district committee or conference hoped to establish itself as a focal point for "neighborly" association between classes, insuring at the same time through its coordinating function that unwise relief policies did not subvert the visitor's efforts to influence the character and ambitions of the poor.

The new era in philanthropy dawned in Buffalo, New York, in 1877, when an English Episcopal clergyman, S. Humphreys Gurteen, proposed the formation of an agency patterned after the London Society for Organizing Charitable Relief and Repressing Mendicancy, established in 1869. He assured the citizens of Buffalo that charity organization promised the only solution to their city's benevolent chaos, characterized by the indiscriminate relief policies of overlapping private charities and a municipal outdoor relief system which presumably encouraged indolence, pauperism, and fraud. The economic crisis of the 1870's, with its spawn of tramps and beggars, unemployment and mounting relief bills, guaranteed a receptive audience for Gurteen, whose efforts resulted in the formation of the Buffalo Charity Organization Society in December 1877.

Charity organization spread rapidly in the next decade and a half, particularly in the larger urban centers of the East and Midwest: New Haven and Philadelphia in 1878; Boston, Brooklyn, and Cincinnati in 1879; New York in 1882. By then, twenty-two societies existed in cities comprising a total population of more than six million. The corresponding figures a decade later were ninety-two societies and a population of more than eleven million.[2]

The swift expansion of the charity organization movement represented one response of a troubled middle class to the social dislocations of the post-Civil War industrial city, but the theory and practice of scientific philanthropy had numerous antecedents in the nineteenth century. In the 1820's, Thomas Chalmers, a Scottish clergyman, had adopted a district plan of organization in his Glasgow parish of St. John, placing the relief work of each district under charge of a deacon. Stressing the importance of cultivating provident and frugal habits among the poor, Chalmers anticipated the charity organization principles of friendly visiting and the subordination of alms to character reformation. In the United States the New York Association for Improving the Condition of the Poor (AICP), established in 1843, not only served as a model for many general relief societies in the 1840's and 1850's, but developed principles which approximated charity organization in all but name.[3] The AICP divided Manhattan Island into districts corresponding to city wards, placing each under the charge of an advisory committee responsible for relief and the recruitment of friendly visitors. The Association, however, did not regard itself simply as an efficient relief agency, but as the coordinator of New York's multitudinous charities. Although it never developed a satisfactory registration and coordination system, it did anticipate the cooperative ideals of the later charity organization societies. No charity organization leader was more convinced of the moral roots of poverty than Robert M. Hartley, an AICP executive. More than alms, the poor needed supervision to help them avoid the snares of intemperance, indolence, and improvidence. To carry out its work the AICP relied in its early years upon a corps of friendly visitors whose function was to investigate each appeal for assistance, to distinguish between the worthy and unworthy poor, and to insure that relief would be blended with a judicious mixture of moral exhortation.

Ten years after the formation of the AICP, a poor-relief experiment was introduced in Elberfeld, Germany; this exerted an important influence on the development of charity organization principles. Again the district plan was critical, with each district under charge of a visitor or "Armenpfleger." Visiting was a compulsory municipal duty, and each Armenpfleger assumed responsibility for four families. The visitor received applications for assistance directly and was required to see every family at least once every two weeks. The case conferences or district advisory committees of the charity organization societies were anticipated in Elberfeld by conferences of visitors for mutual consultation.

Whatever the variations in administration or organization, friendly visiting in some form was central to the charitable schemes of Chalmers, the AICP, and Elberfeld. This was true also of the St. Vincent de Paul Society, a Catholic organization founded in Paris in 1833 by Frederick Ozanam, a young law student, and Sylvain Bailly, a journalist. This new society stressed personal service instead of material relief. District conferences rather than individual visitors decided upon any alms necessary to supplement the personal service.

Probably no examples of personal service to the poor had such direct influence upon the London Society, the general model for the American charity organization societies, as the work of Edward Denison and Octavia Hill. An almoner of the Society for the Relief of Distress in London's East End, Denison decided he could not understand poverty or its causes until he shared the life of the poor; and in 1867 he moved into the Stepney slum district, where he promoted sanitary and educational reforms and developed his philosophy of personal service. Although Denison died in 1870, one year after the founding of the Charity Organization Society, his example exerted a potent influence.[4] The friendly rent collecting of Octavia Hill, begun in 1864, also shaped the policies of the London society. Miss Hill was active in its work from the beginning while her associates were conspicuous among the original corps of visitors.

The nineteenth-century leaders of charity organization in the United States were conscious of the numerous European and national precedents for a benevolent system stressing the desirability of investigation, coordination, and personal service; but they considered the systematic implementation of such principles in dozens of cities a genuine innovation. For

4

the first time a truly scientific charity had emerged, not as an isolated experiment in a Glasgow parish or a vision in the mind of a London humanitarian, but as the professed ideal of many societies and of thousands of workers, paid and voluntary.

Charity organization spokesmen like S. Humphreys Gurteen of Buffalo, Robert Treat Paine and Zilpha Smith of Boston, Mary Richmond and John M. Glenn of Baltimore, Oscar McCulloch of Indianapolis, and Josephine Shaw Lowell of New York were missionaries, in the most literal sense, of a new benevolent gospel. They viewed themselves as exponents of a holy cause, priests lighting a path to secular salvation. Charity organization was a crusade to save the city from itself and from the evils of pauperism and class antagonism. "Look abroad over our own city," Gurteen pleaded, "over every large city of the country, and is there not a 'wound' (and oh! how deep and ghastly) visible on every hand. There is the wound of idleness and improvidence—the indisposition to do manfully our appointed task in life, and leading by a direct path to poverty, destitution and want." [5] The New York Charity Organization Society warned that "if we do not furnish the poor with elevating influences, they will rule us by degrading ones." [6] Organized charity was the urban community's surest safeguard against revolution, for it had "preternatural powers for fusing and moulding and tearing down and building up. Surely here, if anywhere, society will find that better thing than instantaneous revolution—gradual regeneration." [7] Charity organization represented, in large measure, an instrument of urban social control for the conservative middle class. Charity organization, and volunteer visiting in particular, were the "only hope of civilization against the gathering curse of pauperism in great cities." [8]

*

The effectiveness of charity organization depended upon

strict allegiance to "scientific" theory and practice. Leaders insisted that charity must be divorced from mere sentimentality and self-gratification and the permanent welfare of the supplicant regarded as the true goal of benevolence. How could charity be love if lacking in wisdom? And how could it be wise if lacking a "thorough knowledge of all component facts"? [9]

In the nineteenth century scientific charity implied, in the first place, the efficient organization of the philanthropic resources of the community. Efficiency depended upon the adoption of those techniques of functional specialization and centralized coordination and administration that characterized the business world. If the old charity involved a literal interpretation of the injunction, "Give to him that asketh," the new charity must insure the "wise and effective administration of the relief already available." The great demand of modern social ethics was organization.[10] Charity organization was sometimes compared to trustification and amalgamation in business. Abram S. Hewitt, for example, saw much in common between the Pennsylvania Railroad and charity organization, for the latter adopted the same principles of "division of labor and of co-ordination of agencies" that had made the Pennsylvania the wonder it was. "Marvellous results" could be anticipated from the "co-ordination of all benevolent agencies under one general organization."[11] Yet business centralization was one example of a more general "spirit of the age," according to John M. Glenn, for such evolution was basic to success in "nearly every form of modern life." "We live in an atmosphere of organization," he argued. "On every hand are great combinations of various sorts, formed because men are learning the disadvantage of isolated action. Whether or not we approve of trusts and trades-unions and similar combinations, and whatever their motives, they rest on a foundation which is sound alike from the business and religious standpoint; namely, the principle of union and co-operation." [12]

As a managerial technique charity organization was both scientific and businesslike, an attempt "to do in charity what is done in commerce and industry—so to arrange its different agencies, and so to coördinate its different forces as to attain a certain end with the least possible waste of energy." But scientific philanthropy had a second dimension involving the consistent application of biological and economic law to problems of individual, family, and social demoralization. The leaders imposed a blend of Malthusianism, Manchesterian economics, Social Darwinism, Romanticism, and the crude hereditary biology of McCulloch and Dugdale upon the Christian love and brotherhood which theoretically inspired all benevolent efforts.[13] The result was a vast amount of rhetoric concerning the importance of a thorough understanding of the background of each case of dependency, combined with a series of preconceived moral judgments and presuppositions about the character of the poor and about human nature.

According to Josephine Shaw Lowell, "human nature is so constituted that no man can receive as a gift what he should earn by his own labor without a moral deterioration." Relief, at best, was a necessary evil suited to those who could not compete in the ceaseless struggle for survival: the aged, infirm, sick, or orphaned. Under any circumstances it had to be discriminating, for the vital work of charity was "to train the mental and moral nature." [14] Any relief, particularly public outdoor relief, pauperized its recipients for it reduced the incentive to work. Once they accepted public relief, the poor considered it the duty of the municipality to support them in idleness; and such relief could not be of short duration for "the barrier is broken down, and rarely, or never, thereafter, is the effort made to do without it." [15] There were only two classes worth considering—the workers and idlers. Public out-door relief augmented the ranks of the parasites at the expense of the producers.

Work was a universal panacea for problem families. The test for worthiness was willingness to labor, however menial or dreary the task. A Conference of the Boston Associated Charities boasted that when the poor first called for assistance, they requested "clothing, money, etc., etc.," but were refused anything except work.[16] In Gurteen's opinion, there was no "room in this busy world of ours for those social drones who prey upon the industry of others, and prefer to beg rather than to work." [17] Labor was a test of character, an index to the moral virtues and limitations of the individual. Intemperance or indolence represented not only personal moral defects but social crimes for they reduced the capacity for honest toil upon which the progress of civilization depended. The highly specialized, interdependent urban community could not exist if it had to support an army of loafers.

Because humans were naturally inclined to laziness, it was suicidal to tempt them over the abyss with relief. The poor must not starve or freeze, but neither must the worker be deprived of the incentive to labor by the prospect of readily obtainable alms. Deviations from this policy would lead to degeneration in the form of a permanent pauper class, for the "biological condition" of individual and racial development was effort, and "the being which is fed without expense of effort becomes a parasite, and loses powers of locomotion and initiation." [18] The New York Charity Organization Society warned that "honest employment, the work that God means every man to do, is the truest basis of relief for every person with physical ability to work," and "the help which needlessly releases the poor from the necessity of providing for themselves is in violation of divine law and incurs the penalties which follow any infraction of that law." [19]

Nevertheless, many charity organization societies compromised with the economic and biological imperatives to avoid relief in favor of work. A charity organization society had to supply relief in cities where no other agency did, and it was sometimes expedient in attracting popular support. Many persons could not understand why they should contribute money to an agency which failed to distribute it among the poor. Most important, the same pressures which originally inspired the charity organization societies to eschew relief forced them to modify their principles. The pauperism and vagrancy which they hoped to discourage through stringent relief policies were not simply expressions of individual moral perversity, but phases of labor mobility in a growing industrial economy. Those problems were real and disturbing; but benevolent stinginess could no more cope with them than could liberal or indiscriminate relief. Poverty was rooted in structural changes in American economic and social life with consequences too complex and far-reaching to be affected significantly by any form of relief policy.

By 1893, only 25 out of 54 societies for which information was obtained by a committee of the National Conference of Charities and Correction reported that they gave no relief from their own funds. Another survey in 1900 revealed that 51 out of 75 societies dispensed relief.[20] It was more difficult than the founders had realized to distinguish between worthy and unworthy, when no amount of effort could raise the income of a family to a subsistence level or when dips of the economic cycle sharply reduced employment opportunities. The strong environmental emphasis of social reformers in the early twentieth century helped modify the obsessive concern of charity organization workers over the dire moral consequences of relief. Some of them adopted the view that relief, properly utilized, actually possessed constructive possibilities for personal or family rehabilitation, although they often remained firmly opposed to the public outdoor variant. It became clear that relief could not be altogether avoided, and that the real problem was to define the criteria for a normal standard of living as a basis for rational, systematic policy.

Rounding out their benevolent program, the charity organization societies stressed the necessity of painstaking investigation and treatment of individual cases. Paradoxically, their leaders expounded sweeping generalizations about human nature and poverty, and simultaneously insisted upon careful examination into the background of each supplicant. It was "characteristic of the new or scientific charity as opposed to purely emotional philanthropy that it regards poverty as an evil to be assailed in its causes. It does not merely pity poverty, but studies it. It believes that a doctor might as well give pills without a diagnosis, as a benevolent man give alms without an investigation." [21] Like any science, "social therapeutics" presupposed observation and classification.

The unrelenting emphasis of the charity organization societies upon investigation and a full understanding of the facts surrounding each case evoked severe criticism from more sentimental and reform-minded contemporaries. Suspicion often marked the relation between the settlements and charity organization societies. Jane Addams of Hull House referred to the honest outrage experienced by many people who came into contact with them: "When they see the delay and caution with which relief is given, these do not appear to them conscientious scruples, but the cold and calculating action of the selfish man." Robert Hunter criticized the "Don't, don't" or "Hamlet" mentality, and James O. S. Huntington roundly condemned the societies for establishing standards of truthfulness and hard work for the poor which apparently did not apply to the rich.[22] In answer to such criticisms, the charity workers reaffirmed the need for investigation in the atomized urban community where all men were strangers and stressed the primacy of gradualism over radical reform. Mary Richmond warned her co-workers not to "permit themselves to be swept away by enthusiastic advocates of social reform from that safe middle ground which recognizes that character is at the very centre" of social problems.[23]

It was unlikely that Miss Richmond's colleagues, the agents and visitors of the charity organization societies, would be stampeded into drastic social action. Their focus upon the individual case and upon the moral roots of dependency precluded any such possibility. A typical day in the work of a district agent of the Boston Associated Charities, for example, was largely devoted to investigation, advising visitors, and listening to the woes of individuals or families in need of assistance. She seemed little concerned with broad issues of social melioration.

The day of one such agent began with a refusal of aid for a sick woman in the district because of alleged intemperance. Then an appeal for fifteen cents from an "undoubted tramp" was denied and the supplicant advised to earn his keep at Stephen's Lodging-house. Learning from a visitor that a woman "known to be good and industrious" was ill, the agent authorized a fifty-cent contribution for food. Referrals from the Children's Aid Society and a dispensary physician were brought to the attention of the agent who also sent two cases of her own to the officers in charge of vagrancy: a boy of eight found selling newspapers, and a woman with a baby caught begging. She turned down a request from a young woman for money to help pay the rent, claiming that the applicant was one of a family of six, only one of whom was willing to work. Next came a referral to the Society for the Prevention of Cruelty to Children of parents whose offspring and lodgings were "unspeakably dirty"; the agent claimed that the mother was intemperate and that she gave liquor to her child of one-and-a-half. A prescription was filled for a family, sewing obtained for a needy client, and an extension of time procured for a woman and child who had been placed in the Temporary Home for Working-Women. The day ended with an examination of reports which had been requested from the police and a dispensary, and a consultation with a lawyer concerning a man unjustly deprived of his wages.[24]

*

The charity organization societies distinguished between the investigation and administrative responsibilities of the paid agent and the treatment responsibilities of the friendly visitor.[25] The latter was the focal point of the entire effort, the sole justification for the complex machinery of scientific benevolence. Coordination of the community's charitable resources, the labors of the registration bureau, the work of the paid agent, the deliberations of the district committee, and case conferences were all designed to stimulate and increase the effectiveness of visiting. The most thorough and efficient district secretary was a failure unless she could attract volunteers and retain their interest.

The societies discerned no incompatibility between scientific charity and voluntary service. On the contrary, the ultimate goal—the prevention and cure of poverty—depended wholly upon enlistment of the volunteer. Her personal service differentiated scientific benevolence from mere alms. Rejecting alms as an expression of the benevolent instinct, the charity organization societies swung to the opposite extreme and exalted the beneficent potentialities of personal relationship. Efficient charity was essentially a process of character regeneration, not social reform, and involved the direct influence of successful, educated, and cultured representatives of the middle class upon the dependent individual or family. "Marvellous, indeed," Robert Treat Paine, Jr. explained to visitors for the Boston Associated Charities, "it is to find in how many cases some cause of poverty and want exists which you can remove!" The reason was clear: "You go in the full strength and joy and fire of life; full of cheer and courage; with a far wider knowledge of affairs; and it would be indeed a wonder if you could not often see why the needy family does not succeed, and how to help them up." [26]

The urban poor required no resource so desperately as the counsel of an intelligent and kind friend, whose primary qualifications for the work were not technical but personal—"all possible sympathy, tact, patience, cheer, and wise advice." [27] It should not be difficult for the visitor to discern the moral lapse responsible for the social inefficiency of an individual or family and supply the appropriate guidance. This faith of the charity organization societies in the efficacy of friendly visiting reflected a rather naïve optimism about their power to modify the attitudes, behavior, and life-organization of the poor. Men were not rigidly bound to their environment or to the promptings of a subterranean subconscious, but to their own chosen vices and bad habits. Since man was a free agent, he could control his destiny commensurate with his abilities and moral fiber. His lapse into dependency was the result of intemperance, improvidence, indolence, ignorance, or some other personal defect which reduced his social efficiency. Not technical training or scientific understanding of human behavior but moral insight was the desideratum for friendly visiting.

Paid professionals lacked the spontaneity and zeal of volunteers. The "executive labors" of the societies were merely "voices crying in the wilderness, 'There cometh after me that which is mightier than I, the latchet of whose shoes I am not worthy to unloose.'" [28] The society without volunteer visitors was little better than a charitable machine lacking moral purpose and unfit for the fundamental task of helping the poor to help themselves. The paid worker, it was true, offered her skill, experience, and technical know-how to the poor, but the volunteer offered herself—and this offer of oneself was the only foundation upon which to build the friendship between classes which would avert the worst consequences of an urban-industrial society: pauperism, social atomization, class hostility, and the destruction of the family. Friendly visiting was an instrument of social control which assumed not only the right, but the civic duty of intervention in the lives of the poor by their economic and social betters.

The charity organization societies used the word friendship to describe the desired relationship between rich and poor, but did not question the superiority of the visitor. We could not, Mrs. Lowell explained, "be charitable to our equals." [29] The poor were not inherently vicious or mean, but wayward children incapable of discerning their own best interests. Their welfare would be advanced if the rich and prosperous assumed the responsibilities of moral guardianship. The charity organization spokesmen did not claim that friendly visiting would eliminate the class differences so conspicuous in post-Civil War urban society; they did believe that it would reduce frictions and misunderstandings. The poor would realize that the rich were their friends rather than their oppressors, and the rich might benefit from the examples of courage and good cheer displayed by the poor.

"Scientific" philanthropy was fully compatible with a high level of volunteer responsibility because the key relation encouraged was "friendly" or "neighborly" rather than professional. The charity organization ideal was to reëstablish the patterns of social interaction of the small town or village, where the primary group exercised powerful social controls. The charity society was an "artifice," designed to restore the "natural relations" which the city had destroyed.[30] Strangers to each other, the urban masses lacked "ties of blood, sympathy or previous knowledge." [31] "So far have we of the city gone astray from the old democratic social relation of the village," charged the Boston Associated Charities, "that we even take pride in our lack of knowledge of each other and each other's welfare. The latest comer from the country, where he had known every family and child in his town, and been wont to regard them all as neighbors whose interests could not be separated from his own, soon falls a prey to the vast selfishness which, like a vapor, is exhaled from these unnatural conditions. Subtly and imperceptibly it affects him, transforming him from the warm-hearted provincial to the cautious citizen." In their quest for neighborhood and faith in the efficacy of the personal relationship, the charity organization societies personified a Victorian romantic impulse far removed from the sober, scientific philanthropy to which they aspired.[32]

Serving as the substitute for the spontaneous neighborliness of the small town, the charity organization societies would "bring the rich and the poor into real helpful cooperation, by means of neighborhood centers with neighborhood agents." [33] Poverty, pauperism, and other urban social evils could not be cured by alms or by a redistribution of wealth, but by "genuine neighborhood" reëstablished as a feature of civic life.[34] The desire to create an organic unity of groups and classes in the neighborhood was not unique to charity organization in the 1880's and 1890's. Settlement workers promulgated that ethic, for they also believed that the industrial city fostered a pernicious social and racial segregation at variance with democratic ideals.

The view of the district office as a neighborhood community center, serving a purpose comparable to the village meetinghouse or church, could not resolve the ambiguities inherent in the role of friendly visitor. She intervened in the lives of the poor by virtue of a presumptive wisdom and superiority, yet was to conceive of her charges as personal friends. In practice, the superiority ascribed to the volunteer visitor could not be reconciled with the desire to draw rich and poor together as neighbors. Charity organization was the creation of middle-class Protestant Americans, denouncing rigid sectarianism in charitable affairs but inspired by an evangelical sense of mission. Immigrants and workers were not conspicuous as visitors, paid officials, or directors. In a sense, charity organization was more a closing of the ranks against a common threat than a cooperative, equalitarian association of disparate economic and ethnic groups.

The relation between visitor and client may have been personal, but it was not "friendly" in the sense of the informal, natural cohesiveness of peers sharing similar social and cultural backgrounds. Consequently, the visitor saw in her client less an equal or potential equal than an object of character reformation whose unfortunate and lowly condition resulted from ignorance or deviations from middle-class values and patterns of life-organization: temperance, industriousness, family cohesiveness, frugality, foresight, moral restraint. The decline of friendly visiting in the twentieth century was associated with the realization that it had not produced a community cohesiveness or the basis for a satisfactory relationship between the representatives of middle-class society and those who had deviated in one fashion or another. Substituting expertise for moral superiority as the basis of the relationship, social workers perpetuated the charity organization ideal of personal contact and influence in place of material relief, but avoided the fiction that such contact was one of friends and peers bound in neighborhood association.

Exponents of friendly visiting and the neighborhood ethic uncritically assumed that the poor wanted their moral guidance. The New York Charity Organization Society claimed that "the *ideal* of the district office" was "a place known to the poor of the district, where they may come for advice, for help in every kind of trouble; where they may find a friend who will think with them, work with them, struggle by their side, until some means have been found to lift them out of their distress," but the Society did not consider the possibility that the poor had their own friends with whom they had far more in common than with the genteel volunteer visitor.[35] While it was possible to create a satisfactory *professional* relationship between nonequals, such as doctor–patient, or lawyer–client, the charity organization societies assumed they could establish satisfactory personal relationships between "superior" volunteers and "inferior" dependents. It was not surprising that the worker was more likely to turn to his peers for consolation or advice than to the patronizing friend from the charity society.

The immigrant presented an especially difficult challenge, for, if friendly visiting was to succeed as an instrument of urban social control and the neighborhood ethic put into practice, his resistance or indifference had to be surmounted. Yet a conference of the Boston Associated Charities expressed a frustration no doubt echoed by many visitors and other societies: "Until the Italians became numerous, we had at least intelligent means of communication with most of the families we knew. We not only spoke the same language, but they knew what we were talking about when we urged the advantages of temperance, industry, or economical living. Though their acquiescence in our standards might be feigned and though they might never live up to them, we seldom failed to agree in theory . . . [But the Italians] are truly foreigners to us. We do not speak a common language; our standards have no meaning to them, and we may well doubt whether they have any applicability."[36] Although individual visitors might establish constructive relations with families, paternalistic friendly visiting as an organized program of social control was unequal to the challenge of the industrial city with its extensive poverty, its cultural, racial, and ethnic divisions, and the high level of personal mobility which discouraged neighborhood stability.

*

The charity organization societies were not troubled by any inherent weakness in the theory or practice of friendly visiting, not even by the tendency of the paid agent to usurp the functions of the volunteer.[37] Their most frequent regret, on the contrary, concerned the chronic shortage of visitors. In the three decades after 1900, however, the role and status of the volunteer changed. She became increasingly subordinate to the professional not only in charity organization (later family welfare) but in other branches of social work. In the late nineteenth century, social agencies had delegated important administrative and treatment responsibilities to the volunteer; by 1930, her activities were often marginal or else closely supervised. The paid social worker's claim to expertise, the emergence of a professional identity nurtured by schools and associations, and the development of a formal organization or bureaucracy as a characteristic feature of administration were crucial in the devaluation of voluntarism. It had always been limited by prior obligations to family and job; now internal changes in social work resulted in further restrictions.

It was ironic that the charity organization societies of the late nineteenth century, which had revolted against the "officialdom" of existing relief agencies and imbued voluntary service with a semireligious sanctity, were among the leading architects of welfare bureaucracy and professionalization. Their version of scientific philanthropy had stressed the importance of an efficient management of the community's charitable resources and the coordination of the work of private agencies. The federation movement (community chests and councils) which eventually developed represented an effort to achieve the philanthropic coordination which the charity organization societies desired so ardently. At the same time, those societies labored to discover efficient principles of management for individual agencies involving the training and use of paid staff members, supervision of volunteers, and the duties and responsibilities of the executive staff. The increasing interest in social agency administration and community-wide coordination had important consequences for professional and voluntary service.

Blended with the apotheosis of the volunteer by the charity organization societies, were the first faint expressions of interest in a professional self and in professional education. As early as 1893, Nathaniel S. Rosenau of the Buffalo Society questioned the right of the "superannuated clergyman," "unsuccessful merchant," or "political favorite" to serve as manager of a charitable society or institution. It was necessary that persons "take charge of this work who are specially trained, who have a calling for the work, and who mean to devote themselves to it." [38] The distinction would grow in importance between a trained in-group devoted to raising the standards of professional service, and an untrained out-group. Five years after Rosenau's plea, the New York Charity Organization Society inaugurated formal social work education when it established its Summer School of Philanthropy in 1898.

Training in social work implied the existence of a skill. That was the basis on which any profession distinguished its practitioners from the layman. The growing conviction among social workers in the early twentieth century that they possessed a skill to be acquired by formal education and experience was important in explaining the emergence of a professional identity; and here too the charity organization societies played a significant role. Although handicapped by their stress on moral therapeutics and a tendency toward crude classification (worthy, unworthy, drunkard, pauper, deserter), charity organization leaders did espouse the need for a differential approach. The background of each case (at least in theory) had to be investigated, and the factors resulting in dependency discovered. Case records had to be kept, demonstrating the steps in investigation and treatment, not only as a guide to the agent or visitor, but as a basis for future research into the causes of poverty and of individual and family demoralization. Facts and more facts were needed, according to a Conference of the Boston Associated Charities, for "two-thirds of the errors in charity work arise from misinformation or lack of information. In thorough preliminary investigation, followed by an intelligent, sympathetic searching into the facts on the visitor's part, lies our chief strength as a practical body of scientific workers." [39]

Mary Richmond's casework classic *Social Diagnosis* (1917) was in part a sophisticated expression of this passion for "facts" proclaimed by the Boston Society as early as 1886. Modern social casework would emerge when the quest for facts became rooted in a less moralistic, more dynamic conception of human behavior. More than any other category of social workers, caseworkers believed that they had at least the beginnings of a scientific knowledge base as well as a specialized skill, technique, and function which differentiated them from the layman or volunteer. Casework formed the basis of a professional identity and forced upon social agencies a consideration of the roles of professional and volunteer.

There was a wide disparity between the professed standards and goals of social work theorists and the day-to-day work in agencies. By the criterion of objective achievement, "scientific" social work remained an elusive ideal rather remote from reality. It did not follow that the efforts of caseworkers and others to establish social work on a scientific professional basis were meaningless gestures. The fact that they had become dissatisfied with their status and equated progress with professionalization and science merits attention. Even if professionalization was not associated necessarily with substantial scientific achievement and control, it was unquestionably associated with changes in the definition of social work functions, the organization of social work services, and the values and institutions of American society. The professionalization of social work is perhaps better understood in relation to these changes, especially the development of a professional subculture, bureaucratization, and specialization, than to any unique social work knowledge base rooted in science.

Chapter II

From Friendly Visiting
to Social Diagnosis

T HE core of any profession is a special skill applied to a special function. In social work the quest for professional status was closely related to the efforts of caseworkers after 1900 to limit, define, and clarify their particular knowledge base and techniques. Long before group work and community organization emerged as self-conscious specialties, caseworkers had launched an intensive examination of their occupational role.

The functional specialization which developed in the early twentieth century was instrumental in shaping the caseworkers' aspirations. Their employment in several institutions whose effectiveness had been limited by a failure to consider the social environment of clients or patients was a decisive episode in the evolution of social work as a profession. Although specialization was apparent before 1900, and well advanced in larger cities like New York and Boston, social workers thereafter penetrated a series of existing institutions which had ignored the social conditions influencing health and behavior. The knotty problems of adjustment which social workers confronted in these institutions sparked a search for the expertise which differentiated them from other members of the staff and justified claims to professional status. Equally important, charity organization and children's aid societies had been groping toward investigation techniques and methods of diagnosis and treatment which would result in an understanding of the unique problems of each client.[1] This differential approach was frequently undermined by the paternalistic moralism characteristic of nineteenth-century philanthropy and by the lack of any science of human behavior. In different ways, psychology, psychiatry and psychiatric social work, school and medical social work modified the tendency toward categorization and contributed tools needed for "scientific" social diagnosis.

The motto of the Boston Associated Charities had been "Not Alms But a Friend." In the early twentieth century a different concept evolved: neither alms nor a friend, but a professional service. A new view of poverty, stressing environmental causation and exploitation, became incompatible with the friendly visiting ideal. Social workers could not so readily reconcile scientific philanthropy with presumptions of moral superiority in a period when the poor were considered the victims of a hostile environment. A new relationship had to justify interference in their lives; the visitor had to demonstrate a greater claim to authority than class affiliation. The answer seemed to lie in the establishment of a professional relationship in which the social worker's authority rested upon a superior expertise.

*

The work of the friendly visitor in the nineteenth century was sanctioned by an organization established to eliminate pauperism and dependency; her motives coincided with those of the agency. Social work in more specialized settings created unique complications for it had to be related to the primary institutional service and structure. Medical social service, one of the first casework specialties, faced a particularly acute problem of integration. It was an innovation toward which many administrators and physicians were hostile, lukewarm, or indifferent. The hospital was among the most authoritarian and conservative of social institutions, impatient with frills or luxuries having no direct relation to medical diagnosis and treatment. The medical social worker, hard-pressed to justify her existence, could not remain indifferent to questions of professional function or skill. If, as she claimed, the physician and patient often required her services for accurate diagnosis and effective treatment, she had to explain just what her contribution was and how it differed from nursing. Concerned with her status in the hospital hierarchy, she self-consciously scrutinized her function, skill and technique, knowledge base, and relation to patient, medical profession, and hospital administration. In the process she allied herself with the other social workers struggling to establish a profession.

Some individuals and organizations had tried to consider the personality and social environment of the patient in relation to medical treatment before Dr. Richard C. Cabot introduced medical social service at Massachusetts General Hospital in October 1905.[2] As early as the 1850's Elizabeth Blackwell, founder of the New York Infirmary for Women and Children, had visited patients at home and had hired another worker to train mothers in housekeeping and child care. Under the leadership of Dr. Annie S. Daniel, appointed Physician in Charge of Out-Patients in 1881, the Infirmary pioneered in efforts to link medical care with hygienic instruction and improvement in living and working conditions. Around 1890, Dr. Henry Dwight Chapin of the Post-Graduate Hospital in New York organized a volunteer committee for follow-up work with babies; in 1894 this committee hired a paid worker to supply milk and instruct mothers in infant hygiene. The English "Society for After Care of Poor Persons Discharged Recovered from Insane Asylums" was the model for the Subcommittee on After-care of the Insane established by the New York State Charities Aid Association in 1905. Another group which took account of the social environment of the patient was the Ladies Auxiliary of the Lying-In Hospital in New York, whose agent after 1898 visited the homes of dispensary patients at the time of confinement; and visiting nursing services attached to hospitals, boards of health, and settlements stimulated interest in the connection between sickness and living conditions.

Of all the limited experiments in social medicine, none so closely approximated the work begun at Massachusetts General as the "Lady Almoner." Charles Loch, secretary of the London Charity Organization Society, had long shared with hospital administrators a concern over the abuse of medical charities by individuals who minimized their ability to pay. Medical social service in England began in 1895 when the Society placed one of its district secretaries in the Royal Free Hospital to investigate the financial circumstances of patients and to link medical charities with other community agencies.[3]

Seven years after the first Lady Almoner began work, a novel experiment in social medicine was introduced at Johns Hopkins by Dr. Charles P. Emerson, who combined friendly visiting with medical education. Emerson decided that students could better understand the medical problems they encountered in the wards if they knew something about the patient's social environment. Since a majority of the Baltimore Charity Organization Society's executive committee were also connected with Johns Hopkins, Emerson readily won permission to use the Society's facilities. He arranged special district board meetings for the students, where hospital cases were assigned and discussed. Although Cabot, who visited Hopkins in 1903, had become interested in the work of these student boards, Emerson was actually less concerned with medical–social diagnosis and treatment than with improving the quality of medical training.[4]

Cabot's own medical–social experience exerted the most direct and persuasive influence. As a director of the Boston Children's Aid Society for a decade, he had been impressed by the casework of its paid agents, who made "careful studies . . . into the character, disposition, antecedents, and record of the child" and who supplemented their investigations by consultations with schoolteachers, physicians, and others who might provide clues to special problems and needs. The casework method, "the focussing of effort on the part of many experts upon the needs of a single child," intrigued Cabot, who later defended it as the basic tool in medical social service.[5] As a consulting physician to the State Industrial School for Girls, he acquired additional understanding of this method and gradually realized that if it could benefit delinquent girls and children from broken homes, it might contribute to hospital care as well.

Cabot had been appointed Physician to Outpatients at Massachusetts General in 1898. As the sick and handicapped poured into the clincs and dispensaries, a sense of futility and impotence overwhelmed him. Dozens of patients whirled past "like shooting stars—out of darkness and into darkness." He had no time to deal with persons, only with "disembodied diseases." How much of this illness, he wondered, could be traced to social conditions, such as "vice, ignorance, overcrowding, sweatshops, and poverty."[6] The hospital did not really treat the sick but only isolated physical symptoms, and often failed to cure patients who returned to the same social environment which had produced their illness.

In 1905 the average hospital clinic, the entering wedge for medical social work, was poorly equipped for long-term systematic treatment of disease or for preventive medicine. It functioned, in large measure, as a teaching center and as a base for aftercare of discharged ward patients. Hospitals assumed few preventive or educational responsibilities, partly because their administrators were concerned primarily with "important housekeeping responsibilities, such as refrigeration, laundry service, floor covering and accounting." [7] Dr. Charles Emerson remembered the hospital in the early twentieth century as clean and efficient in a deadly way. Its cold professionalism "repelled the patient rather than attracted him." [8] Physicians ignored the social environment, overlooking a potentially useful aid in diagnosis and treatment, while administrators concentrated upon the internal organization of their complex institutions.

Along with the hospital's bleak efficiency went increasing pressure on its facilities. No longer a place of last resort where the sick went to die, it had become the nucleus of the community's medical resources and talent. The medical specialization of the late nineteenth century led to the rapid proliferation of clinics and departments whose staff physicians and surgeons, with the help of such technical advances as X-rays, anesthetics, and diagnostic laboratories, provided the most skilled services available. Urban growth and social pathology provided another stimulus to the establishment and use of hospitals. Immigrants and workers poured into the unsanitary, congested tenement or slum environments, and fell victim to dysentery, pneumonia, typhoid, cholera, and, above all, tuberculosis. Industrial accidents and diseases claimed their toll in an age just launching its crusade for protective factory legislation. Immigrants and workers crowding the hospital clinics might comprehend a dispensary physician's diagnosis of tuberculosis, but not necessarily the relevance of his prescription—plenty of sunlight, fresh air, ventilation, and high standards of personal hygiene to protect others. If he did understand the prescription, he could not always carry it out. How could the immigrant father supporting a family on a subsistence margin take a six-month rest or move into better ventilated quarters? The hospital by 1905 had become more popular, more efficiently organized, but not, Cabot believed, more effective in curing disease or relieving its most tragic social consequences.

Cabot instituted social service to overcome the hospital's depersonalization and isolation from the social roots of disease. The physician needed the social worker to insure full and accurate diagnosis "through more careful study of the patient's malady and economic situation." And, like the agents of the Boston Children's Aid Society who grasped every social resource which might benefit a single child, the social worker would improve the physician's treatment by "organizing the resources of the community." [9] Some of the early social service referrals at Massachusetts General suggested the responsibilities Cabot envisioned for the new department. One physician referred a case with this observation: "Patient is married—wife and child to support. Too sick to work. No money. Has some kidney condition as yet undetermined." Another doctor wondered what social service could do for his patient: "This man probably has T.B. of one or both kidneys. We cannot tell until 6 weeks have elapsed. He is to come here at least twice a week meanwhile and ought not work." Another physician referred what looked like a possible mental case: "This patient tells us stories of abuse at home by his sons. He is depressed and moody—Can you tell us what the conditions are there?" And Dr. Cabot requested assistance for a patient with a heart condition: "Working too hard. Does washing. Can she be relieved of some of her work?" [10]

In extending services to individuals who required more than straightforward medical advice, the hospital caseworker helped socialize her institution; and the facts she accumulated in daily work shed light on the social origins of disease—housing, living, and working conditions. From the beginning, Dr. Cabot hoped that medical social work would contribute to the development of preventive medicine. Through casework the community could better understand and control the environmental conditions which undermined health and delayed the recovery of the sick. [11]

Tuberculosis became a focal point of concern in hospital social work. A preventive campaign against this disease had been launched before Cabot's experiment. In Massachusetts, Dr. Edward O. Otis, Dr. Vincent Y. Bowditch, and Dr. Charles Millet had tried to acquaint the public with methods of care and prevention; in 1903 they helped organize both the Boston Association for Relief and Control of Tuberculosis and the Cambridge Anti-Tuberculosis Association. New York became the center of another militant assault upon the "white plague." Dr. Hermann M. Biggs, chief of the Health Department's bacteriological department had been trying since the 1890's to reduce the ravages of a disease causing thousands of deaths a year in the metropolis. He encouraged Edward T. Devine, general secretary of the Charity Organization Society, to establish its Committee on the Prevention of Tuberculosis in 1902. Two years later the Society helped launch a National Association for the Study and Prevention of Tuberculosis. The martial, well-organized tuberculosis crusade, with its stress upon the relation between disease and living conditions, anticipated Cabot's social medicine ideals and prepared a climate of opinion which encouraged their acceptance.

Social casework in the medical setting was not an easy concept for many physicians to grasp. Trained to diagnose and treat specific organic diseases, they did not consider it their responsibility to worry about a patient's job, relations with wife and children, and similar personal circumstances. Almost two decades after Cabot introduced medical social service, one physician still maintained that the "over-worked hospital doctor cares nothing for 'case work,' his interest lies in curing disease." [12] It had required all of Cabot's enormous personal influence and professional prestige to launch social service at Massachusetts General. Not only were the administration and many physicians skeptical, but social workers themselves did not unanimously accept the need for hospital social service. Although she later became a staunch ally, Alice Lothrop, general secretary of the Boston Associated Charities, originally advised Cabot that a district committee could handle the work.[13] For a long while the administration at Massachusetts General prohibited social service in the wards, restricting it to the out-patient department; it was not officially incorporated into the hospital organization until 1919.

In the critical first two decades, when medical social work labored to define its place in the hospital hierarchy, its survival depended upon the prestige and power of sympathetic physicians and administrators. Cabot, the patron saint of this movement, often lectured and wrote on behalf of the service, attempting to convince doubtful colleagues that social work would improve and not interfere with medical services. A select corps of socially minded administrators welcomed it as a necessary link to the patient's social environment.[14] Medical social service also required the support of influential laymen able to attract funds and win the approval of trustees. Cabot had wisely courted the support of Mrs. Nathaniel Thayer, the wife of a trustee, who later became a trustee herself and a member of the Social Service Supervisory Committee selected by Cabot and Ida Cannon in 1909.[15] Hospital social workers realized that the continued backing of these groups depended ultimately upon their own performance. They were conscious of their uncertain status and sensed that their professional aspirations, if not their very survival, were contingent upon the quality of their services and a satisfactory relation with the hospital's medical staff. Looking back to the first decade of medical social work, Ida Cannon pinpointed the insecurities and challenges confronting her colleagues: "A few physicians and laymen saw the possibilities of our usefulness in improving the care of patients but most doctors and administrators were either indifferent or considered us intruders in an already complicated organization. We had to find our place in the institutional organization and demonstrate a special and useful function different from and sustaining to the service of doctor and nurse." [16]

It was not entirely clear at first whether hospital social service had more in common with nursing or social work. Logically, it seemed that a person serving physicians and sick in a hospital setting should have nursing training. If they had chosen to emphasize a nursing role, medical social workers might have simplified their problem of organizational status; physicians and administrators could understand a kind of social nursing in contrast to social casework, which ostensibly had little relation to medical theory and practice. Nursing could be reconciled with the sundry administrative tasks assigned medical social workers in the early decades: assisting at the admission desk, investigation of a patient's financial condition, dispensary management, and miscellaneous services such as transporting patients or furnishing information to social and municipal agencies. Many of the early medical social workers were, in fact, nurses. A survey of 61 social service departments by a committee of the American Hospital Association in 1920 revealed that 193 out of 350 salaried workers had nursing experience; and of the 61 head workers, 36 were nurses.[17] It is not surprising that the original nucleus of medical social workers was drawn from the group of women most familiar with hospital routine and most accustomed to dealing with physicians and sickness.

Yet deliberately and self-consciously, these nurses set about to obliterate their former occupational identity and to emphasize casework as their special function. Far from being a mere extension of nursing, casework in the hospital was proclaimed as generically distinct, with different and more constructive goals. It aimed to "release the energies of the individual in the best direction possible." In contrast to nursing, it tried "to give the man, dependent from whatever cause, new incentives to self-help and development." Nursing training was useful but could not "suffice for successful medical-social work." [18]

The refusal of medical social workers to identify themselves with nursing had other than functional roots. The nurse occupied a distinctly subordinate status in relation to the physician. An assistant, pure and simple, with no pretentions as a creative practitioner, she was a poor status symbol for aspiring professionals. The physician became the medical social workers' model. Accepting his superiority in medical affairs, they eagerly sought his acquiescence in their claims to superiority in social diagnosis. Their efforts to assume an identity distinct from the nurse was one manifestation of the desire to establish social work as a field offering creative professional career opportunities for women. It was certainly as respectable as the traditional female occupations of teaching and nursing and had the advantage of potential comparison with medicine, law, the ministry, and other high prestige vocations.

The enlistment of medical social workers marked an important stage in the development of professional social work. A casework limited to the charity organization and child welfare societies provided too narrow a base for professional development, associated as it was with problems of relief and economic dependency. Medical social work added an entirely new institutional setting in which to explore the implications of casework theory and practice.

Medical social service invigorated the quest for professional skill and technique. Here was a "new and special service that demands new and special instruction and expertness." [19] Ida Cannon and others, determined to secure a useful and respected place in the hospital hierarchy, insisted that "human kindness alone cannot solve tangled social problems." Their contribution did not "lie especially in a sympathy with patients in immediate distress of mind and body"; the good physician, nurse, or layman had this. It consisted rather of "an enlarged understanding of any psychic or social conditions which may cause the patient distress of mind or body. Character, human relationships, and community life are the fields of her study and effort." [20] The insistence that kindness and a desire to serve were no substitutes for skill and technique paralleled similar claims of family social workers. Both groups in the years before World War I struggled to create an image of professional competence, based upon casework skills differentiating them from volunteer and layman.

Skilled casework practice depended ultimately upon training, and no group of social workers expressed a greater passion for professional education than those in the hospitals. Ida Cannon asserted she would not rest until she could "do something toward developing the training that will fit women to share with the skilled men of the medical profession the great responsibility that social medicine is now placing upon us all." [21] The lack of uniformity in training standards and casework practice greatly disturbed medical social work leaders. Women entering the field from teaching, social work, and nursing were exposed to various apprenticeship systems in the hospitals. The "indiscriminate use of untrained people" resulted in a "lack of standards" which threatened to discredit the entire work.[22] Social work was a "special art with knowledge and skill not attached to any other profession," and it could not tolerate mediocrity.[23]

The interest of hospital social workers in special training programs was stimulated by their close association with the medical profession. In contrast to the systematic curriculum of the best medical schools, training in medical social service and other specialties seemed woefully informal and casual. The lack of standards meant that no director or supervisor could assume a minimum competence when hiring new workers; it was necessary to "study each applicant and her professional history in relation to the job and the other members of the staff."²⁴ How could the physician regard the medical social worker as a colleague under these circumstances?

By 1912 medical social work had barely begun to define its function, skills, or the elements of a professional curriculum. Nonetheless, only seven years after Cabot had established social service at Massachusetts General, the new department cooperated in organizing a one-year course at the Boston School of Social Work.²⁵ This pioneer course required ten months of supervised work in a hospital, combined with school lectures and conferences. The availability of the course soon encouraged a more selective hiring policy at Massachusetts General. An experienced Atlanta social worker wrote for a volunteer appointment in the Social Service Department, hoping to fit herself for a paid position. Miss Cannon informed her that volunteer work would not qualify her for a regular staff post. She could volunteer, if she wished, to test her aptitude for medical social work, but would have to attend the course if she hoped to join the department.²⁶

The New York and Philadelphia schools of social work followed Boston's lead in including medical–social training in their curricula; and by 1920 medical social workers had defined some of the minimum criteria for a satisfactory training program. Any student planning to enter hospital social service had to acquire at least a rudimentary scientific knowledge base, including "the social elements of disease, or of the chief groups of diseases dealt with by hospital and dispensary social workers; and the problems of hygiene and public health which are related thereto."²⁷ The medical social worker needed training in casework technique: interviewing, the preparation of records, the accumulation and evaluation of evidence, and the ability to handle delicate personal situations. An adequate course had to be "long enough and sufficiently thorough to produce a real impression on the personality."²⁸ It had to eliminate personal prejudices or idiosyncrasies which interfered with efficient performance of the task—one of the most important functions of professional education in any field.

This conception of skilled professional service, rooted in medical science and performed in a specific institutional setting, eroded the older friendly visiting ideal and forced a re-evaluation of the volunteer's role in social work. The view of charity as "simple friendliness," Cabot explained, had become outmoded. It savored too much of paternalism, moral righteousness, and class distinction. The only valid form of superiority in a democracy was the superior knowledge of the expert, which involved "not a particle of sense of shame on the one side or of condescension on the other." If a neighborly or friendly relationship could not exist in the heterogenous urban environment, then the "relationship of mutually acknowledged experts is the best alternative." [29] "The most precious asset" in casework, according to Ida Cannon, was the "capacity for putting oneself in another's place, and at the same time seeing the situation objectively." Subjective, moralistic evaluations of patients interfered with the purpose of casework in the medical setting—restoration of health. The hospital social worker dealt only with sick persons, not sinners, and she resented the assumption that even venereal disease implied "immorality on the part of the patient—an assumption followed by routine approach to the question from a moral point of view." [30] Moral preconceptions became a liability as functional specialization helped shift the casework focus. "Scientific" philanthropy implied a quest for function and organizational relationships, skills and techniques, and scientific knowledge base, within specific institutional settings.

*

Shortly after Cabot had extended social work into the hospital, a second casework specialty emerged. Visiting teaching arose in response to inadequacies in mass public education, which educational reformers believed had lost touch with the individual child. Like the physician who saw only a disease, not a person, the schoolteacher saw only a mind, not a child. Yet the school could not ignore the relation between the child's scholastic performance and his social environment if it wished to fulfill its obligations. It had to establish contact with the family and community which affected the child's life more profoundly than an institution where he spent only a short part of the day.

Settlements and civic organizations, rather than social case-workers, developed the earliest forms of school social work.[31] In New York City in 1906, Hartley House, Greenwich House, College Settlement, and Richmond Hill House co-operated in sponsoring two visitors for three school districts. Mary Marot, a teacher and resident of Hartley House, was particularly active in promoting the new service. Early the following year the Public Education Association of New York established a committee on visiting teaching and assumed responsibility for the work.[32] The Association employed Jane Day, a colleague of the prominent educator, Julia Richman, and slowly enlarged the staff until by 1912 it had reached seven. The efforts of the Association's visiting teachers attracted the interest of Superintendent of Schools William H. Maxwell, and with his support the Board of Education officially incorporated the practice into the school system in 1913.

Boston launched its program of school social work in 1907 when the Woman's Education Association and the Boston Home and School Association sponsored visitors, followed by the West End Neighborhood Association two years later. Several settlements joined in the work after 1909. In Hartford, Connecticut, the initiative in socializing the school came from the director of the Psychological Clinic, who engaged a visitor in 1907 to assist in obtaining children's histories and to carry out social adjustments necessary for treatment. A fourth early experiment began in Philadelphia in 1909–1910, under the auspices of the Child Welfare Committee of the Friends' Quarterly Meeting, the Juvenile Aid Society, and the Juvenile Protective Association.

Like medical social workers, visiting teachers desired official status rather than informal affiliation, and beginning in 1913 boards of education began to confer it. By 1921 visiting teaching had been established by boards of education in such diverse communities as Newton, Massachusetts; Mount Vernon and Utica, New York; Mason City, Iowa; and Fargo, North Dakota. Altogether in 1921, approximately ninety individuals in twenty-eight communities served as visiting teachers. School social work received a considerable boost in numbers and prestige when in 1921 the Commonwealth Fund decided to sponsor it in connection with its five-year Program for the Prevention of Delinquency. With the Fund's assistance, a National Committee on Visiting Teachers was established and affiliated with the Public Education Association in New York. The National Committee, in cooperation with local boards, launched school social work in thirty communities in the hope that it would be permanently adopted.

A visiting teacher on the staff of the Public Education Association described her function as "socializing the school and individualizing the child." Mass public education needed the social worker to guarantee proper "adjustment of conditions in the lives of individual children, to the end that they may make more normal or profitable school progress."[33] The visiting teacher represented a response to the depersonalization of the public school in the complex urban community. In the past, and "even at the present time in smaller communities, the teacher knew her Toms and Dicks, both in and out of school, their capacities, their handicaps, their dislikes, their probable outlook for the future." [34] The village teacher and school formed part of the network of primary-group associations and were integrated into the community's social structure. The teacher in the crowded urban public school, however, often represented a social or ethnic class different from that of her pupils and their parents; and the school itself, particularly in the immigrant district, became an island isolated from the social life of the neighborhood. The child's school experience, in short, was divorced from his social environment. The function of the social worker was to integrate them.

The many-sided progressive education movement pursued a similar objective. It labored to expand the school curriculum to satisfy the individual aptitudes and needs of children, normal or handicapped, focused attention upon the child as a unique personality who had not only intellectual but physical and recreational needs, and sought to relate the school to surrounding family and neighborhood life. [35] The interests of progressive educators and school social workers intersected at another important point. Along with many social reformers of the Progressive era, both viewed the child as a key to the problem of urban social control. The ethnic and class divisions of the urban community troubled the Progressive generation no less than the spokesmen for the nineteenth-century charity organization societies, and the public school assumed special significance as an instrument of acculturation. It was the one American institution which reached the majority of children, exposing them to a common educational experience and range of middle-class norms; through its influence over the future generation the public school might assist the community in transcending the atomization caused by industrialization and immigration. If rightly used, it would ensure the Americanization of immigrant children and the nurture of a law-abiding, respectable generation of citizens. The public school was our "greatest child-welfare agency." It came into contact with practically every child and was, therefore, the "logical place to detect symptoms of future inefficiency, whether they be departures from the mental, social, or physical standards." [36] Visiting teachers frequently stressed the preventive aspects of their work; they discovered deviations from the normal before they became deformities. [37]

In theory, the visiting teacher dealt with those for whom neither the attendance officer, school nurse, nor classroom teacher was equipped. The teacher or principal referred children whose educational experience was obstructed by deficient scholarship, demoralizing home conditions, misconduct, physical defect, and similar handicaps. After an examination into the background and personality of each child, the visiting teacher used whatever personal influence or social adjustments were necessary to insure efficient performance. She relied upon casework as her major technical resource.

Like their counterparts in the hospitals, school social workers vehemently denied that ordinary good will sufficed. The importance and delicacy of the task required a substantial skill and knowledge base nurtured by education and training. "It must be recognized," proclaimed the official professional organization of visiting teachers in 1921, "that the visiting teacher has by now developed a real technique of social case work as applied to school and that this technique is only acquired by training plus experience." [38] Those concerned with the education of the visiting teacher argued that she should have some acquaintance with psychology, mental testing, mental hygiene, sociology, dietetics, biology, medicine, and industrial conditions. [39] One study of visiting teaching in Rochester concluded that the work demanded application to behavior problems of a special technique, and background in psychology, educational theory and practice, and community resources.[40] Like medical social service, visiting teaching helped shape the social caseworker's image of herself as a skilled professional representing a social institution.

Family casework traced its ancestry to the activities of the paid agent and friendly visitor of the charity organization society.[41] It was not suddenly introduced into a social institution whose effectiveness was hampered by its isolation from the social environment of its clients. In this sense, family social work lacked the same stimulus to define its professional function and knowledge base. Equally important, the specific institutional settings of hospital, school, or mental clinic, with their clearly defined service goals of education or cure of the sick, shaped the activities of the social worker and encouraged the growth of an objective, nonmoralistic attitude. The functional specialization of the early twentieth century nonetheless played a significant role in reshaping the charity organization worker's definition of her role.

The emergence of specialists in medical, school, and psychiatric social work in addition to child care meant that no one had assumed responsibility for the most important institution of all—the family. This was the nuclear social institution through which the community transmitted its moral, cultural, and spiritual heritage. It gradually dawned on charity workers that specialization had made them the experts on family adjustment; and, as environment superseded moral defect as an explanation of dependency, they perceived their task to be the discovery of internal and external pressures which interfered with normal family life. Poverty was only symbolic, effect as much as cause, of a breakdown of cohesion or of an unsatisfactory relation to other social institutions.[42]

Encouraging a liberation from abstract moral–economic categories were the clues to diagnosis acquired from other casework specialties. Medical social work suggested the possibility that behavior dismissed earlier as shiftlessness or indolence might have organic origins, and it generally directed attention to health as a basic factor in diagnosis. Visiting teaching pointed to the school as an important source of data about the children of the family and their special problems. Psychiatry and psychiatric social work alerted the visitor to the possibility of mental defect or disturbance as an explanation for the client's situation. Functional specialization provided important tools for differential diagnosis and encouraged the belief that charity organization meant less an uplifting the poor than expert authority on the dynamics of family life.

By 1920 some family caseworkers looked back to the early charity organization era with embarrassment. The societies had relied too much upon standardized diagnosis and treatment. "It is only in the last fifteen years," claimed Mary Richmond, "that social case work in families has contrived to slip from under the domination of the economists. Though case work always demanded a method in sharp contrast to wholesaling, its earlier period was shaped too often by whole-salers." A period of analysis had succeeded the period of broad generalizations about "relief, about family life, about desertion, widowhood, immigrants, and the rest." [43] In the opinion of some social workers in the early twentieth century, differential casework required a degree of skill and knowledge of human behavior and community resources that the untrained or volunteer did not possess. The day is near, observed Frederic Almy of the Charity Organization Society of Buffalo, "when social workers like doctors will have to pass an examination before they are allowed to practice upon the lives of the poor." [44] Increasingly after 1900, one caseworker combined the roles of agent and visitor, which meant that the volunteer performed no distinctive function superior to that of the paid worker. Training rather than function now measured the difference between paid and volunteer work, and the purpose of training was to develop skill in differential diagnosis. This became the critical point of comparison between the philanthropy of the nineteenth and twentieth centuries.

The ideal of differential casework affected the attitude of family social workers toward relief, the old bugaboo of the charity organization societies. Many family social workers wished to scrap not only generalizations about worthy and unworthy poor but also those about the inherently pauperizing tendency of relief as well. Relief could be a useful tool in treatment, "as efficient an agent in the removal of certain forms of dependency as the substitutes which have been recommended in its place." There were "specific forms of poverty in which material relief, and material relief alone" could help.[45] Money could "be made quite as spiritual in its effects as the alms of good advice." "Constructive relief" was "one of the new slogans of charity."[46] Edward T. Devine summarized the new attitude when he described relief as society's obligation to those "unable to maintain the standard of living which is accepted by the community as normal."[47] Relief, in this sense, represented the difference between a family's income and the amount the agency or social worker thought necessary for a family to satisfy its basic needs.

The concept of differential casework affected attitudes toward several categories of dependents. The charity organization societies had regarded the tramp and vagrant as the quintessence of social irresponsibility and moral turpitude. Laziness and work were the standard diagnosis and treatment. Family social workers in the twentieth century realized that the personal and social roots of pauperism were complex and that no generalization could be offered without careful study of the vagrant, for even in this group the individuals presented striking contrasts in "matters of physical and mental health, of training, temperament, and moral standards."[48] Differential casework was even more imperative in handling deserters and their families. Although the charity organization societies had been confident that "some indulgent habit is at the bottom of most desertion," family social workers in the twentieth century viewed desertion as a complex social problem that required skill and delicacy in treatment.[49] There was "no one cause or group of causes underlying breakdowns in family morale." Desertion was a "symptom of some more deeply seated trouble in the family structure." Each case had to be studied individually and, if humanly possible, any resort to court action avoided. The charity organization societies had been too quick to demand "wherever a desertion law existed, that the deserted wife go at once to court and institute proceedings against her husband," steps which destroyed any possibility of reconciliation.[50]

The diagnostic clues contributed by medical, school, and psychiatric social work not only helped shift the emphasis in charity organization from moral supervision to the accumulation of comprehensive social data, but also refined the differential casework evident in child welfare before 1900. Always alert to psychiatric and medical developments which might assist its staff in understanding the personality and special problems of dependent children, an agency like the Boston Children's Aid Society personified progressive casework ideals and practice in the early twentieth century.[51]

The Society urged for each child a "careful recognition of moral, temperamental, personal considerations as well as those relating to environment." [52] Differentiation was indispensable in the case of foster care; not every family could satisfy the requirements of every child. The Society condemned false economies which ignored the child's special problems and handicaps—such as placing several unrelated children with the same family or placing one in a free foster home which could not satisfy its "real needs." A good society would not transfer children from home to home because families were not "selected and used with discrimination" in the first place, and would not overload the caseworker with more children than she could learn to know intimately. The children's aid society not only had to consider the "exact physical and mental condition of each child in care," but had to keep track of his relation with his foster parents, who also needed training and supervision. Although one of the most successful practitioners of differential foster care, the Boston Children's Aid Society nonetheless warned against it as a panacea, for some children presented unique personal or disciplinary problems which foster parents could not handle.[53]

The Society's high regard for casework skill evolved directly from its emphasis upon differential treatment, and it urged contributors to "consider the maintenance of a high standard of service essential, even if such means a definite limiting of work."[54] Not quantity, but quality counted, and the Society tried to restrict each worker to forty or forty-five cases. Natural endowments alone could not insure the kind of skilled professional service it demanded. The worker had to be trained, in the "professional social-work schools," if possible, or by the Society, which developed a two-year program designed to transmit that "understanding, proper interpretation and treatment of individuals in need which is the task of the trained social worker."[55] The Society viewed with alarm the Home Service sections of the Red Cross, established in 1917 to care for families of servicemen, because the new horde of volunteers threatened to destroy the high standards built over the years. At best, the volunteers were fitted for only "the most carefully supervised work." "All that we count as precious in the way of good standards of case work will be very quickly scrapped if large responsibilities for inquiry and treatment are to be speedily placed on the shoulders of those who have not been trained to act with balanced hearts and minds and who are not most carefully directed."[56]

Dr. Cabot had marveled at the ability of agents of the Boston Children's Aid Society to exploit any community resource which might benefit the child. In keeping with this tradition, the Society joined forces with Drs. Healy and Bronner who had come from Chicago in 1917 to head the Judge Baker Foundation. With the help of these psychologists, the Society believed that "really scientific principles of conduct diagnosis and treatment are at last being worked out." [57] Healy had previously directed the Psychopathic Institute in Chicago, organized in 1909 to supplement the work of the Chicago Juvenile Court. Founded in 1899, the Court was the first to combine probation, separate hearings, and a special judge in the legal treatment of youthful offenders. Healy's work in Chicago and Boston, involving the careful mental and physical study of each child referred from the Court, along with the preparation of detailed family and social histories, greatly influenced children's and family casework. Mary Richmond singled out the combination of Juvenile Court and Psychopathic Institute (along with charity organization and medical social work) as decisive factors in the evolution of casework. No single figure made a greater contribution to social work theory than Miss Richmond, and what she extracted from juvenile court work and the others was a theory of differential casework. This concept is central to any understanding of her relentless effort to refine casework techniques and establish standards which "imperfect now, are being advanced to a point where they can be called professional." [58]

Like many others of her generation, Miss Richmond entered social work in an offhand manner. She had been a clerk in a publishing house, a bookkeeper in a stationery store, and a hotel office assistant before, in answer to a newspaper advertisement, she became assistant treasurer of the Baltimore Charity Organization Society in 1889.[59] Two years later she was promoted to general secretary, a post she held until 1900 when she left to direct the fortunes of the Philadelphia Charity Organization Society. Although Miss Richmond had remarked, somewhat naïvely, in 1890 that "only two things are necessary in order to do good work amongst the poor; one is much good will, and the other is a little tact," she exhibited interest in training programs almost from the start.[60] She launched a series of "educational conferences" for Baltimore friendly visitors in 1893, hoping to improve their work through systematic analysis of case histories. In 1897, in a paper read before the National Conference of Charities and Correction, she called for the establishment of a training school, and in 1905 she became editor of the Field Department of *Charities and the Commons*, formed by several societies to extend charity organization to new cities and encourage an exchange of case records, publicity, and publications.

In 1909, when the Russell Sage Foundation established the Charity Organization Department to take over the work of the Field Department, Mary Richmond left Philadelphia to become its director. Until her death in 1928 she devoted herself and the resources of the Russell Sage Foundation to raising standards of casework practice. One device she used was the publication of case histories in the Departmental *Bulletin* from 1911 to 1915. These were sent to agencies and schools of social work as teaching guides, and Miss Richmond, ever anxious to stimulate interest in standards, requested comments and criticisms from workers and staff conferences. Beginning in 1910, she sponsored an annual "Charity Organization Institute," which brought together each summer in New York City twenty to twenty-five practicing social workers. Through seminars and special committee projects, the Institute provided an opportunity to trade information and improve skills. Beginning in 1915, Miss Richmond headed a similar project—the "Supervisors' Conference"—for assistant secretaries and casework supervisors.

Social Diagnosis

In two influential books she summarized her experience and philosophy. The master idea behind both *Social Diagnosis* (1917) and *What is Social Case Work?* (1922) was differential casework as the foundation of social work skill and technique. The earlier book was a technical treatise, in which the author tried to formulate the common elements of casework whatever the institutional or agency setting. She interpreted social diagnosis as "the attempt to make as exact a definition as possible of the situation and personality of a human being in some social need—of his situation and personality, that is, in relation to the other human beings upon whom he in any way depends or who depend upon him, and in relation to the social institutions of his community." [61] The social worker's unique skill—in contrast to the physician, minister, lawyer, teacher, friend, neighbor, or ordinary layman—involved her ability to base treatment upon the expert collection and interpretation of social evidence. Social evidence she defined as "consisting of any and all facts as to personal or family history which, taken together, indicate the nature of a given client's difficulties and the means to their solution." In minute detail Miss Richmond analyzed the many potential sources: client, family circle, relatives, medical record, school, employer, printed documents, neighbors, and social agencies. Following her investigation and accumulation of social evidence, the social worker would subject it to a "critical examination and comparison" and from this devise an "interpretation and the definition of the social difficulty." [62]

Miss Richmond revolted against any dualism which separated mind from body, man's spiritual or social needs from his material ones. Instead, she substituted for the categories of the nineteenth century a "theory of the wider self" which interpreted man as the "sum of his social relationships." Distinguishing between individuality and personality, she argued that the former, the biological inheritance, did not change and could not be influenced by the social worker. Personality embraced individuality and "social heritage and environment," which could be modified. Casework consisted of *"those processes which develop personality through adjustments consciously effected, individual by individual, between men and their social environment."* [63] Four processes constituted the marrow of casework technique: insight into individuality, insight into the social environment, "direct action of mind upon mind," and "indirect action through the social environment." [64] None were unique to social casework, but their skilled use in combination marked, presumably, the emergence of a genuine professional technique.

Since each person was the sum of his individuality and social heritage, the guiding principle of casework was to treat unequal things unequally. Such "differential social treatment" demanded "special social skill," whatever the institutional setting: school, workshop, hospital, court, or mental clinic. Skilled, differential casework, emphasizing client participation, eliminated once and for all the patronizing overtones associated with philanthropy in the past. An "administrative process which does different things for and with different people" and which included client participation as a vital part of the process was truly democratic. Social workers had learned the futility of the nineteenth-century tendency to do things to and for people. Human beings were not passive animals, devoid of will and purpose. The best casework enlisted the client's help.

Functional specialization had stimulated the quest for professional skills among all categories of social workers, but no one was sure exactly how the specialties combined to form a profession. In *Social Diagnosis* and *What is Social Case Work?* Mary Richmond attempted to explain the unity of social work despite practice in a variety of institution or agency settings. It applied to problems of human maladjustment a differential casework, based upon the accumulation and interpretation of social evidence. Social evidence was a unique form of insight into the human personality, different from that of the psychiatrist, psychologist, or any other group concerned with human relations and added a "new power in the world." [65]

*

One of the founders of the Boston Associated Charities observed in 1915 that "philanthropy is becoming a business and a profession." Social agencies had begun to "shut away the layman from any active connection with their function," crushing him beneath a "magnificent and thoroughly perfected machine." [66] The charity organization societies in the nineteenth century had inaugurated a new era in philanthropy when they defined benevolence as intelligent, efficient service meant to restore the poor to self-sufficiency, and not an opportunity for the rich and well-born to store up credits in heaven or to exercise their altruistic instinct. Yet they had not doubted that scientific philanthropy could be reconciled with voluntarism. As questions of skill and technique influenced the thinking of social workers after 1900 the status of volunteers became insecure and ambiguous, although they continued to exercise important responsibilities. The value of voluntary service was seriously questioned in a period of functional specialization and presumptions of expertise.

Despite the efforts of Mary Richmond, Zilpha Smith, and others of an older generation to strike a balance between paid and volunteer service, younger social workers were shedding allegiance to the principle of widespread lay participation. Charles R. Henderson of the University of Chicago objected to those "young and inexperienced" salaried agents who underestimated the "value of the judgment of men and women who have learned much of human nature by contact with the world, even if they have not read books and heard lectures on 'scientific charity,'" and Mary Richmond criticized a "certain opinionated and self-righteous attitude in some of the trained social workers," who viewed themselves as a "complete and satisfactory substitute for the volunteer." [67] The heritage of philanthropy clashed with the desire of the paid worker to insure efficient agency service and acceptance of her claims to leadership; she was the trained social technician upon whom an urban-industrial society depended for guidance in the application of science to problems of social control. Even though Edward T. Devine, general secretary of the New York Charity Organization Society, maintained that the friendly visitor should not be crowded out of social work, he also argued that not everyone was suited to charity work, and that "good motives" did not always coincide with the "interests of humanity." A "picked band of a hundred devoted, trained and capable workers, especially adapted to the task in hand, will not only accomplish more than a thousand untrained, unassorted volunteers, but they may actually do more to develop the genuinely spontaneous charitable tendencies of the whole population." [68] Devine did not rush to Mary Richmond's defense when his old mentor, Simon Patten, sharply criticized her idealization of volunteer personal service. [69]

The devaluation did not take the form of outright rejection because of the long tradition of voluntarism in American philanthropy and because professional social workers needed the power, influence, and financial support of volunteers. In Boston, for example, many volunteers who served as directors, trustees, members of supervisory or advisory boards, and even found time for friendly visiting, came from a single social group. "A gathering of the clans at tea time, lunch, or dinner,"—Lees, Cabots, Jacksons, Lowells, Putnams, Higginsons—"could resolve itself into a council of social agencies." [70] Social work needed such links to the community power structure. The problem was never how to eliminate volunteers but how to define their task in a way that satisfied the professional ego. In practice, this implied restrictions upon their administrative and treatment responsibilities, and a reversal of agency or institutional leadership roles.

The charity organization societies in the nineteenth century had considered the paid worker, literally, as the agent of the friendly visitor and of the volunteers on administrative or district committees. She was viewed essentially as an investigator and adviser to volunteers.[71] Her success was measured in part by her ability to stimulate volunteer service. As interest in professional skills developed after 1900, the paid worker considered herself a creative practitioner rather than the servant of her volunteers. Her expertise neutralized any superior social status of agency volunteers.

Traditionally viewed as a duty of the citizen in a democratic society, voluntarism was becoming instead a privilege granted by philanthropic agencies to those who accepted their discipline. The volunteer had to realize that "the supervisor, the trained worker, makes her work her main objective, not a mere side issue, and therefore has a moral right to make certain demands on the volunteer." The latter had "no conceivable right to indulge her own idiosyncrasies at the expense of the work."[72] Ida Cannon demanded "promptness and regularity" from volunteers as well as paid workers, and insisted that the "supervision of volunteers should be painstaking."[73] The New York Charity Organization Society in 1919 established a committee to examine the volunteer problem. This committee agreed that, although friendly visiting had its values, it should not become a cloak concealing a "type of case work that is not in line with modern development." It urged a volunteer service which "accepts training and gives adequate and regular amounts of time." As a result of the committee's report, the Society appointed a secretary to recruit and train volunteers. They were placed on a one-month probation and, if accepted, took a three-month course followed by an examination and a supervisor's report on field work. Even if a volunteer satisfied the academic requirements, she was barred from casework if she had performed poorly in the field. Out of sixty-six volunteers who took the course during the first year only twenty-six survived and received the Society's certificate.[74] Increasingly the professional welcomed the volunteer only to the degree that she submitted to agency supervision and accepted a supporting role under the paid worker's leadership.

*

Social work's emergence as a profession resulted not only in a devaluation of voluntarism but in a chronic tension between public and private welfare. In minimizing the desirability of relief in favor of character rehabilitation and close personal supervision of the poor, the charity organization movement discredited public assistance. Charity organization leaders convinced themselves and countless Americans that public outdoor assistance was incompatible with efficient, scientific philanthropy because it pauperized the recipients. Unaccompanied by satisfactory investigation and rehabilitation procedures and accepted by the poor as a right, public relief disrupted the social and economic order by reducing all incentive to work.

This legacy of suspicion provided one explanation for the philanthropic division of labor which prevailed until the Great Depression. Only a small percentage of state and local welfare budgets was channeled into outdoor relief in contrast to institutional care. In 1915 public funds covered only 20 to 25 percent of all expenditures for outdoor assistance. Despite the expansion of state assistance programs for special categories of dependents (children and the blind and aged), in the first three decades of the twentieth century, as late as

1929 all but 3 percent of state welfare budgets was applied to institutional care.[75] Relief remained a significant responsibility of private agencies until the 1930's, when social security and vast public assistance expenditures on all levels of government shifted the balance.

Logically, the professional aspirations of social workers should have encouraged efforts to discard the relief function, associated as it was with the Lady-Bountiful and religiously inspired benevolent tradition from which they had rebelled. Its retention testified, in part, to the tenacious belief that public welfare was residual in character, best suited to handle categories of dependents requiring long-term institutional supervision. Public welfare concentrated upon the "unprofessional" tasks of classification, determination of eligibility, and routine surveillance in contrast to social diagnosis.

The values and institutions associated with the professionalization of social work were generated primarily in the private sphere. Individuals connected with public welfare lent their support, but the organized system played a subordinate role in defining the professional norms and creating the supporting institutions. Significant developments occurred in public welfare in the early twentieth century, but they were marginal to professionalization. Leaders of the organized social insurance movement like I. M. Rubinow either were indifferent to professional status or, like Sophie Irene Loeb and Hannah Einstein, were bitterly critical of private philanthropy whose scientific aspirations and objections to public assistance they equated with heartlessness, ignorance, and pretentiousness. On the other hand, progressive public welfare leaders like Gertrude Vaile of Denver and L. A. Halbert of Kansas City imitated the rhetoric of private philanthropy in an effort to enhance the prestige of public assistance. They maintained that public welfare could be as efficient and adept at differential casework as private agencies claimed to be. Their position was defensive and their program shaped in the private image. "I realize," Miss Vaile conceded, "that the private charities have been justified in the distrust of public relief." Explaining that Denver was working hard to "change the old archaic county agent office for doles of coal and groceries into a real department of social service along the lines of the charity organization society," she urged the private charities "not to stand aloof from the public charities in distrust or indifference but to stay with them." [76]

In retrospect, it would seem that the contempt, or at least suspicion, of government welfare associated with the emergence of social work as a profession proved unfortunate for all concerned. The vast expansion of public assistance functions and expenditures beginning in the 1930's was superimposed upon a long tradition of disdain totally incongruous with the political and economic power assumed by the public welfare sector.

Chapter III

Mind and Matter:
Psychiatry in Social Work

A MAJOR source of irritation to social workers anxious to elevate their professional status consisted of those "many popular misunderstandings of social work, which identify it with nursing, with mental testing, with occupational therapy, with neighborliness." [1] Psychiatry in the early twentieth century played a significant role in strengthening the social worker's conviction that she offered a distinct and valuable service which required specialized skill and training. Important links were forged between psychiatry and social work before the Freudian penetration of the 1920's. Toward the end of the nineteenth century a new kind of psychiatry, receptive to social service, launched a new casework specialty and a quest for professional function and skill in new institutional settings.

Stressing the probability of a multiple causation in delinquency and dependency and the need for comprehensive physical, mental, psychometric, and social examination of deviant individuals, psychiatry paralleled social work in an evolution toward differential casework. It developed what social workers regarded as comparatively sophisticated methods, providing them with an important working model and standard of comparison. Psychiatry was also evolving a dynamic interpretation of human behavior comparable to the efforts of social workers to understand the individual as a product of his environment rather than as an independent moral agent who diverged from or adhered to fixed moral norms. Psychiatry and social work in the early twentieth century shared a common interest in scientific understanding and control of behavior through casework practiced by a professional, technical elite.

Just as Richard Cabot, a physician, had taken the initiative in promoting medical social work, so psychiatrists in rebellion against prevailing institutional methods of care for the mentally ill labored to integrate therapy with environment. A social psychiatry had emerged, identified with such men as Adolf Meyer, August Hoch, C. Macfie Campbell, William A. White, Thomas W. Salmon, Elmer E. Southard, James J. Putnam, and William Healy. In conjunction with the organized mental hygiene movement, it substituted a clinical, empirical approach to mental illness for the institutional isolation and custodianship of the latter nineteenth century. Adolf Meyer, one of the most influential spokesmen for social psychiatry, described the contrast. "Important things had happened in the years that immediately preceded and followed the opening of the twentieth century. In place of the passive descriptive psychiatry of the older tradition, limited to 'insanity' and 'asylums,' and the mainly prognostic-dogmatic, diagnostic-nosological newer psychiatry of Kraepelin, concerned with classification rather than therapy, a biological, dynamic psychiatry which included the whole of human nature had arisen to pledge itself to research and teaching, based on an interest in daily work with patients." [2]

Psychiatry in the last quarter of the nineteenth century had progressed little beyond institutions for the insane, despite the emphasis upon a moral or milieu therapy in the earlier part of the century. Organic theories and therapies were stimulated by an increase in neurological knowledge and the conviction that physical origins could be discovered for mental activity. The crowding of hospitals with immigrants and others encouraged the substitution of minimal custodial care for the "moral treatment" of the past. In remote, isolated asylums, superintendents and physicians guarded their wards and performed autopsies to discover the brain lesions or other organic defects which they assumed caused mental illness. Preoccupied with the physiological roots of insanity, they practiced little therapy with the living patients. Treatment usually consisted of the administration of such drugs as hyoscine, paraldehyde, morphine and chloral, or hydro- and electrotherapy. Few distinctions were made between the organic and functional disorders, such as hysteria and neurasthenia. The latter became a "garbage can of mental medicine," discrediting the patient as a malingerer subject to treatment by placebo.[3] Psychiatrists had to train themselves because medical schools generally ignored mental disease. Benjamin Rush's *Medical Inquiries*, first published in 1812, remained the only systematic treatment of the subject until 1883 when William A. Hammond and E. L. Spitzka, both neurologists, published new texts. Research "was confined almost exclusively to the anatomy and pathology of the nervous system," and the chief instruments of psychiatric research were the microscope and sectioning knife.[4] Institutional psychiatrists devoted much attention to static classification schemes; and even those were crude until Meyer and others introduced Emil Kraepelin's descriptive psychiatry in the 1890's. Basing his nosology upon clinical rather than logical views and building upon Pinel's broad categories of mania, melancholia, and dementia, Kraepelin developed the concept of dementia praecox (schizophrenia) and introduced manic-depressive as a disease group. Kraepelin, moreover, accounted for changing syndromes in mental illness, noting that diverse and varied symptoms appeared in the course of a single case.

Although Kraepelin's descriptive psychiatry was useful,

it did not explain why mental illness originated, how it could be prevented, and how it could be treated or controlled. In the 1890's and afterward, a number of psychiatrists including Adolf Meyer had begun to wrestle with those fundamental questions. Born in Switzerland in 1866, Meyer received his medical degree in 1892 from the University of Zurich. A specialist in neurology, he saw no future in Switzerland and decided to come to America, where he planned to combine practice with research in comparative and clinical neurology. After a short stay in Chicago, he accepted the position of pathologist at the state mental hospital at Kankakee, Illinois, where he began "hewing a way to personality-studies, to a scrutiny of life situations and dynamic developments." In 1895 he transferred to the Worcester, Massachusetts State Hospital, where he eventually became clinical director. There he developed methods for compiling comprehensive clinical histories based upon uniform mental and physical examinations of patients. After seven years, Meyer became director of the Pathological Institute of the New York State Hospitals. He transferred the Institute from Manhattan to Ward's Island, the site of the state hospital, and soon organized a clinical department in order to combine the Institute's pathological research with examination of living patients. Always interested in teaching facilities for psychiatry, Meyer gave courses to physicians and internes which included methods for the systematic examination and study of mental patients and techniques in the histopathology of the central nervous system. In 1909, a year after Meyer had succeeded in changing the name of the Pathological Institute to the Psychiatric Institute, he accepted the directorship of the Phipps Psychiatric Clinic in Baltimore.

Although trained as a physician and neurologist, Meyer rejected any extreme organic interpretation of behavior. Yet he did not view mental activity as the product of a "peculiar form of mind stuff"; mind, he insisted, was a *"sufficiently organized living being in action."* Mental activity was best understood in its "full meaning as the adaptation and adjustment of the individual as a whole." [5] The "psychobiology" which Meyer developed focused upon the interaction of the total human organism with concrete life situations. "Man is fundamentally a social being. There are reactions in us which only contacts and relations with other human beings can bring out. We must study men as mutual reagents in personal affections and aversions and their conflicts; in the desires and satisfactions of the simpler appetites for food and personal necessities; in the natural interplay of anticipation and fulfillment of desires and their occasional frustration; in the selection of companionship which works helpfully or otherwise." [6] Psychiatry could not restrict itself to the mental institution or pathological laboratory. It had to reach out into the community, where family and other personal ties shaped man as a social being. The psychiatrist had to understand this pattern of relationships, past and present, and link it with a clinical examination of the patient's physical and mental condition.

For Meyer a basic flaw of nineteenth-century institutional psychiatry had been its isolation. Cloistered behind asylum walls, obsessed with classification and the organic origins of mental disturbance, it lacked a sound clinical and empirical base. It studied brain lesions of dead patients instead of working back to the community where "things have their beginnings." [7] As long as psychiatry ignored the social environment of patients, it could not contribute to the prevention or effective cure of metal illness. "Just as bacteriology studies the water supply and the air and food of communities, schools, and homes," Meyer explained, "so we psycho-pathologists have to study more effectively the atmosphere of the community and must devise safeguards in the localities from which the patients come, and to which they are to return." [8] The Freudian psychiatrist William A. White agreed with Meyer that the individual could not be considered "apart from the environment, and this impossibility is especially to be borne in mind when the individual is considered as a social unit and his reactions are considered from the standpoint of the social level." And like Meyer, White rejected any interpretation of emotions or intellect as self-contained entities. The human being was an "organism, a biological unit," and any mental disorder had to be diagnosed and treated as a malfunction of the total personality.[9]

Psychiatric progress, in Meyer's opinion, depended upon the development of a comprehensive system of psychiatric services in each community, active not only in treating and preventing mental disorder but in education and research. The mental hospital would be the nucleus of any such system, but it had to be socialized like Cabot's general hospital. He envisioned small state hospitals linked to extramural psychiatric services in one or a few manageable districts, instead of grim, inaccessible fortresses located in remote corners of the state. Research and teaching as well as custodial and therapeutic institutions, they had to maintain close contact with the patient's home and social environment. Otherwise, they would lack the facts needed to "reconstruct the patient's life." The success of the socialized mental hospital depended ultimately upon the "organization of social work and home visitation." The physician, Meyer declared, "*must* work as a social force and he has happily learnt to do so with the help of the social service worker." [10]

Central to any scheme for the "hygienic socializing of the community" was the dispensary or clinic, which included on its staff not only physicians but social workers skilled in investigation and in the guidance of patient and family. Closer to the people than the state hospital, the clinic was valuable as a preventive and educational agency. It could assist in training the public to recognize symptoms which, if treated in the mild or incipient stage, could be cured more readily than the severe psychoses. Special mental hygiene associations would serve as useful adjuncts, providing for emergency cases, assuming some responsibility for after-care, and advising both individuals and community agencies on the placement of mental patients. Meyer viewed the public school system as a critical element in any community mental hygiene program. As early as 1895 he had complained that "mental abnormalities and mental diseases in childhood have been little studied so far," and he saw in the school a golden opportunity to detect and treat mental illness.[11]

The systematic, coordinated psychiatric districts which Meyer envisioned did not materialize, but psychiatry after 1900 did break loose from its cramped institutional boundaries.[12] A few state hospitals hired psychiatric social workers as did several of the new psychopathic clinics, and the organized mental hygiene movement which developed after 1909 directed attention to environmental factors in the prevention and treatment of mental illness.

*

Detention wards had been established at Bellevue Hospital in New York in 1879 and in the Philadelphia General Hospital in 1890, but the first psychopathic ward in a general hospital which included treatment along with confinement and observation appeared at Albany Hospital in 1902 (the year Meyer became director of the Pathological Institute). In 1906 the first university psychopathic hospital opened at the University of Michigan, followed a few years later by the Henry Phipps Clinic at Johns Hopkins in Baltimore. The first psychopathic hospital connected with a state mental institution opened at the Boston State Hospital in 1912 and included an out-patient department.[13] The independent clinics—the Juvenile Psychopathic Institute in Chicago (1909), and the Judge

Baker Foundation in Boston (1917)—represented a fourth variety of extramural psychiatry, closely allied with the juvenile courts. The Boston Psychopathic and the Phipps Clinic also participated in child guidance while the Westchester (New York) County Department of Child Welfare established a guidance clinic in 1918.[14]

Many of the clinics and hospitals included a psychiatric social worker among their personnel. The social psychiatrist like Meyer considered her "one of the fundamental and most important factors of progress in psychiatry." Social service was the "agency which reaches into the home and makes it its duty to supervise the conditions outside of the hospital and the activity of the patient in relation with the family and the community." [15] Once again a social work specialty emerged because certain physicians and administrators felt a need to link their institutions with the special environment of patients or clients and insure more effective diagnosis and treatment.

Meyer's wife was among the first psychiatric social workers for about 1904 she began to visit Manhattan State Hospital patients in the wards and at home. The New York State Charities Aid Association launched a more substantial service in 1906 when it formed after-care committees and hired a paid agent. The committees found work for mental patients and performed any other social services which promised to aid in rehabilitation.

A second pioneer experiment occurred at Massachusetts General under the guidance of Dr. James J. Putnam, chief of the Hospital's neurological service. Interested in the problems of psychoneurotic patients, he had supported Cabot's program of medical social service and in 1906 took the initiative in creating a special division of the Social Service Department to deal with mental patients. Putnam hired Edith N. Burleigh as his assistant in 1907. A former mental patient, Miss Burleigh was a trained social worker and acting headworker at

Denison House Settlement. She was joined by Antoinette Cannon, a Bryn Mawr graduate, and Katherine Burrage, a teacher of clay modeling. Putnam raised the money for Miss Burrage's salary and the equipment needed for a clay modeling class, which he viewed hopefully as a method to arouse new interests, powers of concentration, and "social consciousness" among mental patients. Putnam patterned his manual therapy after Grohmann's experiment in a Zurich sanitarium and Dr. Herbert J. Hall's "School of Handcraft" at Marblehead, Massachusetts. The social workers visited patients' homes in order to establish a "friendly relation." Putnam found in this policy a "fresh endorsement . . . of the value of skilled friendly visiting and the careful study of home conditions as a supplement to the physician's work among dispensary patients and as a means of making his directions to them effective." [16]

In both New York and Massachusetts the experimental, privately sponsored social service led eventually to official acceptance in the state hospital system. In New York, the Manhattan and Central Islip state hospitals assumed responsibility in 1911 for the after-care work of the State Charities Aid Association. The association had been anxious to have the work placed on a "professional basis" in order to insure completeness and thoroughness as well as community education in the principles of mental hygiene.[17] In 1913 the state legislature broadened the scope of social service when it authorized each state hospital to establish an out-patient department with a physician and social worker. Psychiatric social work forged ahead in Massachusetts in 1913 when the Danvers and the Boston state hospitals added social workers to their staffs, and the Boston Psychopathic Hospital organized a social service department under Mary Jarrett.

A few additional testing grounds for psychiatric social work had appeared before 1920. The State Charities Aid

Association contributed a social worker to cooperate with Dr. August Hoch at the Cornell Clinic of Psychopathology in New York City, and in upstate New York the Laboratory of Social Hygiene added a social worker to round out its staff of psychiatrist, psychologist, and sociologist. Located at Bedford Hills and directed by Katherine Bement Davis, the Laboratory focused upon problems of delinquency. Outside of New York and Massachusetts, social work began at the Phipps Clinic in 1913 and the State Psychopathic Hospital at the University of Michigan in 1916. Much of the extramural psychiatry and psychiatric social work of this early period was concerned with problems of juvenile crime and delinquency. The undisputed leader in this field was William Healy, and his work at the Juvenile Psychopathic Institute was probably more familiar to social workers than any other practical experiment. Through Healy, in large measure, the principles of social psychiatry entered the mainstream of social work thought.

Born in England in 1869, Healy received his B.A. from Harvard in 1899, and in 1900 his M.D. from Rush in Chicago. After a year as assistant physician at the Wisconsin State Hospital, he became associate professor of nervous and mental disorders at the Chicago Polyclinic, where he served from 1903 to 1916. In his work he encountered many young patients, including choreics, epileptics, and hysterics, whose symptoms included "conduct difficulties." Healy began to sense the futility of punitive measures in home, school, or court and thought a program of research into the causes of delinquency might assist in the "common sense application of scientific knowledge to the treatment of human beings."[18] He expounded his ideas at a conference at Hull House in 1908 called by the Juvenile Protective Association. The conference members included Julia Lathrop and Allen Burns, whose knowledge of proceedings at Chicago's Juvenile Court and boys' division of the municipal court had led them to the conclusion that a mere physical examination explained little and limited the Court's effectiveness. Healy convinced the conference of the importance of research, and with the help of a grant from Ethel S. Dummer set out on a tour of exploration. He found no research clinics and only two places where psychological testing was added to a physical examination—Lightmer Witmer's clinic for retarded children at the University of Pennsylvania which had been established in 1896, and Henry H. Goddard's Research Laboratory at the Vineland, New Jersey, School for the Feeble-minded. He reported his findings to Julia Lathrop, who also consulted William James, Adolf Meyer, and James R. Angell, Professor of Psychology at the University of Chicago. When Mrs. Dummer agreed to finance a research project for five years, Miss Lathrop requested Healy to head the projected Juvenile Psychopathic Institute.[19]

Although Healy "from the first . . . had decided not to be unduly influenced by current theories concerning the essential nature of any proportion of offenders," he did test many of them. One of the most popular was the degeneracy theory identified with Cesare Lombroso. Healy patiently photographed hundreds of heads, measured hundreds of crania, and tracked down other alleged "stigmata of degeneracy." He found the Italian criminologist's theory no more convincing than others which traced all delinquency and crime to bad heredity. Defective traits appeared in the family background of many delinquents, but he found no evidence that criminal traits were directly inherited. Healy considered the evidence for and against numerous other theories: that enlarged or infected tonsils and adenoids caused delinquency or retardation, or that delinquency derived from refractive errors, from peripheral irritations such as impacted teeth, from cigarette smoking, from phimosis, from intracranial pressure. He reached only one solid conclusion: "Collecting data from case after case soon showed us that the whole concept of the causation of delinquency could not possibly be so simple as previous writers had made it out to be. The causative factors, as I termed them, were always multiple. Even the same types of factors played their parts in varying degree in different cases and were interwoven, often in intricate fashion." [20]

A few psychiatrists and psychologists had spent some time at the Institute, as had several juvenile court judges, including Edward F. Waite of Minneapolis, Charles W. Hoffman of Cincinnati, and Harvey H. Baker of Boston. During the first five years, Healy lacked social service personnel although he tried to develop "psychiatric insight" in social workers attached to cooperating agencies and in a few volunteer social workers. In 1914, when Mrs. Dummer's financial support ended, the Institute officially became the Psychopathic Clinic of the Juvenile Court. It received its funds from Cook County and a social worker was assigned from the probation office of the court. Healy undoubtedly exerted his greatest influence upon social workers through his writings, particularly *The Individual Delinquent*. Social workers, Mary Richmond declared, read *The Individual Delinquent, Pathological Lying,* and *Honesty* with "more interest" than any others relating to child study, while the first transcended problems of delinquency and constituted a "text-book for all engaged in the study of human beings." [21] They learned from Healy no simple solution to problems of social deviancy and control, but the importance of multi-causal, differential diagnosis as the foundation of scientific casework. Social workers had to discard preconceived theories about behavior and investigate each case empirically and objectively, considering the relevant mental, physical, and social facts.

*

The close relationship between psychiatry and criminology in the early twentieth century was paralleled by developments in the field of mental defect. Widespread public interest in control of the feeble-minded had important consequences for social work. The alarm over the menace of the mental defective alerted social workers to the possibility that a client's behavior might reflect not an obstinate reluctance to accept good advice or an innate moral perversity, but a subnormal mentality. The mental test became a significant weapon in the caseworker's scientific arsenal. "It seems hard to believe," Healy recalled, "that when we started our clinic there were no standardized mental tests for even the most general classifications." [22] The development of such tests received considerable attention from Healy and his staff at the Psychopathic Institute, and they originated a number designed to measure reasoning ability.

The feeble-minded had not always been viewed with fear and alarm. Until the last quarter of the nineteenth century, teachers like Samuel G. Howe and Hervey B. Wilbur were optimistic about their ability to educate mental defectives and help them achieve some measure of self-sufficiency. Superintendent of the first training school in America for mental defectives, which opened in South Boston in 1848, Howe applied the physiological method of instruction developed by Edouard Seguin. A pupil of Jean Itard, Seguin believed that the feeble-minded could be educated through a system of sensorimotor training, and his system exerted considerable influence in America and Europe.[23] By 1889 the relative failure in educating the feeble-minded in both public and private institutions resulted in a general abandonment of the idea. The mentally defective, like the insane, were tucked away in custodial institutions and forgotten.

Then in the early twentieth century the development of psychological testing, the resurrection of the Mendelian laws of inheritance and August Weismann's discovery that acquired traits were not transmissible, abruptly ended their oblivion. Scientists and laymen came to fear that the "best material out of which to make criminals, and perhaps the material from which they are most frequently made, is feeble-mindedness." Social workers, wrestling with problems of dependency, were informed that the feeble-minded constituted an "undue proportion" of every category of dependency. Large numbers of defectives could be found "in the school, in our juvenile courts, in our almshouses, in our insane hospitals, in our reform schools, in our homes for cripples, in our asylums for the blind." They multiplied in "brutal ratio" in contrast to better stock, and drowned society in a wave of prostitutes, alcoholics, paupers, criminals, and other undesirables.[24]

The alarm with which Americans viewed the feeble-minded resulted in part from an unqualified acceptance of the psychological test as a measure of mental deficiency. Simon and Benet had devised and published in 1905 a series of objective tests, followed in 1908 by a more refined set graded by age. Healy and Henry H. Goddard, director of the Research Laboratory at the Training School for the Feeble-minded, Vineland, New Jersey, were among the first to use them. Following a trip to Europe in 1908, Goddard published accounts of the tests; he found a close correlation between the mental age of Vineland inmates revealed by the tests and grading based upon institutional observation. He formulated a classification scheme, presented in 1910 before the American Association for the Study of the Feeble-minded, which included the idiot (mental age up to two years); the imbecile (three to seven years); and the moron (eight to twelve years).

With Goddard's encouragement, psychologists and others applied the tests outside of institutions for the feeble-minded, in schools, prisons, and almshouses. It was distressing to find, according to the tests, that many children considered slow learners were really morons, and that many dependents, delinquents, and criminals were mentally retarded. One typical study of feeble-minded women concluded that "illegitimacy, attempted murder, theft, forgery, arson, prostitution, drunkenness, destitution and disease are salient features of the social careers of these incompetents." The climax of the rage for mental testing occurred during World War I when statistics demonstrated that 47.3 percent of white men drafted were "feeble-minded." [25] This astounding figure suggested that something was wrong with the tests or their interpretation, and that mental age revealed by a psychological test alone was not an index of mental competence. Before the reaction came in the 1920's many Americans were convinced that feeble-mindedness prevailed among the general population far more than had ever been suspected, and that mental deficiency accounted for an enormous percentage of crime and other forms of social deviation.

Americans would have been more confident of their ability to control the feeble-minded were it not for the scientific pessimism arising from the new eugenics movement. Not only were the mentally deficient more prevalent than anyone had realized, but they bred prolifically and transmitted their traits to their offspring. Gregor Mendel's laws of heredity had been resurrected around 1900 by Hugo de Vries and two other European biologists. At the same time a eugenics movement was beginning in England under the leadership of Sir Francis Galton, a scientist and statistician who first devised the term.[26] As interest spread both in Britain and the United States, scientists and laymen considered the possibility of a program of negative eugenics, or repression of defective stock, as a means of control.

In the decade after 1908 numerous studies, reflecting the eugenic interpretation of mental deficiency, traced the pedigree of degenerate stock. Goddard's *Kallikak Family* was

69

among the most influential and representative of these works, and revealed the despair associated with the problem of mental defect. Working on the assumption that the "human family shows varying stocks or strains that are as marked and that breed as true as anything in plant or animal life," Goddard traced the progeny of Martin Kallikak, a Revolutionary War soldier. He had seduced a feeble-minded girl, whose illegitimate son, Martin Kallikak, Jr., became the fountainhead of 480 descendants. Goddard claimed definitely that only 46 of these were normal, while 143 were feeble-minded; the rest were unknown or doubtful. He warned, ominously, "there are Kallikak families all about us," who multiply at double the rate of the normal population. Recognition of this fact was the key to many social problems. No amount of reform would eliminate urban slums as long as mental defectives lived and bred in them, for "mentally defective people . . . can never be taught to live otherwise than as they have been living." [27]

Fear of the feeble-minded and exaggeration of the problem in social control which they posed resulted in a campaign for sterilization laws. Like child labor or housing reform, the biological eradication of the feeble-minded was part of the Progressive social reform program. In 1907 Indiana became the first state to enact a sterilization measure, and by 1926, twenty-three others had passed such laws. Goddard did not think they really met the challenge, for they applied only to inmates of institutions. Somehow, he insisted, "we shall have to come to the point of authorizing a commission of physicians to carry out this practice, wherever, in their judgment, it is advisable." [28]

Social workers and social-minded physicians like Cabot and Putnam soon realized the implications of mental defect for casework. Cabot suggested that "probably many of the prostitute class are feeble-minded and *should*, therefore, be taken out of the community and put under permanent custodial care." Dr. Putnam, referring to the "remarkable family histories and family trees worked out by Dr. H. H. Goddard," noted that there were "degrees of mental and moral irresponsibility which though apparently slight are really far more common and far more serious in their results than we used to believe, both for the individual and the community." [29] The Boston Children's Aid Society, wrestling with the problem of unmarried mothers, saw one answer in the "proper institutional restraint" of feeble-minded girls and women. The community paid an enormous sum each year, the Society complained, "in allowing low-grade defective girls and women to bring into the world equally defective children." [30] Edward T. Devine, of the New York Charity Organization Society, lauded the eugenics program as one "with which social workers may sympathize and in which they should clearly cooperate." He envisioned a reduction of the "total social burden" if the community prevented the "feeble-minded, the insane, the incorrigibly criminal, and the hopelessly ineffective" from breeding. [31] Mary Richmond looked to the school for "evidence" which would "play an important part in the discovery and segregation of defectives." The community had to comprehend the danger involved in leaving a child with "no moral sense" in the midst of normal children. [32]

Like social psychiatry, concern over the problem of mental defect helped alert social workers to the possibility that some form of mental disturbance, rather than moral perversity, lay at the root of a client's difficulties. The drive to expose and repress the feeble-minded did not, however, seriously undermine the social worker's faith in the possibilities of personal and social regeneration through scientific casework. Even though the mentally defective were larger in numbers and considered a greater social menace than in the past, they constituted a special category of dependents, distinct from the vast majority who could benefit from the skilled ministrations of the caseworker. For the feeble-minded alone, psychiatrists and social workers reserved a pessimistic, biological determinism.

*

The National Committee for Mental Hygiene included institutions for the feeble-minded among its surveys and investigations and established a Division on Mental Deficiency in 1917. Its primary concern, however, was the preservation of mental health and the establishment of adequate facilities for care of the mentally ill. It devoted its resources to elevating institutional standards, expanding extramural psychiatric services, and developing programs of community enlightenment. Through its educational and publicity efforts and interest in environmental conditions which affected mental health the Committee helped link psychiatry not only to social work but to the broader Progressive reform movement. With their interest in the "total organism," social psychiatrists considered a wholesome physical and social environment as a key to mental hygiene, and found themselves committed to the improvement of living and working conditions.[33] Abraham Myerson spoke of the new alliance between psychiatry and fields like "criminology, social hygiene, the employment phase of economics, the distribution of charity and social relief."[34] What good was it if a patient improved under the influence of the simplified, but artificial, environment of the hospital, and then returned to "conditions more or less the same as those under which he broke down before?"[35]

The National Committee for Mental Hygiene had been founded in 1909 by Clifford W. Beers, a former mental patient. A Yale graduate in 1897, Beers had been severely shaken by his brother's epileptic seizure three years earlier, and feared that his own breakdown was only a matter of time. His distress increased after the brother died in 1900, and, following an attack of grippe which intensified his depression, Beers jumped out of a window in a vain attempt at suicide. He then experienced paranoic delusions, arising in part from guilt feelings over the abortive suicide, and viewed everyone as an actor in a drama leading inexorably to his own destruction. Unable to cope with him, Beers' family placed him first in a private sanatorium run for profit, then in a private non-profit institution, and finally in a state hospital. In all three places he found the physicians and attendants ignorant at best, cruel at worst.[36] Even before his release from the state hospital in September 1903, he had determined to arouse the conscience of the world, a decision strengthened by a reading of Hugo's *Les Misérables*.

In 1905 Beers began work on a book outlining his experiences as a mental patient. William James, who read the manuscript, was deeply impressed by the author's sincerity and determination, but Beers also wanted the endorsement of a practicing psychiatrist familiar with state hospital conditions. Dr. Stewart Paton recommended Adolf Meyer to whom Beers sent the manuscript along with a statement of his plans for reform. Meyer was eager to assist, for he had long "wished that some organized auxiliary movement for better care and treatment for the insane and for the prevention of mental disorders might be inaugurated in this country."[37] Assured of a respectable sponsorship, Beers published his classic *A Mind That Found Itself* in March 1908, and launched the Connecticut Society for Mental Hygiene in May. The book's favorable reception led to the establishment of the National Committee in February 1909.

Lack of funds restricted the work during the first three years, but in 1912 a gift from Henry Phipps, patron of the Johns Hopkins psychiatric clinic, enabled Beers to expand its operations and influence. The Committee acquired Dr. Thomas W. Salmon as its medical director. He was an experienced psychiatrist who had been affiliated with the United States Public Health Service as an examiner of immigrants and had worked in state hospitals. With Salmon's help, the Committee assumed undisputed leadership of the organized crusade for mental hygiene and improved institutional care of the insane. Like many other social reform movements of the Progressive era—child labor, social insurance, minimum wage, workmen's compensation, housing, public health, social hygiene, or factory legislation—the National Committee poured great energy into a campaign for public education.[38] The public had to understand that rational, scientific social action could nurture mental health, and that trained physicians, social workers, and other experts could show the way. Then, as Healy explained, "we may look forward with complete assurance to a morrow when a vastly greater scientific spirit shall invade social effort."[39]

Complete and accurate information on existing conditions was the foundation for any campaign of public enlightenment or legislative reform. The Committee compiled a summary of laws relating to the commitment and care of the insane, as well as a directory of all institutions accommodating the mentally disturbed, feeble-minded, epileptic, and alcoholic. It gathered data on facilities for psychiatric instruction and on psychiatric clinics. After surveying methods of care and treatment of the insane, it exposed "incredible practices." "Mentally sick men and women were often sent to almshouses to be confined in iron cages in damp, gloomy quarters, abandoned to filth and misery. Strait jackets and other forms of mechanical restraint were the rule rather than the exception, and the care of patients usually was relegated to men and women of no professional training or ability."[40] The National Committee for Mental Hygiene sponsored several studies designed to uncover the prevalence of mental abnormality among selected groups or within a selected area. Bernard Glueck examined 608 consecutive admissions to Sing Sing Prison and concluded that about 30 percent were mentally defective. In 1916 the Committee supervised a study of mental disease in Nassau County, Long Island, and, with the help of a Rockefeller Foundation grant, began a study of the mental factors in delinquency at the Children's Court in New York City. Two years later, at the request of the New York City Board of Education, the Committee examined the mental problems of children in a truant or probationary school.

The facts compiled through its surveys and investigations served as the basis for the Committee's educational efforts. It sponsored lectures, prepared numerous magazine articles, and distributed pamphlets to physicians, nurses, relatives of mental patients, and others. Under Dr. Salmon's direction, in 1912 it prepared a mental hygiene exhibit for the Fifteenth International Congress on Hygiene and Demography, held in Washington, D.C. Including material on the "incidence, cost and social significance of mental disease and mental deficiency and the fields of preventive effort," the exhibit was later displayed in other cities. Supplementing the National Committee's work and testifying to the growing popularity of mental hygiene among physicians and laymen, were various state divisions. By 1918 seventeen state committees for mental hygiene existed, and another had organized in the District of Columbia.

The prestige of the National Committee for Mental Hygiene increased enormously during World War I when it played a central role in the establishment of psychiatric services for members of the armed forces. Following a trip to Europe by Dr. Salmon in 1917 to study the effect of "war neuroses," the Committee worked out plans to eliminate the mentally unfit before induction, to treat those who developed mental disorder while in service, and to rehabilitate them after release. With the Committee's assistance, a Division of Psychiatry, Neurology and Psychology was created and staffed within the Army Medical Corps, and an elaborate training and hospital program organized.[41] Dr. Salmon, who served as Senior Consultant in Neuro-Psychiatry to the American Expeditionary Forces, supervised the establishment of psychiatric wards in military hospitals in Europe.

After the war, the Committee continued its efforts to secure psychiatric care for servicemen. It dispatched Dr. Douglas Thom to various cities to gather information for the federal government, and to secure cooperation between the Red Cross and the federal and local agencies responsible for psychiatric treatment. The Committee also appointed an agent to assist communities in obtaining trained psychiatric social workers. A number of psychiatric social workers served under the auspices of the Red Cross, which had been designated by the United States Public Health Service and Bureau of War Risk Insurance to organize medical social service in hospitals and district offices.[42] By 1921 about eight Red Cross chapters, located in such cities as Cleveland, Cincinnati, Louisville, Detroit, and Chicago, had established some form of psychiatric social work. The Red Cross appointed psychiatrists to several administrative divisions responsible for ex-serviceman relief.[43] World War I not only enhanced the prestige and hastened the acceptance of psychiatry in America by demonstrating its value in a period of national emergency, but brightened the prospects for psychiatric social work as well.

*

Social psychiatry represented a form of casework rooted in an understanding of the patient's social environment in addition to his mental and physical condition. The patient had to be studied "not merely as an individual composed of a number of organs each of which is liable to structural disease or damage but still more as a unit of a social organization in which he must so behave as not to menace his relation with, and the welfare of, the group of which he is a member." [44] Social work and psychiatry shared the common goal of understanding and control based upon a differential diagnosis, upon an accurate and comprehensive insight into the individual patient's needs, and treatment adapted to this insight. Just as the social worker struggled to substitute a differential casework for the standardized, moralistic casework inherited from the nineteenth century, the psychiatrist rebelled against a simple organic-pathological interpretation of mental disorder, in which classification took the place of empirical, scientific analysis. "Psychiatric experience," Meyer complained, had "suffered from veritable debauches in unwarranted systematization." Modern psychiatry had no use for the "routinist" satisfied with a "few diagnostic signs." [45] Healy in *The Individual Delinquent* warned against the "predictable inadequacy of social measures built upon statistics and theories which neglect the fundamental fact of the complexity of causation, determinable through study of the individual case." [46]

Psychiatry and social work were both beginning to account for behavior in functional-historical terms. White explained that each "psychic event" had a history. Behavior was dynamic, a ceaseless effort to adapt to the pressures and tensions of the environment. [47] Antisocial behavior did not necessarily signify moral perversity, but the symptomatic expression of an unresolved mental conflict or unsatisfied inner need. The functional interpretation of behavior had important implications for casework, for it helped reshape the social worker's attitude toward dependency and delinquency. Casework could not be professional if moralistic prejudices obstructed "scientific conceptions of the nature of social maladjustment." [48] Good casework required objectivity, the establishment of a professional relationship between worker and client in which the word "sin" did not obtrude. Not even syphilis could justify a self-righteousness which threatened to diminish the worker's professional reserve and insight. "No worker with the faintest trace of the moralistic point of view," according to Maida H. Solomon, "can be successful in handling either the syphilitic or his family." The caseworker dealt with a sick individual, not with a convenient object for a lecture or moral sermon, and she was obliged to maintain a "scientific spirit" in addition to an "impersonal and cool attitude." [49]

The psychiatric social worker, like her medical counterpart, was in close contact with physicians and conspicuously aware of casework as a "scientific discipline and of dependency as a form of social maladjustment rather than a punishment for sin." [50] The close association with physicians, however, created troublesome function and status problems, as it did for medical social workers. Early leaders in psychiatric social work who claimed special skills which distinguished them from the psychiatrist had to justify their independent professional role, and explain why psychiatric social work was the "most subtle and difficult of all case-work," requiring a "social knowledge and technique the psychiatrist necessarily lacks." [51]

Through the social examination the caseworker was said to preëmpt a field and develop a skill "impossible for the busy physician." [52] The psychiatric like the medical social worker deplored any confusion of casework with nursing. Without training in "social technique," the nurse had nothing to contribute to the psychiatrist beyond her assigned work. By contrast, the trained social worker was equipped to serve as the psychiatrist's consultant, selecting the "psycho-social material" necessary for diagnosis and helping patients who required a "readjustment of social conditions or personal re-education." [53]

In the training school for psychiatric social work established at Smith College in 1918 Mary Jarrett found confirmation of the "growing belief" that social work was becoming a "profession that will eventually demand academic and practical training comparable with education now required for the established professions." [54] As early as 1914 Miss Jarrett and Elmer E. Southard, director of the Boston Psychopathic Hospital, had instituted a six- (later eight-) month training course. With the outbreak of World War I and the increased demand for psychiatric social workers, the Smith College course was established under the auspices of the National Committee for Mental Hygiene. It included lectures on psychology, sociology, and social psychiatry as well as field work in the form of bi-weekly clinics at the Northampton State Hospital. Schools of social work in New York, Chicago, and Philadelphia incorporated courses in mental hygiene and psychiatric social work in their curricula during the war period.

The emergence of psychiatric social work not only reinforced the quest for skills and technique in casework, but foreshadowed major changes in the entire structure of theory and practice. Although even the psychiatric social worker still admitted that casework involved the "adjustment of individuals with social difficulties," she sometimes minimized the client's social environment as a factor in diagnosis and treatment in her zealous efforts to permeate all casework with the psychiatric point of view. [55] Was not the "study of personality" a "requisite of all effective case work?" [56] Prophetically, Mary Jarrett announced in 1918 that "we see case-work about to pass into a psychological phase." "Personality," in contrast to "environment," promised to dominate the interest of future social workers. [57] In support of her belief, Miss Jarrett argued that 50 percent of the cases cited by Mary Richmond in *Social Diagnosis* presented "clearly psychiatric problems," while another 15 percent suggested the possibility of a "psychopathic condition." [58] Jessie Taft anticipated the eventual establishment of a "new psychological foundation for all case work." [59] The

79

psychiatrist encouraged this development. "The principles of mental hygiene and the technique of dealing with human problems which psychiatry has evolved" deserved a wide application in social casework, "even where no clear-cut psychiatric issue presents itself." [60]

*

Before the 1920's, none of the influences shaping the character of professional social work—functional specialization, differential casework ideals, mental hygiene, social psychiatry, or psychiatric social work—deflected the attention of caseworkers from the client's social environment. Although services to individuals rather than leadership in the reform crusades of the Progressive era constituted the primary function of the caseworker, and the inspiration for the professionalization of social work, casework before the 1920's retained an interest in the living and working conditions of the client.

In practice, casework meant anything designed to influence behavior and improve the client's welfare. It implied something as simple as a pair of eyeglasses for the youngster troubled by headaches or something as complex as the breakup of a family and the foster placement of the children. Casework services included a summer outing in the country for the tenement child or a new job for the man depressed by his inability to support his family. It involved relief for dependent widows, a stay in a tuberculosis sanatorium, training in budgeting and household management for the housewife, or guidance for the young girl falling under the allure of the dancehall. For medical social workers, as at Massachusetts General, casework could mean a program of hygienic instruction, the training of mothers in infant feeding, the referral of patients to outside agencies for financial aid or convalescent care, the establishment of tuberculosis classes, or an investigation into the living conditions of working girls. Casework might involve an examination of the family and neighborhood environment of the schoolchild who seemed moody and disinterested or the instruction of friends and relatives on the after-care of released psychiatric patients. In addition to concrete services, the caseworker was alert to the implications of "wholesale" legislative reform for her own work as, for example, the predicament of the family whose income was restricted by the enactment of a child labor or tenement sweatshop law. If such laws created excessive hardship for workers and immigrants they would be discredited. Mary Richmond explained the relation between social reform movements and casework in this fashion: "The adapting of these large measures to the needs of the Jones family and to the needs of the newer importations whose names are more complicated than Jones; the realization of the neighborhood point of view and of the neighborhood difficulties which stand in the way of an immediate acceptance of our sanitary and other programs—these are a very important part of the process of assimilation, a very important part of the prevention which really prevents." [61] In these broad terms social casework did link up with the settlement movement and crusade for social justice in the Progressive era. The social worker concentrated upon services to individuals, but she viewed the individual for purposes of diagnosis and treatment as rooted in a social environment which explained both his personal limitations and potentialities. Most of her concrete services focused upon the environment, adjusting the client to its disciplines and pressures.

All the casework specialties before the 1920's reflected, in some measure, an interest in neighborhood life and structure as a particular facet of the environment. The nineteenth-century charity organization ideal of the district office as a kind of neighborhood center carried over into the twentieth century. Agents, visitors, or district committees could serve the poor most effectively if they thoroughly understood the neighborhood in which the lives of most immigrants and workers centered. Mary Richmond contrasted the "older type of charity agent" who sat at a desk dividing the poor into categories of "worthy" and "unworthy" with the new type who not only worked with the so-called undeserving but knew "like a book the district in which he or she works—its schools, its doctors, its clergymen, its industrial opportunities, its charitable people; and [was] quick to use all of these in giving poor people a lift upward." [62] The visiting teacher also viewed her work in relation to the neighborhood environment of child and school. The school was not simply an educational but also a social institution, with a "social responsibility toward its children," and a "social place in the community." Indeed, work with children, according to Mary Richmond, was the most effective means to "discover neighborhood conditions and deal with them." [63]

Medical social work had originally developed because the hospital had ignored the "relatedness of all phases of man's social life." The Social Service Department at Massachusetts General devoted much attention to the patient's home and neighborhood environment in order to understand his difficulties and treat them effectively: "To act as a link of connection between the hospital and the outside world and so *to make sure that the good done in the wards shall not be undone in the first weeks at home* is one of the tasks which our social workers have tried to do whenever they have been able to get in touch with cases about to be discharged." [64] Despite her interest in the patient's mental life, the psychiatric social worker before the 1920's was concerned with problems of social environment. She gathered data for the psychiatrist, linked the mental institution with the community or neighborhood network of "schools, charitable agencies, recreation centers, employment agencies, hospitals and churches," and assumed responsibility for after-care or adjustment of the discharged patient to his social environment.[65] Hopefully, the psychiatric socal worker dealt with the patient "in his social setting as intelligently and constructively as the physician deals with him in the hospital." [66]

Social work had achieved a rough kind of balance prior to the 1920's. Scientific, professional casework, in the eyes of leaders like Mary Richmond and Ida Cannon, implied diagnosis and treatment based upon unique insights obtained through skilled accumulation and interpretation of "social evidence." Yet the social worker did not entirely ignore problems of mental defect or disturbance. Mary Richmond was familiar with the work of Meyer and Healy, and referred to several other psychiatrists and neurologists in *Social Diagnosis*.[67] She included, of course, "insight into individuality and personal characteristics," as well as "direct action of mind upon mind," in her analysis of the casework process. It is clear that a critical decision facing social workers around 1920 was whether to continue along the lines of the psycho-social casework expounded by Mary Richmond and being practiced or whether to embrace the psychotherapy which some psychiatric social workers were beginning to view with favor.

Whatever the choice, social work had been radically modified. Functional specialization launched an intensive quest for skill and technique in casework and contributed to the notion of social work as a profession. The status of the volunteer diminished, relative to the nineteenth century, when charity organization leaders viewed friendly visiting as the keystone of philanthropy. Trained, paid social workers in the twentieth century asserted their leadership prerogatives and welcomed the volunteer if she accepted a supporting role under their direction. Disturbed by the contrast between their professional aspirations and the historic affiliations of philanthropy with charity, sentimentalism, and paternalism, social workers began to redefine their relation to the client. They had not entirely liberated social work from the moralism and paternalism of

83

friendly visiting, but they had become dissatisfied with the older tradition. The "new *professional attitude*," compounded of "authority and impersonal friendliness," was to be similar to the "ideal attitude" in such established professions as medicine, education, and theology. The social worker had begun to view herself as the professional representative of an agency or institution rather than of a class. "On the whole," Mary Jarrett explained, "we believe the best results come from teaching the patient to look upon the social agency or the hospital as the source of help and direction, medical and social. . . . We have found the point of view to be of more importance than the personality of the worker."[68] The friendly visitor's personality had been the essence of her contribution. She had been dispatched not as an expert in investigation or the handling of relief, but as the representative of a middle class which elevated the poor by virtue of its "high moral standards," its "trained intellect," and its "refined tastes."[69]

The failure of friendly visiting suggested to social workers, particularly in the larger urban centers where the problems of social control were most acute and where a functional specialization had progressed furthest, that social casework required training and leadership by a paid, professional corps. Only such specialists in "social adjustment" could salvage the wreckage and prevent needless demoralization. In this sense, social work reflected a more general interest in a technical and scientific elitism which developed during the Progressive era. The Progressives favored the expansion of democracy and economic opportunity, but many of them also assumed that the preservation of democracy and the salvation of the industrial city depended upon the wisdom and guidance of the expert. "Lovers of mankind were to be found in every age," Simon Patten noted, "but effective improvers of mankind are of a newer generation."[70]

Chapter IV

Inner vs. Outer Need:
Psychiatry and Fragmentation

THE evolution of social work in the 1920's disturbed Eduard C. Lindeman, a reflective educator interested in group relations and community life. A professor at the New York School of Social Work, with a background in the cooperative movement and community and rural organization, Lindeman feared that professionalization and bureaucratization had transformed the social worker from the "embodiment of sentiment" into the "symbol of technique." Social work had become "dehumanized," a compound of hardness, cynicism, and jargon; it had lost the enthusiasm and compassion of the past. Abraham Epstein, a long-time crusader for social insurance, voiced a similar opinion. Having become "too practical to be passionate," social work no longer possessed a "spiritual equilibrium." Thanks to her infatuation with technique, the social worker had not only transcended charity and preventive reform but "social panaceas and far-visioned dreams" as well.[1]

Such sweeping generalizations obscured the fact that social reform and legislation continued to occupy the attention of many social workers. Numerous individuals and organizations of the Progressive era remained active in the 1920's, providing an important link with the prewar humanitarian crusade.[2]

"Technique" was not necessarily incompatible with social action, as the Progressive generation of reform experts like Florence Kelley, Lawrence Veiller, and the Goldmark and Abbott sisters, demonstrated. Lindeman and Epstein objected, in reality, not to expertise or to a total abandonment of social action but rather to a fragmentation of the social work community which left the reformer isolated in comparison to the Progressive era. The absorption of Freudian doctrine and a general interest in psychotherapy contributed to a shift in caseworkers' orientation from social environment to mental process. They identified themselves with the psychiatric clinic team rather than the social meliorist, who seemed a bit old-fashioned.

Even if the average social worker was unequipped to apply psychiatric theory, she conceded its superiority to mere "social diagnosis" and environmental manipulation. In the 1920's she continued to concentrate upon services to individuals rather than reform. But a new conception of "scientific" casework developed, rooted in Freud and the mysteries of the psyche, personality, and emotions. The psychiatric social worker emerged as the queen of caseworkers, for if her point of view was relevant to all casework, then no group was better qualified by training and experience to speak for the profession. Her prestige soared once social workers no longer assumed without hesitation that men necessarily lived up to their environment.

*

Freudian doctrine trickled slowly into America. Before the 1920's it had attracted the attention of the Greenwich Village intelligentsia and of a small American medical group including Morton Prince, Frederick Peterson, William A. White, Smith Ely Jelliffe, James J. Putnam, A. A. Brill, and Ernest Jones of Canada. Brill, who was especially prominent as a proselytizer among the pioneers, attended the first class of physicians trained by Dr. Meyer at the Pathological Institute on Ward's Island, and spent several years at the Central Islip (Long Island) State Hospital. He became dissatisfied with the ineffectual treatment of the functional disorders in the first decade of the twentieth century; and in seeking an alternative to the "dry, descriptive psychiatry of the German school" as well as the organic-pathological tradition, Brill became interested in the hypnotic therapy launched by Mesmer and applied in nineteenth-century Paris by Jean Martin Charcot. In search of the enlightenment, he went to Paris in 1907, accepting an appointment at the Hôspice de Bicêtre, whose director, Pierre Marie, had impressed Brill with his work on acromegaly and aphasia. Disappointed by the lack of interest exhibited by French psychiatrists and neurologists in the earlier experiments of Charcot in hypnotism and suggestion, he contemplated quitting psychiatry altogether, but was dissuaded by his mentor, Dr. Frederick Peterson, who advised a trip to the Zurich clinic where Bleuler, Jung, Meier, and others were studying and applying Freudian theory. Freud's psychogenetic interpretation of the functional neuroses came as a revelation: "It had never occurred to me before I studied psychoanalysis that it was possible to obtain any information about a patient which transcended his own conscious knowledge." The same revelation, coming later to social workers, helps explain the impact of Freudian psychiatry. Once alerted to the effects of the unconscious, it seemed to many social workers that environmental manipulation had been based upon rationalistic assumptions having no relation to the dynamic factors in human motivation and behavior.[3]

In 1908 Brill arranged to translate Freud's works into English. The following year he published "A Case of Schizophrenia" in the *American Journal of Insanity*, describing the psychoanalytic method of therapy. In September of 1909 Freud delivered a series of lectures at Clark University at the invitation of G. Stanley Hall, its president and a well-known psychologist. This important event stimulated interest in psychoanalysis among American physicians. The following year Dr. Morton Prince of Boston, who had founded the *Journal of Abnormal Psychology* in 1906, established the American Psychopathological Association which included most physicians interested in the psychogenetic origins of mental illness. Brill then organized the New York Psychoanalytic Society, and in 1913 Jelliffe and White launched the *Psychoanalytic Review*, the first journal dealing with the subject in the English language.

Prior to World War I, social workers exhibited little awareness of Freud. He was not mentioned by Mary Richmond in either *Social Diagnosis* or *What is Social Case Work?* Any reference to Freud in social work literature was rare though the Social Service Department at Massachusetts General knew of him through Dr. Putnam. Putnam had brought Freud to the hospital after the Clark University conference and was rewarded by a "storm of abusive criticism." Nonetheless, he impressed upon social workers the fact that "service was to be founded upon understanding, and understanding upon science, and psychoanalysis was the scientific method by which to understand personality and therefore a person." [4] As psychoanalytic concepts gradually filtered down from medical circles to social workers and the general public, it seemed that mankind had finally discovered the key to scientific understanding and control of behavior.

With some exaggeration no doubt, a prominent social worker recalled that her colleagues in the 1920's "peered anxiously into the faces of their comrades with the unspoken question: have you been psychoanalyzed?" [5] Just as some social workers in the twentieth century looked back with dismay at the categorical paternalistic philanthropy of the nineteenth century, others found little to commend in the pre-Freudian era. "How sterile our work was before Freud and how fertile it has become through his genius," remarked one social worker from the perspective of 1940.[6] If reality was rooted not in the objective environment but in the individual's emotional and intellectual perception of that environment, and if men had grossly overestimated the power of reason to direct behavior, then caseworkers wrestled with superficialities if they concentrated upon external manipulation instead of the client's psychic life. "The most daring experimental case-workers," Jessie Taft reported, "have all but lost connection with social obligation and are quite buried in their scientific interest in the individual as he has evolved through his own unique growth process." [7] Realizing the significance of emotional and unconscious factors in human behavior they were prepared, for the first time, to treat their clients effectively.

Freud's influence in the 1920's could not be gauged simply by the number of social workers who incorporated psychiatric techniques in their work. A truer measure was the growing conviction that insight into emotions and psychic life was the key to skilled casework, and in this development the child guidance clinic played a crucial role. It emerged in the 1920's as an experimental laboratory, demonstrating to social workers the potentialities of psychiatrically oriented casework. Equally important, the clinic did not deal with narrow problems of economic dependency and relief but with universal problems of mental health and emotional adjustment. In identifying herself with psychiatry and the clinic team, the social worker sought to obliterate the stigma of charity associated with her efforts in the past. The clinic became the agency through which the psychiatric social worker achieved her preëminent position in the 1920's and impressed upon any skeptical colleagues the fact that social casework was a form of therapy.[8]

*

Although William Healy developed the comprehensive mental, physical, and social diagnosis at Chicago's Juvenile

Psychopathic Institute, he had worked primarily through court referrals and had not systematically explored the principles of clinic organization. At the Judge Baker Foundation, however, Healy and Augusta Bronner after 1917 drew many cases from sources outside the courts and incorporated the social worker as a permanent member of their team—providing a model for the Commonwealth Fund child guidance clinics of the 1920's.

Boston social workers, judges, physicians, and other professionals had first become interested in the possibility of a clinic in 1912 and 1913, when Healy explained the work of the Psychopathic Institute in summer lecture courses at Harvard. Judge Baker of the Juvenile Court, who came twice to Chicago for enlightenment, ardently desired a clinic as did his successor, Frederick Cabot. The plans matured in 1916, when Miss Bronner visited Boston and was assured financial support from Galen Stone, and professional support from Judge Cabot, Jessie Hodder of the women's reformatory, Edith Burleigh, Frances Stern, head of the food clinic at the Boston Dispensary, J. Prentice Murphy of the Children's Aid Society, and Herbert Parsons, head of the State Probation Commission. Most important, Healy and Bronner were assured the full cooperation of the Boston children's agencies, the most progressive in the country, as well as the support of other social agencies. The prospect of such cooperation, which they had been unable to acquire in Chicago, was a decisive influence.

From the beginning in Boston, they accepted referrals not only from the juvenile court and social agencies, but from public and private schools and even individual families. Instead of depending upon probation officers as at Chicago, they acquired Margaret Fitz, an experienced school visitor, as a full-time staff social worker. Healy and Bronner invited referring agency workers to their staff conferences and established a training service which included students from the Simmons and Smith schools of social work.[9] The Baker Clinic anticipated the close links between social work, child guidance, and psychiatry which would develop through the Commonwealth Fund program in the 1920's.

In creating its program for the prevention of delinquency, the Commonwealth Fund was inspired by motives similar to those of Healy and his supporters in Chicago and Boston. "The wide employment of unintelligent methods of dealing with delinquents and criminals, the persistence of the punishment theory, the fact that a very large proportion of criminals begin their unsocial careers in youth and that many children are impelled toward delinquent conduct through lack of wisdom and understanding on the part of parents, teachers, and others—all these things pointed to the outstanding need for a better comprehension of the entire situation, for the placing of emphasis upon the checking of wayward tendencies early in their development, and more concretely, for the development of methods and processes by which results of this character might be secured." [10]

The Commonwealth Fund launched its experiment in cooperation with the National Committee for Mental Hygiene. Dr. Thomas Salmon, medical director of the National Committee, presented the Commonwealth Fund with a formal appeal for support in November 1920. He recommended the establishment of a Division of Delinquency under the National Committee's supervision, a proposal which received the Commonwealth Fund's sympathetic consideration and resulted in the organization of a temporary advisory committee which convened at Lakewood, New Jersey early in 1921. The committee, including Dr. Healy, Augusta Bronner, Bernard Glueck, Dr. Salmon, and J. Prentice Murphy, now director of the Philadelphia Children's Bureau, formulated a series of recommendations and conclusions.[11] It proposed an expansion of facilities for study and treatment of individual delinquents, coupled with a training program for medical, psychological, and social work personnel. To correct the lack of understanding by teachers and educational authorities which often transformed incipient conduct disorders into delinquency, the committee also recommended the dissemination of the "present scientific conception of disorders of conduct and their treatment," and an increase of casework services in schools.[12]

Dr. Salmon discussed the Lakewood proposals with the Commonwealth Fund directors in April 1921, and in November the Fund officially launched a five-year program for the prevention of delinquency. Four divisions were set up: a Bureau of Children's Guidance under the auspices of the New York School of Social Work, a Division on the Prevention of Delinquency of the National Committee for Mental Hygiene, which was responsible for the demonstration child guidance clinics; a National Committee on Visiting Teachers, affiliated with the Public Education Association of New York; and a Joint Committee on Methods of Preventing Delinquency which coordinated and interpreted the program.

The Commonwealth Fund program profoundly influenced social work. The divisions worked closely with social agencies and hastened the acceptance of a psychiatric point of view among caseworkers. A large number of psychiatric social workers received their training in the child guidance clinics and became consultants in family agencies and other non-psychiatric settings. Social workers who referred agency cases to child guidance clinics and helped carry out the recommendations witnessed the translation of mental hygiene from an abstraction to a working reality. In Jessie Taft's opinion, "it would be hard to overestimate what social case work owes to the leadership of these stations for practical research in human behavior." Through the child guidance clinic, the caseworker

has become "intimately associated with the clinical psychologist, the psychiatrist, and the psychoanalytic school of
thought." [13]

The child guidance clinics established by the Division on
the Prevention of Delinquency of the National Committee
for Mental Hygiene were temporary, and would be succeeded, it was hoped, by permanent ones organized by the
communities. With varying degrees of success, the clinics
concentrated upon treatment of individual clients, cooperation with social agencies, exposure of gaps in the network
of welfare services for children, and training of the clinic
team.

The first clinic, opened in St. Louis in April 1922, worked
out the ratio of one psychiatrist, one psychologist, and three
social workers.[14] It initially accepted many cases from the
juvenile court, but later turned to other community agencies
in the hope of detecting personality disorders in their earliest
stages. A program of preventive mental hygiene, it discovered, did not begin in the courts, but in the school, family,
and social agency. Successful treatment depended upon the
cooperation of outside agencies and upon the skill of their
casework personnel in following recommendations. The child
guidance clinic, therefore, had reason to arouse the interest
of social workers in psychotherapy, and its personnel aggres-
sively expounded their belief that the social worker who
"passes beyond 'relief work' to 'case-work,' as it is ordinarily
defined . . . enters a field in which the mental-hygiene factor
bulks large and in which she has need of the data and techniques of psychiatry." [15]

The importance of community cooperation in fulfilling
the promise of child guidance was borne out by experience
in the one rural clinic at Monmouth County, New Jersey,
where expenses were met by a grant from the Laura Spelman
Rockefeller Memorial Fund. Headed by Dr. Christine Leon-

ard, the clinic team found its work hampered by the shortage of welfare agencies and trained social work personnel typical of many rural districts. In subsequent demonstrations at Norfolk, Virginia, Dallas, Minneapolis-St. Paul, Los Angeles, Cleveland, and Philadelphia, community education and training of social work personnel became as much a clinic function as case treatment. The Norfolk clinic sponsored a social service exchange, initiated mental hygiene surveys of local institutions, and supervised the field work of Smith College students and volunteer social workers. The clinic staff in Dallas worked very closely with local agencies through participation in case conferences, supervision of volunteers assigned by the cooperating groups, and lectures. In Minneapolis, the clinic accepted a number of Smith College students for field work training, and transferred many treatment responsibilities to social workers assigned to the clinic for training in mental hygiene. The Los Angeles clinic, although handicapped by a deficiency of existing welfare services, benefited from the cooperation of a progressive juvenile court under the leadership of Miriam Van Waters and from an active mental hygiene program in the schools. Cooperation between the clinic and local agencies was particularly close in Philadelphia where many cases were agency rather than court or school referrals.

The Cleveland clinic experienced little difficulty in winning cooperation and the acceptance of the doctrine that psychiatry was fundamental to casework practice. The Associated Charities had formed a Mental Hygiene Committee in 1919, five years before the demonstration clinic opened. In 1920, Helen Hanchette, assistant general secretary, informed the executive committee that "psychiatry . . . is giving us new light on our methods of dealing with people. In the past our approach has been from the standpoint of externals. In order to really bring about better adjustments in the lives of our clients, it is necessary to understand the deep-seated motives for human conduct . . . After we learn more of the meaning of people's attitudes of mind, the possibilities of more effective treatment by the casework method seem unlimited." [16] To stimulate interest in mental hygiene among staff workers, the committee disseminated "descriptive material about mental disorders" in the Associated Charities *Bulletin.*

The clinic engaged in a variety of educational and consultation services to illustrate the values of psychiatric insight through the medium of child guidance. Clinic personnel, including Dr. Lawson Lowrey, gave lectures and seminars at Western Reserve's School of Applied Social Sciences, and established a system of decentralized consultation services for the Associated Charities, a children's agency, a school, and a summer camp. Associated Charities workers presented cases to the clinic staff for help in diagnosis and treatment and attended clinic case conferences. The clinic assigned special workers to Associated Charities districts for consultation purposes, and in the summer of 1925 clinic personnel participated in district staff meetings. Cleveland social agencies assigned a number of workers to the clinic for several months. Within the Associated Charities these workers later formed the nucleus of a special unit which assumed supervisory responsibilities, carried select caseloads, and held weekly meetings with the director of Cleveland's permanent clinic to discuss their cases.

Edward D. Lynde, secretary of the Associated Charities, summarized the implications of child guidance in a paper before the National Conference of Social Work.[17] The clinic demonstrated the "universal value" of casework to the "average man." It proved that, although casework had been identified with problems of economic dependency in the past, it was in reality a helping device applicable to all classes and all varieties of need. The clinic focused upon the individual child, contributing to the caseworker's responsibility for "individualization in diagnosis and treatment," and staff conferences (which included cooperating social workers) brought the entire resources of agency and community to bear on each individual case. This was the antithesis of shallow, standardized, routine casework, and induced the "other agencies to go more intensively into the problems which they bring." Child guidance demonstrated the value of psychiatry and psychology in casework. These disciplines insured a "deeper insight into all human behavior," and suggested the wisdom of including psychiatric consultation in all cases. In short, clinic organization and service goals formed a professional model which social agencies might well emulate.

The influence of the child guidance clinic was not restricted to demonstration cities like Cleveland. Books and pamphlets publicized the work while psychiatric social workers and others who had participated carried the gospel of mental hygiene to other communities. A field consultation service established in 1923 assisted other communities in developing child guidance programs. The National Committee for Mental Hygiene continued the consultation work after 1925. Through these activities, such communities as Macon, Memphis, Richmond, Birmingham, Indianapolis, Milwaukee, New Orleans, and Houston were introduced to child guidance principles. When the Commonwealth Fund's program ended in 1927, the National Committee established a permanent Division on Community Clinics.

The child guidance clinics developed no rigid pattern of staff relations and responsibilities. The psychiatrist was the leader, and possessed ultimate authority in determining treatment, but of necessity he had to depend upon staff and cooperating social workers to carry out decisions. Although social workers were expected to handle environmental adjustments, such as recreational opportunities or school transfers, they also assumed some responsibility for therapy. In this sense, the clinic was a laboratory in which social workers applied psychiatric concepts in casework under supervision. They became "conscious of the technical problems involved in therapy through the interview." Association with the psychiatrist enriched their techniques and some became "accomplished" psychotherapists, usually centering their "direct therapeutic efforts on the mother." This was natural because "responsibility for social study of the family" forced social workers to "enter into some degree of relationship with the parents, while the psychiatrist, in his role as 'doctor,' was in immediate charge of the 'patient'—the child." [18] The clinic needed the mother's cooperation and understanding in order to succeed with the child; social workers, therefore, had to interpret the clinic's work and insure that emotional obstacles, such as the mother's fear that the clinic might subvert her own authority over the child, did not undermine its effectiveness.

Not all children referred required intensive psychotherapy; and sometimes the clinic lacked time or personnel to treat all cases intensively. Staff and cooperating social workers necessarily provided a wide range of environmental adjustments. But these did not arouse any particular interest among social workers, who had long been accustomed to such procedures. By contrast, they viewed the clinic's application of mental hygiene and psychiatry to casework as a revolutionary innovation with vast promise for professional, scientific casework. Study of the client's emotional life was an alternative to the socio-environmental, "superficial" casework of the past. Mental hygiene, social workers now suspected, was basic to all casework because no sharp line separated the "normal" from the "abnormal"; everyone's behavior reflected his emotional needs and represented a more or less successful effort to satisfy them. Behavior was neither good nor bad, but functional. The nonmoralistic casework relationship rooted in functional specialization and social psychiatry received additional impetus from Freudianism and from the child guidance clinic.

Porter Lee, director of the New York School of Social Work, and Marion Kenworthy, of the Bureau of Children's Guidance, expounded an extreme version of the identity between social work and psychiatry. In their view, the "practice of psychiatry, psychology, and social case work respectively overlap each other and . . . no sharp dividing line can be drawn at the present time between their respective fields." Any division of responsibility in child guidance clinics was arbitrary and administrative rather than scientific or "based upon completely logical distinctions in their inherent functions." [19] Lee and Kenworthy's interpretations sprang from the experience of the Bureau of Children's Guidance, established under the Commonwealth Fund's program. The Bureau accepted 591 cases in the five and a half years of its existence, but did not really serve as a community clinic. Directed by Dr. Bernard Glueck, its real purpose was the education and training of social workers, and, in particular, the creation of psychiatric social workers.

As in other child guidance clinics, social workers at the bureau participated in therapy. Each new case was assigned by the supervisor to a student, who prepared the social history. Only after its completion was the child seen by the psychiatrist and psychologist. The psychiatrist treated the child, but the social worker under his supervision handled parents, teachers, and other community representatives in the hope of influencing their attitudes. Lee and Kenworthy considered this ability to shape attitudes a key skill in casework: "When one considers that environment is to a large extent expressed through personality it becomes apparent that lack of adjustment to one's environment is largely a lack of satisfying relationships to other persons. Hence, attitudes become important focal points of treatment." The ability to affect attitudes depended upon the social worker's skill in establishing a satisfactory relationship with others through utilization of the "facts and concepts of psychiatric and social science," along with an "ingenious and imaginative use of a multitude of minor devices, emphases, suggestions, etc." [20]

When the Commonwealth Fund program ended in 1927, the Bureau of Children's Guidance was succeeded by the Institute for Child Guidance (1927–1933). New York social agencies experienced an uninterrupted ten-year exposure to child guidance in operation. The Institute had no difficulty in finding cases. One hundred and forty-eight were transferred directly from the defunct Bureau of Children's Guidance, and "by 1927 social agencies, schools, and the public were so conscious of the value of child guidance that requests for service came readily." The Institute developed an elaborate training program for psychiatric social workers, in which student supervision was divided between staff social workers, a supervisor for the New York School of Social Work, and another representing Smith College. Once again, social workers received an opportunity to apply casework therapy under psychiatric supervision. The Institute was not original in learning that child guidance often involved treatment of the mother; but it departed from previous technique "when the social worker entered so intensively into the role of therapist and the mother so consciously into the role of patient that the relationship was one of mutual agreement and the problems of the child were excluded from direct attention." [21]

Although the work of the Institute for Child Guidance and other clinics suggested that psychiatry was relevant to all casework, some practitioners like Charlotte Towle espoused an extreme Freudian view. Miss Towle observed that "we must meet the basic emotional needs of the individual through the worker-client relationship in terms of parental needs." This relationship was essentially a "parent-child one." Those who came for help experienced a "deep-lying need to be guided by a parental hand," forcing the social worker to "identify and to play in secure fashion the mature parent role in social leadership." [22]

*

Like the child guidance clinics, the visiting teaching sponsored by the Commonwealth Fund directed attention to the psychiatric foundations of casework. Visiting teachers were placed in five schools associated with the Bureau of Children's Guidance and assigned for three-year demonstration periods in various communities. [23] The demonstrations were supervised by the National Committee on Visiting Teachers, affiliated with the Public Education Association of New York. Howard W. Nudd, director of the Association, also served as chairman of the National Committee. Reflecting the general opinion of psychiatrists and social workers, Nudd considered the school's understanding of the child's emotional life as important as any purely pedagogical or environmental adjustments; therefore, he argued, the visiting teacher's training had to include the principles of psychiatry and psychology. Only then would she be in a position to aid the school in developing the child's "attitudes and traits of character." [24]

From the mental hygiene viewpoint education implied, not a narrow focus upon intellectual attainment, but the child's evolution into a balanced, emotionally stable, and creative personality. The classroom teacher had to understand that the acquisition of intellectual skills was less important than emotional rapport. It was the teacher, Glueck explained, not "some impersonal educational process to which the child has to adjust primarily, and his joys and sorrows as a human being as well as his successes or failures as a pupil are largely determined by the nature of this contact." [25] Jessie Taft agreed with this evaluation and criticized the average teacher's failure to understand the role of mental hygiene in education. The teacher had to develop a "vital psychology" which penetrated beneath symptoms to the purposive or functional roots of behavior. It might relieve her feelings to label a difficult child as "liar, thief, truant," but such labels obscured the inner tensions and conflicts which exploded in overt deviant behavior. The teacher had to realize that "if only one factor in a child's maladjustment at school can be changed, the attitude of the teacher will usually be found to be the most important and its alteration most immediately effective in bringing about improvement."[26] Just as the child guidance clinic learned that therapy with the mother was often fundamental to treatment of the child, the visiting teacher learned that the personality and emotional attitudes of the classroom teacher affected her own casework. Whatever the school social worker might accomplish with the child, his school adjustment was "in the last analysis, effected directly by the teacher."[27]

The Commonwealth Fund program advanced the notion that the school was a kind of mental hygiene laboratory in which the visiting teacher became a pivotal figure: "Probably three-fourths . . . of unfortunate children can, under the observation and management of a visiting teacher trained in social and psychiatric case work, be brought into normal relations with the school."[28] A few schools even hired psychiatric social workers (who were moving into family agencies to serve as consultants, supervisors, and "super" caseworkers) to perform the visiting teaching work. By 1929 the child guidance program of the Newark Board of Education included, besides a psychiatrist and psychologist, five psychiatric social workers. Two private schools, the Glenwood (Illinois) Manual Training School and the Lincoln School in New York City, had added psychiatric social workers to their staffs.[29] In the 1920's the concept of the school as a mental hygiene laboratory extended to the high school and university. The La Salle (Illinois) High School established a Bureau of Educational Counsel in 1923 with a psychiatric social worker in charge, and in 1926 Yale University employed one for its mental hygiene department.[30]

Like the Commonwealth Fund, the White-Williams Foundation of Philadelphia labored in the 1920's to stimulate the school social worker's awareness of the emotional roots of behavior, and assist her in incorporating psychiatric insight in her training and technique. Anna Beach Pratt, the Foundation's director, emerged as one of the most influential interpreters of theory and practice in the field. She organized an elaborate teaching and supervisory program in cooperation with departments of education and sociology, schools of social work, and social agencies at a time when few facilities for training in school social work existed. She upheld visiting teaching as a professional specialty distinct from teaching and requiring advanced technical preparation. Most important, she emphasized to educators and the public that school social work was a means of individualizing the child—of understanding his unique problems and personality—in the face of the pressures for standardization exerted by a system of mass public education. Intellectually alert, attuned to progressive ideas emanating from social work, education, and the behavioral sciences, Miss Pratt explained that the child's school performance was no self-contained intellectual affair, separable from his emotional needs and personality. The White-Williams Foundation developed its casework, vocational guidance, and scholarship program on the assumption that not only must teachers and parents "understand the emotional make-up" of pupils, but that the child's growth into a "well-integrated personality" depended also upon "intellectual insight and emotional adjustment in relation to their own problems, on the part of all who come in contact with him."[31]

Those who stressed the school's responsibility for shaping

the child's emotional life invariably associated psychiatry with a nonauthoritarian, individualized approach to behavior, typical of child guidance from Healy's Psychopathic Institute down to the Commonwealth Fund program. This emphasis upon scientific, objective analysis was a major contribution of child guidance to the theory of professional casework. If the social worker was akin to the "scientist working in a laboratory," she could not allow personal prejudices to cloud her professional judgment. [32] "Moral prejudice and social taboo should yield to a scientific and therefore sympathetic consideration of those factors in each child's life which are thwarting active social expression of the instinctive energies." [33]

The problem of sexual behavior was one such taboo and a source of possible misunderstanding between visiting and classroom teacher. "Like other case workers," visiting teachers were "accustomed to meeting these problems in children and to considering them frankly in their relationship to the entire situation." [34] But what if a more squeamish classroom teacher interpreted a child's normal sexual curiosity as evidence of immorality, and resented the social worker's failure to acquiesce in her judgment? The teacher might even resent the social worker's desire for an "impersonal hearing of the child's own story" whatever the trouble, construing the social worker's impartial appraisal as a threat to her authority.

Such differences of opinion confirmed the visiting teachers' conviction that they were professional specialists with a function separate from that of the school personnel. They were never reluctant to identify themselves with medical figures like doctors and psychiatrists, but just as hospital social workers were quick to dissociate themselves from nurses, they were anxious to evolve an identity separate from the classroom teacher. This was true even before World War I, but the Commonwealth Fund program of the 1920's with the mental hygiene content it poured into casework led to fresh affirmation of professional independence and skill in school social work. No matter what courses classroom teachers took in normal school or college, they would not qualify as social caseworkers "any more than the present courses in hygiene and psychology have made them doctors or psychologists." [35] They would always depend upon the social worker's "specialized technique" in handling serious behavior disorders.[36] The school needed the visiting teacher to link it with the child guidance clinic, where the most refractory behavior problems could undergo intensive scientific diagnosis and therapy.

In their presumption of professional expertise applied to the understanding and control of behavior, visiting teachers in the 1920's reflected an attitude common to the broader fields of child guidance and social work.[37] No doubt, as Lindeman and Epstein feared, social work had lost its sentiment and spontaneity. But, having committed herself to the attainment of professional status, the social worker was perfectly willing to exchange such virtues for what she hoped was scientific effectiveness. In a striking passage Jessie Taft revealed the social worker's vision of control founded upon scientific insight: "The position of the case worker is at once the most thrilling and the most terrifying in the whole gamut of scientific or semi-scientific undertakings which seek to gain social control in terms of the behavior of the human organism. There is no turning back. The choice lies not between doing or not doing, but between doing on a more or less sentimental and subjective level, which leaves the results to Providence or doing as courageously and consciously as possible whatever is done, however inadequate the equipment, struggling for a greater and greater scientific understanding and reduction of the intuitive field to a minimum." [38]

*

A wide discrepancy between theory and practice characterized the social work of the 1920's, a fact acknowledged and regretted by contemporary leaders in the field. The average social worker, whatever her setting, usually confronted a caseload too large to permit the differential social diagnosis envisioned by Mary Richmond, let alone the intensive examination and therapy symbolized by the child guidance clinic. Equally important, the average caseworker was unequipped by training or experience to apply effectively the mental hygiene or psychiatric insight which presumably constituted the very foundation of scientific social work. It would take a "long time" for "the approach, the objectives, and the philosophy of mental hygiene . . . to permeate and displace the present primarily economic, legal, or health approach of the average non-psychiatric social case-worker." [39] And after an embarrassingly critical study of case records, Maurice J. Karpf, director of the Training School for Jewish Social Work, concluded that social workers exhibited little skill in the use of social, psychological, or biological science. This was true whether the "attitudes, emotional states, personality and personality traits" of the client were involved, or the "care of his health, the care he gives his children, his standard of living, the adequacy and inadequacy of his housing, and a host of other types of important problems and situations." As a *coup de grâce*, Karpf noted that social workers' judgments were "largely subjective, individualistic, and unverifiable," exhibiting more evidence of "common sense concepts and judgments" than scientific knowledge or technique. [40]

It might be well to emphasize once again, in the light of Karpf's study, that we are dealing with the professionalization of social work in terms of changing aspirations and organization of services rather than objective scientific achievement. Social workers undoubtedly acquired a proficiency and dexterity in certain operations, such as the preparation of case records, and this, combined with a terminology drawn from

psychiatry and psychology may have obscured a largely subjective performance. The crucial development between 1880
and 1930, however, was the emergence of the belief that social
work was heading toward a scientific understanding and control of behavior and at the same time clarifying its distinctive
professional function. This belief both triggered and sanctioned significant changes in social work institutions and in
the relation between paid worker and volunteer.

In a famous address before the National Conference of
Charities and Correction in 1915, Abraham Flexner had
drawn blood from social work's vital center—the aspiration
for professional status rooted in scientific knowledge and
discipline. He denied that social work could ever become a
genuine profession, claiming that it lacked a specific skill
applied to a specific function. Flexner described the social
worker as the "intelligence" which "mediates the intervention
of the particular agent or agency best fitted to deal with the
specific emergency." She possessed no uniquely professional
skill, but called upon the "specialized agency, professional or
other," equipped to handle the problem. [41] He viewed the
social worker as a kind of traffic director who guided the
client to the appropriate community resources or mobilized
them on his behalf.

Apparently Flexner did not consider the possibility that
liaison and resource mobilization in a complex urban society
was a professional function requiring considerable skill and
specialized training. Drawing his models from the traditional
professions like medicine, law, and the ministry, he did not
recognize that the ability to mobilize the many specialized
services of a community on behalf of a single individual or
to serve as liaison among social groups and institutions was
a pivotal task in modern society and no less "professional"
than any other. The transfer of many responsibilities from
the family and primary group to organized social agencies

and the extreme specialization of the twentieth-century urban community had resulted in a "progressive differentiation," in an "intricate network of interdependent, specialized parts" which confused the individual seeking assistance and produced a fragmentation of groups and functions.[42] Whoever accepted the responsibility for liaison, communication, and the nurture of "community coherence" therefore performed a vital service.

Social workers interpreted their role differently. By the 1920's they tended to minimize the integrating and coordinating function in favor of human relations skills or therapy based upon an understanding of individual growth processes. Equating professional achievement with scientific knowledge and control of behavior through psychiatry, they devaluated their liaison and mobilization task. Like Flexner, social workers failed to realize that the opening of lines of communication between individuals, classes, and institutions, and community resource mobilization, could be defended as legitimate "professional" responsibilities.

Casework had always been a helping technique which focused upon the individual personality and problem. It was a "retail" approach, as Mary Richmond put it, which served as a necessary complement to the "wholesale." Whether scientific or not, it was one resource among others in society to which troubled individuals could turn for assistance or reassurance. This emphasis upon individual service supplied a basic continuity between the casework of the 1920's and that of an earlier period. At neither time were caseworkers reform leaders, but during the Progressive era the individual helping process was more closely related to social reform than it was subsequently because caseworkers more readily accepted a liaison and mobilization function. Since they attempted to understand the individual in terms of his social situation and environment, they considered coordination of community services and creation of new welfare resources indispensable to the helping process. Social work was a "great crusade for human betterment in which case-by-case personal contact with people in poor circumstances would not only raise individual families to a higher level but would furnish data for far-reaching reforms. The favored classes, learning to know their poor neighbors personally, could never thereafter be indifferent to the causes of poverty, disease, and crime, or fail to support needful reforms." [43]

A significant shift in emphasis occurred toward the 1920's when social workers "became accustomed to thinking of psychiatry as a key to unlock all the mysteries of personality in all kinds of circumstances. Circumstances became less important . . . than the kinds of people exposed to them." [44] The welfare field had fragmented, isolating the reformer or community worker and reducing social work's capacity for united social action just prior to the Great Depression of the 1930's. The prestige accorded psychiatry by all varieties of social workers in the 1920's might well have aroused feelings of frustration and inadequacy in the caseworker mired in the backwaters of environmental manipulation. Perhaps its greatest impact upon social work was to deflect attention not only from the liaison and mobilization function, but from any alternatives to a clinically oriented relationship therapy.

The hard-pressed medical social worker, still struggling to carve out her niche in the hospital organization, continued to express some interest in social environment typical of the pioneering years.[45] Yet medical social workers were not immune to the influences affecting the thought of their colleagues, and in the late 1920's and 1930's they addressed themselves to the implications of mental hygiene for their work. A committee of the American Association of Hospital Social Workers agreed that the caseworker's task included "mobilization of measures for the relief of the patient and his associates," but, significantly, it denied that community and public health work, or improvements of conditions in industry and education were among the worker's main purposes. The committee did maintain that treatment of "personality problems" was as "appropriate" for medical social workers as treatment of social relationships.[46] "We have appreciated the tremendous influence that psychiatry and psychology have had on social work," reported Ida Cannon, and to illustrate the point medical social workers began searching for the emotional complications of illness and the elements of a relationship therapy.[47]

Edward C. Lindeman observed in 1926 that "no social agency would dare make an appeal to one of the large financial foundations today without including somewhere in the budget an item for individualistic mental hygiene even if orthodox family case work was the intended function. Psychiatric social work . . . is the current fashion."[48] Family agency executives embraced mental hygiene with unqualified enthusiasm, as if the purpose and function of casework shone forth with brilliant clarity after the obscurity of a long night. The general secretary of the Springfield (Illinois) Family Welfare Society noted that "consideration and development of personality has always been an important part of social case work, but better understanding of mental hygiene has made clearer to us the importance of stressing personal relationships."[49] Edward D. Lynde of the Cleveland Associated Charities argued that "psychiatry has unquestionably added depth and richness to social case work,"[50] and developments in family casework, according to the general secretary of the New Bedford (Massachusetts) Welfare Society, indicated a trend of advance toward "inner content" rather than "outward routine." Personality occupied the "center of the picture," with "material factors as background on the canvas."[51] The general secretary of the Milwaukee Family Welfare Association explained, in this connection, that economic and health problems were receding in favor of "more subtle factors of mental health, personality, character, and the forms of treatment which these require."[52] Beatrice Z. Levey of the Chicago United Charities described psychiatric social work as "transmuted family case-work."[53]

Attuned to mental hygiene, family agencies now discovered that many of their clients were mentally and emotionally disturbed. The general secretary of the Louisville Associated Charities urged social workers to alert themselves to the symptoms of constitutional psychopathology: "impulsiveness, suggestibility, emotional inadequacy or emotional excess, egotism, overestimation, bombastic talk, and irritability,"[54] and the casework supervisor for the Cincinnati Associated Charities regretted that "comparatively few laymen realize what a large percentage of the people on the lists of social agencies, are suffering from mental ill-health." She observed that 22 percent of the agency's cases in 1920 exhibited an obviously "unhealthy mental condition," and that the figure would probably reach 80 percent if all clients were subjected to psychiatric analysis.[55]

Through psychiatry, family social workers could reconcile the relief function with their professional aspirations, and in an evaluation of casework practice for the New York Charity Organization Society, Grace Marcus pointed the way. Miss Marcus argued that the caseworker had to accept the reality of the client's obsession with money, which was the key to his physical survival, and an emotion-laden symbol in American life. Financial dependency in a competitive, capitalist society which equated wealth with status, implied personal inadequacy and unworthiness; the client who applied for relief might therefore carry a burden of guilt or inferiority. He had surrendered his claims to respect, equality, and independence, and was afflicted with the psychological burden of failure.

Inner vs. Outer Need

Yet the social worker could not permit the client's concern with money problems to undermine casework goals and relationships. The skilled caseworker accepted relief as a factor in the relationship, but used it to promote her therapeutic objectives. Relief provided an "excellent entree into the confidence and good will of the clients," and permitted the client to divert his attention to nonmaterial affairs by insuring his physical survival. In authorizing relief, the caseworker had to divest herself of any assumption that financial assistance automatically resulted in chronic dependency. She had to reject, once and for all, the cherished charity organization principle that relief necessarily caused a deterioration of character, and instead determine whether economic dependency reflected a more basic emotional disturbance. Otherwise she could not distinguish between the "controllable and uncontrollable factors producing the financial dependency." The granting or withholding of relief might have only the most superficial relation to the client's permanent rehabilitation, on the one hand, or continued demoralization, on the other. "From a professional point of view," Miss Marcus explained, "relief is expended fruitlessly when casework has not succeeded in discovering those personal and environmental assets and limitations of the clients which must be considered before they can be motivated to practical goals, or when casework has overestimated the possibilities for recovery of clients who now possess none, or when it has not developed the techniques necessary to stimulating the clients to an independence far more satisfying than the possession of relief." [56] In the course of diagnosis, it was important for the social worker to recognize that financial dependency might reflect an emotional dependency rooted in the client's childhood and family experience. Unless casework came "to the rescue" with its "impersonal, practical objectives," there was danger of establishing an unproductive parent-child relationship in which the client interpreted the giving or withholding of relief as the bestowal or denial of affection.[57]

Psychiatry could imbue even the relief function with professional dignity. These problems of emotional dependency and mental disturbance which the caseworker confronted in relief were common to all men and all classes, and she handled relief as one tool in a basically therapeutic relation. With one stroke, the trained family caseworker in the private agency distinguished herself from the public welfare agency with its routine determination of eligibility limits, from charity, and from the layman or volunteer unaccustomed to the subtleties of casework.

Miss Marcus warned that a successful integration of financial assistance and professional therapy depended upon the social worker's objectivity, upon her ability to exclude her own attitudes toward money and relief from the professional relation. To insure that her emotions and prejudices did not color this, she had to subject herself to "professional analysis and discipline."[58] One notable consequence of the psychiatric and psychoanalytic influence in the 1920's was to direct the social worker's attention to her own emotional life. "Many potentially promising workers and outstanding leaders," Charlotte Towle explained, "have recently been or are now being analyzed." Others, not analyzed, felt the "need of identification with the analytic trend."[59] If casework represented not environmental manipulation or mobilization of community resources, but a helping process based upon a dynamic relation between worker and client, the worker's personality was surely a subject of professional concern. The caseworker, ideally, had to strive for a professional detachment in which her own biases did not intrude. Even if such detachment proved impossible, the caseworker, according to Virginia Robinson, was responsible for the "development of self-consciousness in relationships, a constant process of analysis of herself and the other in interaction." [60]

The psychiatric point of view found many vigorous champions in the 1920's, but none so zealous or uncompromising as Miss Robinson. Her book, *A Changing Psychology in Social Case Work,* published in 1930, sharply contrasts with Mary Richmond's *Social Diagnosis.* Miss Robinson was not only critical of the past, but somewhat condescending. "I should like to put forward . . . the conviction that all social case work, in so far as it is thorough and in so far as it is good case work, is mental hygiene. Case work not founded on the point of view of personality and adjustment for which mental hygiene contends is simply poor case work, superficial in diagnosis and blind in treatment." [61] In her extreme version of casework as psychotherapy, Virginia Robinson personified the fragmentation which had occurred in social welfare. She abstracted casework almost entirely from its roots in the client's social environment and cultural milieu and placed it squarely in the camp of the psychiatrists and psychologists. Her historical interpretation of social work was a morality play in which psychiatric heroes like Healy, Meyer, Hoch, Freud, and Rank revealed the true word and saved social work from eternal damnation in the hell of the "old sociologic approach," with its quaint assumption that since agency clients had been "deprived," the provision of "environmental opportunity" might change their behavior.[62]

In Miss Robinson's estimation, social work came of age in the 1920's, when interest shifted from the environment to the meaning of experience within the individual psyche. There was no reality external to the individual, and therefore no objective environment to analyze and manipulate. Social workers could dispense with the elaborate investigatory process described in *Social Diagnosis,* and concentrate instead upon the client's interpretation of his experience. His own story, his personal reality, possessed greater significance for the caseworker than factual verification in the Mary Richmond tradition.

For facts, environment, and social situations, Miss Robinson substituted the therapeutic relationship. A client appeared at a social agency searching out a relationship through which to realize his "ego trends." The person who voluntarily sought help unleashed constructive "ego forces" and was basically (even in the case of economic deprivation) in quest of a personal relationship able to satisfy his psychological and emotional needs. Therapy, therefore, began at the moment of contact between worker and client, and did not await the outcome of social investigation and diagnosis. In developing the relationship, the social worker had to be conscious of the ambivalent quality of human behavior. Behavior patterns could not be reduced to a logical causal sequence. In the course of transference, the worker might become an object of hate and fear as well as affection. The worker not only had to accept this ambivalence in reaction, but she had to limit treatment goals as well. Miss Robinson argued, in a significant departure from casework theory, that treatment was not defined by the client's needs, but by his capacity for growth and change within the casework relationship.

Miss Robinson's emphasis upon limited treatment goals became a key issue in the schism which eventually developed between the Freudian (diagnostic) and Rankian (functional) casework schools.[63] Led by Miss Robinson and Jessie Taft, the functional group centered in Philadelphia. Drawing their inspiration from Rank's "will psychology," they placed unusual stress upon the helping process or relationship as the medium through which the "will" effected vital personality changes. The more deterministic Freudians viewed the casework relationship as an opportunity to reduce the "reality pressures" upon the client and to shore up his ego strengths. From the functional group's point of view, the casework relationship was not shaped by the client's ego drives, but by the agency structure and service. Treatment could not exceed the limits imposed by the client's ability to benefit from the helping process within the agency structure.

It was not until the 1930's that functional casework emerged to challenge Freudian concepts of therapy. Jessie Taft, who had come to Philadelphia in 1918 to head the Department of Child Study of the Seybert Foundation and underwent analysis with Rank in 1926, cites the winter of 1929–30 as the turning point when Rank "launched without previous warning or preparation a new psychology and therapeutic method." Centering in the Pennsylvania School of Social Work and the Philadelphia children's agencies and child guidance clinic, functionalism was significant as an effort to adapt to casework in the agency setting Rank's theory of the reality of the will and his emphasis upon limitations of time and responsibility in the casework relationship. Its originators believed that the practice of limited therapy adapted to the "agency function and procedure" would eliminate the confusion caused by casework's "inability to find its place between pure therapy and public relief." [64] Social workers would acquire a technique which differentiated them from the psychiatrist. The psychiatric influence had produced a casework superior to the older social diagnosis and environmentalism, but it had obscured rather than clarified the social worker's distinctive function.

Yet, in placing extreme emphasis upon the agency as the key to professional progress, the Philadelphia social workers overlooked a truism implicit in their argument: any social work process or function, and any casework, whether Freudian or Rankian, was limited by its administrative setting. The social agency was a bureaucracy, a form of organization which necessarily imposed constraints and discouraged unlimited assumptions of responsibility for service. In maintaining that "the worker's responsibility is mediated by the agency and what it can and cannot do," the functionalist proclaimed the obvious.[65] The professional career and services of almost all social workers were conditioned by bureaucratic imperatives. The functionalists had raised disturbing questions about professional identity but exaggerated the uniqueness of the social agency and its role as a catalyst of change.

The still unhealed schism which erupted in the 1930's had opposing sects and an esoteric vocabulary. Both groups, however, were committed to a casework in which psychiatry played a dominant role. The child guidance clinic had been instrumental in this development. For many social workers, the clinic became a concrete point of contact with psychiatry and a vivid contrast to the superficial, external, and routine work of the overburdened social agency. Unlike the mental hospital, the clinic did not necessarily deal with severe mental disturbance, and offered a working model for the agency handling troubled, but not psychotic, clients. In order to improve the quality and enlarge the scope of their own services, clinic psychiatrists like George S. Stevenson and Lawson G. Lowrey actively promoted the acceptance of a mental hygiene viewpoint in social work. In large measure, psychiatry entered the mainstream of social work theory and practice through the child guidance clinic.

Psychiatry and child guidance promised to eliminate one of the most serious obstacles to the attainment of professional status—the historic identification of the social worker with charity. The psychiatrically trained caseworker was a therapist who dealt with universal problems of emotional disturbance, not simply problems of pauperism, poverty, and economic dependence. As Grace Marcus suggested, even the relief function was professionalized when linked to psychiatric skill. Psy-

Sage Foundation had enabled the school to organize a research department headed by Julia Lathrop and Sophonisba Breckinridge.[45]

In Boston, as in New York and Chicago, social workers rather than educators or academicians took the first steps in developing a formal training program. The Boston School for Social Workers was organized in 1904 by Jeffrey R. Brackett, a native of Massachusetts who had established a reputation for his contributions to public welfare and charity organization in Baltimore. Brackett's interest was undoubtedly stimulated by his membership on the New York Charity Organization Society's Committee on Philanthropic Education. Like Mary Richmond, he believed that the future of scientific, professional social work depended upon its educational facilities. While attending the first Massachusetts Conference of Charities and Correction in the fall of 1903, he broached the subject of a professional school to Frances G. Curtis, a volunteer, and Alice L. Higgins, general secretary of the Boston Associated Charities. These women responded favorably, and with their help a campaign was launched to secure the backing and financial support of Harvard and Simmons College. The instigators of the movement succeeded in obtaining what Miss Higgins described as a synthesis of Harvard's research and the democratic spirit of Simmons.[46] Brackett became the School's first director and Zilpha Smith, who had retired from the Associated Charities, became associate director.

In Philadelphia, interest in professional education was stimulated by J. Prentice Murphy (formerly secretary of the Boston Children's Aid Society) and the child welfare field.[47] The school began modestly in 1908, and was reorganized the following year as the Pennsylvania Training School for Social Workers. In 1916, it was incorporated as the Pennsylvania School for Social Service. Farther west, in 1901, round-table discussions of workers in the St. Louis Provident Association expanded into fortnightly conferences of social workers and public lectures. The social workers of the city organized the St. Louis School of Philanthropy in 1907, whose fifteen-week course was followed in 1908 by a regular one-year course. The school was affiliated with the University of Missouri until 1909, when it became the School of Social Economy of Washington University. The affiliation with Washington University was dropped in 1915, and after a year of independent existence, the rechristened Missouri School of Social Economy transferred back to the auspices of the University of Missouri.

In Cleveland, sentiment in favor of a professional school crystallized in 1913 when a committee representing eighteen philanthropic organizations addressed a petition to the trustees of Western Reserve University. The social workers wanted a school which "should teach the social sciences in direct application to community life and public affairs." [48] Three years later Western Reserve established its School of Applied Social Sciences. Two other schools of social work had emerged by 1918, both in the South. The Richmond School of Social Economy was founded around 1916 in addition to the Texas School of Civics and Philanthropy, located in Houston. The former became the Richmond School of Social Work and Public Health. The Texas School was taken over by Rice Institute in 1918.

The founders of these early schools agreed that social work demanded of its practitioners a methodology which could not be acquired through impressionistic apprentice training. "Whether there be a science in all this or not, the problems are to be studied and solved in scientific ways—by open-mindedness, by use of the teachings of experience, by efforts to see causes and results." [49] The Chicago School of Civics and Philanthropy proclaimed that, because relief had become scientific, social work had "attained recognized professional status and those who lead in it are rightly regarded as scientific specialists." Social work had its own "standards and technique" which required a special educational preparation.[50] But what kind of preparation and how different from apprenticeship? The fact that these early schools were established and controlled by social workers virtually guaranteed a conflict between the ideal of the school as a scientific laboratory, offering a broad professional education while expanding the boundaries of social work theory and research, and the need to satisfy agency demands for trained workers.

In many cases the university affiliation was a formality in terms of financing, faculty, curriculum control, and admission policy—the real affiliation being with the social agencies of the city. They supplied the instructors, the opportunities for field work, and the jobs, and the schools organized their curricula to satisfy the practical demands of the agencies. Although formal entrance requirements and curricula differed, there was a tendency toward extreme specialization and a concrete, practical curriculum which subordinated theory and research to technique. The early schools passed on a legacy of specialized, practical education for social work which became the bane of social work educators and others interested in the development of broad, scientific training. Another troublesome legacy was the role of casework in the curriculum. Casework provided the lion's share of field and vocational opportunities. Equally important, it seemed the most clearly defined technique in social work, and appropriate to the requirements of an educational institution. Like the professional association, the professional school was shaped by caseworkers as an instrument of control in the professional subculture and contributed to making casework the nuclear skill in social work.

The Chicago School of Civics and Philanthropy, although

143

not immune from the pressures toward specialization, practicality, and casework, exhibited a distinctive interest in social research, public welfare administration, and broad professional education, a program largely identified with Edith Abbott and Sophonisba Breckinridge. Both women, distinguished experts in child welfare and labor legislation, resisted agency demands for specialized technicians in the belief that social work's future as a profession depended upon the schools' ability to produce administrators equipped to handle broad problems of legislation and community welfare. Believing in university standards, they succeeded in transferring their institution to the University of Chicago in 1920 as a graduate professional school. Integration with the University evoked criticism from "eastern colleagues" who feared for the survival of casework and field work in the academic milieu.[51] By 1920 influential Eastern schools like the New York School of Philanthropy and the Boston School for Social Workers had proceeded far in the direction of specialization, vocationalism, and casework. They produced practitioners, rather than social administrators, scholars, or theorists. They offered courses in sociology, economics, political science, and community problems like immigration and industry, but these were often related to social work method and technique.

The resignation of Samuel McCune Lindsay as director of the New York School of Philanthropy in 1912 epitomized the uneasy alliance between academician and practitioner which blurred the goals and objectives of social work education. Both groups agreed upon the superiority of school to apprenticeship training, and both agreed that a social work curriculum had to combine the academic and the practical, but social workers placed far greater weight upon field work and the vocational goals of training. A political scientist and professor at Columbia University, Lindsay had succeeded Edward T. Devine as director of the New York School in 1907. He favored the creation of a university professional school on or near the Columbia campus, but was thwarted by the Charity Organization Society's Committee on Philanthropic Education which favored a more limited training school devoted to the improvement of technique in a few areas of social work if not exclusively in the operation of a charity organization society. John M. Glenn of the Committee informed Lindsay that the courses offered were excessively academic, whereas the chief goal of a school of philanthropy was to train workers in the methods and skills needed in charity organization and children's aid societies. Preparation to fill positions in these agencies was, according to Glenn, the real justification for the establishment of social work training schools.[52]

The year Lindsay resigned, the New York School of Philanthropy offered four required courses and a profusion of electives, many of them practical in nature. The required courses included the "scientific basis of social work" as revealed in sociology, economics, psychology, and related subjects; the "essential problems" of personal and family rehabilitation; the problem of neglected and delinquent children; and statistics. The electives included courses in medical social service, immigration, labor legislation, executive and financial management, the delinquent, social settlements, housing, neighborhood activities, the church, and community. Once a week, students meet the director for discussion of "social forces," and the supervisor of field work for conferences.[53]

The core of the curriculum and identifying mark of the school of social work was the provision for field work. Students at the New York School of Philanthropy had to spend four afternoons or twelve hours a week over a five-month period in clinical experience. Two months were spent in a district office of the COS, where the student was introduced to the records and filing system, studied case histories, attended committee meetings, and visited families. The district secretary was responsible for supervision. After two months with the COS, the student was free to specialize, and selected whatever branch of practical work she desired. Beginning in 1911, the School offered a two-year course, but much of the second year was devoted to field work.

The curriculum of the Boston School for Social Workers also focused upon field experience. Course work was almost an afterthought. "With the tendency to specialization, there is a growing technique in each kind of work. The best way of getting technique is by observation and practice with persons experienced in it. The field work, deemed an essential part of the school courses, is chosen with regard to the particular interests and needs of each student. The class work is chiefly to give the foundation of knowledge which all need, and to stimulate independent thought upon any problems." [54] Students attended five or six class exercises a week and divided the year's field work between two agencies. With the aid of a Russell Sage Foundation grant the school added a second year in 1912, devoted primarily to the preparation of district secretaries for charity organization societies. Most of the requests for student placement came from charity organization societies, medical social service departments, and children's agencies. [55]

The presence of the settlement leader, Robert A. Woods, on the administrative board of the Boston School failed to halt the swing toward casework and vocationalism to the neglect of neighborhood work and leadership in preventive social reform. [56] Although Brackett himself was interested in public welfare and preventive work as well as charity organization and casework, and tried to teach that social work dealt not merely with needy individuals but with community conditions and prevention as well, casework satisfied the School's need for a transmissible technique, field-work opportunities, and vocational placement in a fashion unequaled by settlement work or other forms of philanthropic endeavor. One problem with the settlement in these formative years of professional social work education was that it "desired to emphasize what might be called 'mere' neighborliness and to eliminate any tendency to regard the residents who made up its household as more expert in neighborliness than any of their neighbors." [57] The settlement was handicapped too by its belief in residence as the key to neighborhood or social understanding.[58] The assumption that one learned by absorption or immersion did not satisfy the student's desire for a ready-made helping technique such as charity organization and casework offered, and alienated those who wished to help the poor but not necessarily live with them.

From the viewpoint of social work educators the field of social legislation was equally unsatisfactory for purposes of curriculum. At a meeting of school representatives in 1919 it was voted that students should receive instruction in case work, statistics and community service. F. Stuart Chapin, a sociologist and director of the Smith College Training School of Social Work, failed to convince the group that all social workers should be trained in the techniques and methods of promoting social legislation. Unfortunately, Chapin explained to John B. Andrews, secretary of the American Association for Labor Legislation, the educators believed that social legislation lacked the clarity of the other social work techniques and was not suitable for field work. Andrews, citing the difficulty encountered by the Association in filling staff positions, expressed dismay over the "limitations placed upon social workers by their lack of knowledge in social legislation." [59]

The initial contribution of the school of social work was not to lay the foundation for a broad, generalized professional education but to establish casework as the nuclear skill in social work. The number of schools multiplied in the 1920's— undergraduate, postgraduate, and mixed—but their distinctive feature remained casework training through practical field experience. That orientation was the feature singled out most frequently for criticism by sociologists, social work educators, and others who favored a less narrow and specialized approach to professional education. Jesse F. Steiner, in his study of *Education for Social Work,* observed that "however much this group of professional schools may differ as to particular courses they offer, they find a common bond of agreement in their emphasis upon their case-work departments and in their insistence that case-work must form a very considerable part of the training of all their students, no matter in which field they intend to specialize." [60] James H. Tufts complained that the school curricula were "better developed along lines of technique and special training for specific tasks, than along lines of a philosophical view of the social process and social problems." [61] In a third general study of social work education James E. Hagerty argued that the schools were too busy producing specialists and technicians to devote attention to the "most important task they should be engaged in, namely, the education of the leaders, the organizers, the administrators—in short, the executives in social work administration." [62]

The fact that a school of social work up to the 1930's might allot as much as 80 percent of the scheduled hours to field work greatly distressed an exponent of broad professional education like Edith Abbott. Miss Abbott charged that the "academic curriculum of most of the professional schools is now poor and slight and covers in many schools only the various aspects of a single field—case work." The schools produced the technician rather than the "scientific person," whose casework skills were enhanced by an understanding of public welfare administration, social research, law, and government in relation to social welfare, social economics including social insurance, and the history of social experimentation. These constituted "foundation," not background courses.[63]

148

Miss Abbott attributed much of the blame to the social agency, which placed its needs before those of the student and the profession. She pointed bitterly to the "extreme specialization" which the agencies forced upon the schools: "We have not only not been asked, we have, in fact, scarcely been allowed to develop a solid and scientific curriculum in social welfare. Instead of that, we have been asked to provide special 'training courses' for family welfare workers, special 'training courses' for child welfare workers, special 'training courses' for medical social workers, special 'training courses' for psychiatric social workers, special 'training courses' for travelers' aid work, community chest executives, and so on." [64] The educator who favored a broad scientific curriculum resented not only the vocational curriculum which the agency imposed upon the school but its employment of raw recruits who were alloted responsible staff positions after a short apprenticeship. Nothing would give "social work the recognition and status of a profession so long as people find it possible to enter the field without professional training." [65]

With some justification, the social agency replied that the schools did not supply enough social workers to meet the chronic shortage. Although the Milford Conference report endorsed the goal of professional school training for all social workers, it admitted that as of 1929 the schools could not meet the demand, forcing the agencies to "undertake staff training on an apprentice basis." [66] A major challenge to social work education after 1930 was the expansion of its training facilities to supply enough graduates to supplant the apprentice system, and to accomplish this despite higher admission requirements and the organization of a curriculum less specialized and vocational in content.

A second and related task was to standardize admission policy and curricula in order to impose some measure of uniformity so that school training did not become as individualized as agency apprenticeship programs. As an institution of control in the professional subculture, the school nurtured group cohesiveness and identity by exposing neophytes to a uniform acculturation process. This implied the existence of an accrediting body to establish membership requirements for schools, just as the professional association did for individual practitioners. In terms of both acculturation and accreditation, social work education was severely handicapped before 1930. Since one did not have to graduate to find employment, the school did not directly influence every individual who selected the career. Men and women often entered directly from high school, college, or some other vocation. Yet the schools influenced the subculture in one important sense. Like the associations, they helped shape social work as a profession in the image of casework, and at least provided an alternative mode of entry into the professional group—an alternative which social work leaders stressed as the swiftest, most direct, and most opportune channel of advance for those who chose social work as a career. The "professional training school ideal has become such a well-established reality that it will not be many years before those seeking to enter the profession of social work at any point will find that the advantages of special education are so great that they will not be willing to attempt competition without that preparation." [67] The nongraduate and any defenders of apprentice training were placed on the defensive by those who linked professional education to professional status. Despite their limited enrollment, the schools of social work played no small role in elevating casework to the "nuclear skill," the caseworker to the "nuclear image," and professional training to the legitimate mode of entry into the subculture.

Working to expand the influence of the schools as instruments of professional control and acculturation was the Association of Training Schools for Professional Social Work, organized in 1919. The Red Cross had established training courses in home service during World War I in fifteen universities, arousing the interest of educators in social work. Several universities organized schools or departments of social work and it became apparent to social work leaders that some accrediting agency was necessary to prevent anarchy.[68] When the Association was organized in 1919 it included several college and university schools or departments of social work among its seventeen charter members, a membership which increased to twenty-eight by 1929.

The Association (renamed the Association of Professional Schools of Social Work in the 1920's) found it no easy task to impose some measure of uniformity upon this unwieldy assortment of independent graduate schools, undergraduate schools and departments, and university-affiliated graduate schools. The earliest membership requirement simply stipulated a full-year program including course and field work. In time the Association tightened its control over admission policy and curricula. Like those of the AASW, its initial requirements were broad and inclusive, reflecting a compromise with existing confusion and heterogeneity. The rising standards of both associations illustrated the tendency of institutional agents of control in the professional subculture to work toward homogeneity. Not long after the AASW raised its membership requirements to include provision for professional school training, the Association of Professional Schools took the first steps toward standardization of social work education.

In December 1932 the Association adopted its minimum curriculum for the first graduate year of professional education. The curriculum was divided into four groups. Group A contained required courses in casework, and medical and psychiatric information; Group B contained courses in community organization, specialized casework, and group work (two required); Group C contained courses in the field of social work, public welfare administration, child welfare, and problems of labor or industry (two required); and Group D included courses in social statistics, social research, social legislation, and the legal aspects of social work or social aspects of law (one required). These requirements applied to the schools, not to the students. In 1934 the Association took steps to insure that member schools could meet the minimum requirements for new applicants by establishing machinery for inspection and expulsion, and shortly afterward required all member schools to affiliate with a college or university. In 1939 the confusion arising from the mixture of graduate and undergraduate training programs was eliminated when the Association ruled that accreditation would be based upon the establishment of two-year graduate programs (although until 1952 provision was made for institutions with one-year programs).

By 1932, when the Association of Professional Schools adopted its minimum curriculum, social work educators had become more conscious of the professional school as an instrument of acculturation. They were describing education as a socialization process which eliminated personal idiosyncrasies, prejudices, or habits detrimental to professional efficiency, replacing them with attributes compatible with the values of the fraternity.

The new view would eventually dominate the philosophy of social work education. The student had to be purged of "feelings and attitudes, biases, and prejudices that are inappropriate to his particular profession." [69] It became "almost axiomatic in social work education that the self of the student" was "at the very center of his learning and that change in its use takes place during the two years of graduate study," through the student's relation with her supervisor and her "experience of acceptance of professional form" in the social agency.[70] This self-conscious interpretation of social work education had barely emerged by the late 1920's, but it illustrated the manner in which an aspiring professional community attempted to mold and perpetuate a group identity.

The concept of professional education as a growth process affecting personality reflected the psychiatric and mental hygiene point of view which entered social work in the 1920's. Since social work had shifted its focus from the external environment to the "individual's inner problem," there was "no escape from responsibility for the worker's attitudinal equipment as the first concern of training." [71] It had to be shaped in accordance with the norms and values of the professional subculture in order to insure that the student did not use the worker-client relationship as a means of satisfying her own emotional needs. Education as growth also pointed to a solution of the perplexing problems raised by field work in the curriculum. It was admittedly indispensable. Yet social work educators had never been sure just how to relate field to course work in an integrated, meaningful fashion, or how to make it a genuinely educational experience rather than mere exposure to a series of isolated, routine agency tasks. Conceivably, the answer lay in a view of the student's training as a growth process, for if she arrived at a new "orientation, a point of view that will eventuate in technique and that will be organized in knowledge content, then the class and the field are related in the beginning." [72] The personal relationship established between the student and the supervisor, who represented the agency and the profession, made field work an educational experience through which the student matured into a professional person. The supervisor was there to see that the student adjusted her personality and emotional attitudes to the exigencies of the job.

The theory of professional education as growth attained its most systematic formulation in the 1920's through the Bureau of Children's Guidance at the New York School of Social

Work. Porter R. Lee, the School's director, became an eloquent spokesman for the new approach. Lee had succeeded Mary Richmond as secretary of the Philadelphia Society for Organizing Charity in 1909. His executive abilities and interest in social work education led to his appointment as director of the New York School in 1917. He was the first teacher of casework at the Pennsylvania School of Social Work and among the first to use the case method of instruction, familiar to law and medicine, in social work education. No one—not even Mary Richmond—had greater faith in the development of social work as a profession based upon scientific knowledge and technique acquired through training in a school of social work. Technique, he admitted, was no end in itself, but it was the indispensable "factor which rounds out our march towards social justice and every social program must in the end stand or fall upon the quality of its technique." [73] Technique was a stage in an evolutionary process which saw ideals and concepts crystallized into programs, and the programs carried through by skilled social engineers. Lee epitomized a strain of Progressive thought which idealized the expert or technician and which was used by social workers to justify their claims to leadership.

If Lee brought to the New York School of Social Work his evaluation of the social worker as the social engineer in a pluralistic, atomistic society which had witnessed a decline in the authority of traditional institutional controls, he also brought a passion for improving the quality of education so that the school could fulfill its obligations to the student, profession, and community. "If we are to insure the steady development of our standards, we need to consider even more thoughtfully than we have already done the personnel of our profession." Successful social work, Lee continued, "means a higher order of skill than it ever did before." [74] A key to the entire structure of social work education lay in the establishment of a relation between school and agency which guaranteed the student a valuable field experience. The schools should not send the agencies more students than they were equipped to handle, and the agencies should not regard field work as the part-time responsibility of an overworked staff member. Agencies should accept only as many students as could be handled by full-time workers assigned to the task by either school or agency. Lee accepted the implications of this policy: the agency's and school's first responsibility was to those who adopted social casework as a professional career.[75] In their early years the schools had welcomed volunteers as well as paid workers.[76]

During the 1920's Lee advanced from the theory of social work education as training in technique to the theory of social work education as a growth process precipitating changes in personality and attitudes. He observed in 1926 that "in so far as the social worker succeeds by deliberate effort in improving his personality equipment he is, in my judgment, adding to his technical skill. In so far as he makes himself master of the technique of social work I believe he is schooling his personality to express itself in ways that make for sounder, more helpful professional relationships. Technique means nothing but a better organization of one's powers for a particular task."[77] Lee explored the deeper meanings of social work education in *Mental Hygiene and Social Work*, published with Marion E. Kenworthy of the Bureau of Children's Guidance in 1929. The training period, they argued, should result in "certain definite personality developments which are quite as important in the practice of social case work as are experience and education in the more limited sense."[78]

Through the medium of carefully supervised field work the student first experienced and tested her professional self. Representing the agency and profession, the supervisor gradually introduced the student to the accepted procedures and norms of the subculture, insuring at the same time that the student did not experience severe emotional and mental strain. The students needed help as much as the clients, for they had to adjust to a new professional role incompatible at many points with their existing mental and emotional equipment. Those, for example, who were easily shocked and found it difficult to withhold moral judgment had not achieved the objectivity which the "professional obligations of social work demand." [79] The field-work experience offered them an opportunity to develop and test professional capabilities, but the supervisor directed professional growth in a manner beneficial to the clients and served as a necessary source of security and reassurance.[80]

Through field experience directed toward professional growth, the school and agency tightened the subculture's control over new recruits. The assumption that social work demanded not only scientific and technical skill but certain personal attributes acquired through a prescribed educational process emerged as a second limitation upon the spontaneous will to serve. In both cases an effort was made to restrict membership in the practitioner group to those qualified by training and indoctrination.

Chapter VI

Agency and Community:
The Apotheosis of Efficiency

NO development was more significant in explaining the limitations imposed upon voluntarism than the bureaucratization of the social agency. Administrative exigencies shaped theory and practice as much as the concept of professional skill and the emergence of a professional subculture. In his presidential address before the National Conference of Social Work in 1929, Porter Lee had argued that a successful cause tended to "transfer its interest and its responsibility to an administrative unit" which justified its existence by the test of efficiency, not zeal, by its "demonstrated possibilities of achievement" rather than by the "faith and purpose of its adherents." Although some persons deplored the emphasis upon "organization, technique, standards, and efficiency," fervor inspired the cause while intelligence directed the function.[1]

The shift from cause to function, a process far advanced by the end of the 1920's, signified the institutionalization of social responsibility and mutual aid in an urban-industrial society. Believing that social problems were subject to rational analysis and control, but also that their scope and complexity were too vast to be handled by the impulse of benevolent individuals, reformers in the late nineteenth and early twentieth centuries created an immense network of welfare organizations to care for the deprived and maladjusted. Among the consequences for remedial, preventive, and constructive philanthropy were function instead of cause; administrator instead of charismatic leader; rational organization and centralized machinery of control instead of individual impulse and village neighborliness. Gertrude Vaile doubted that great leaders and pioneers like Jane Addams, Robert Woods, Julia Lathrop, or Florence Kelley would appear again. "The whole host of social work," she explained, "has now, through organization and the labor of many, moved forward to occupy positions to which the great leaders heroically blazed the way . . . Indeed, we find in positions of organization leadership persons of executive powers who may or may not have powers of social insight and leadership." [2] Haphazard methods of help, according to another social worker, were ineffective in an "increasingly machine governed and urban civilization." [3] Organization was the key to efficient philanthropy.

The charity organization movement foreshadowed subsequent administrative developments. Its leaders insisted that philanthropy could become a science if social agencies were properly coordinated and if the workers were trained or supervised. The crusade to elevate philanthropy to scientific status and eliminate dependency by discovering and eradicating its underlying causes resulted in the repudiation of spontaneous or sentimental charity and the substitution of the social agency for the benevolent individual as the repository of philanthropic wisdom. The efficiency and effectiveness of the community welfare program required that the impulse of individuals be disciplined, channeled, and filtered through the agency.

In the absence of any firmly established tradition of philanthropy as an endeavor demanding skill and central direction, critics interpreted efforts to restrict benevolent spontaneity as misguided attempts to substitute cold, impersonal machinery for the instincts from which charity sprang. Mornay Williams, a New York lawyer, informed Edward T. Devine of the New York Charity Organization Society, that love superseded method in charitable affairs. He deplored the Charity Organization Society's emphasis upon technique rather than service, and advised that it was preferable to forego investigation and give to an unworthy subject than to stifle the ordinary man's charitable sentiments by prohibiting spontaneous charity.[4] Even a member of the Society's executive committee objected to the red tape in which its charitable labors had become ensnarled; an inordinate amount of the organization's resources was devoted to clerical and statistical work.[5]

After 1900, the emergence of casework and the professional subculture hastened the transition from cause to function in social work. An occupational group aspiring to professional status had arisen with a future closely linked to that of the agencies. Unlike other professions, social work was almost exclusively a corporate activity, with little opportunity for independent practice. To carve out a niche, the social worker had to attain hegemony within the agency; that task was facilitated by bureaucratic pressures nurturing professionalism at the expense of voluntarism.

*

The interests of the social agency and of social work as a professional subculture intersected at several key points, all related to the bureaucratic goal of efficiency. Efficiency was the object of bureaucratic organization, in contrast to democratic organization, where dissent, freedom of expression, and respect for individuality were superior values.[6] One significant measure of the shift from cause to function in social work, then, was the degree to which the efficiency goal influenced agency structure and service.

Formal organization was not necessarily incompatible with a high level of volunteer responsibility in administration and service.[7] Generally speaking, however, social welfare and particularly casework organizations followed the path of least resistance, seeking not the modes of reconciliation but rather justification of their community mandate through efficiency embodied in a trained, paid staff. This bureaucratic imperative of efficiency linked with the professional subculture to limit and control voluntarism; in the eyes of the social worker seeking professional recognition, the agency goal of efficiency and her monopoly of treatment and administrative responsibilities were inseparable. The first generation of paid workers had cooperated with the volunteer in building the framework of organized welfare services, and they never doubted the real or potential contribution of voluntarism. Their successors, less intellectually and emotionally committed to the volunteer and simultaneously embarked upon a quest for professional status based upon technical proficiency and scientific casework, became reluctant to consider themselves the paid agents of volunteer directors and visitors.

The extraordinary success in attracting and retaining visitors which the Boston Association Charities had in the nineteenth century was the product of "twenty years of patient, hard work." These volunteers were not cheap labor. On the contrary, they greatly increased the administrative and supervisory burdens of the agency. Zilpha Smith welcomed them, however, because she believed that their efforts were "for the good of the poor people, for the good of the whole community."[8] She was prepared to subordinate efficiency in the sense of economical, standardized, and rationalized operations to the goal of citizenship participation.

The emphasis began to shift in the first two decades of the twentieth century to the ideal of efficiency, heralding the transition from cause to function. One observer commented favorably upon the brisk, businesslike atmosphere of the New York Association for Improving the Condition of the Poor: "Its watchword is efficiency; the test applied to the individual and to the organization as a whole being economy of administration and the best results with the least expenditure and waste." The Association's achievement resulted from the replacement of "unskilled sympathizers using desultory and spasmodic efforts, with workers who are trained to follow up one effort by another and who are less liable to make mistakes and are less easily discouraged." [9] By 1913 it appeared that the time was near at hand when "no charity can be recognized as efficient that does not employ trained professional workers." [10]

The quest for efficiency and administrative technique in social agency operations paralleled the caseworker's efforts to reduce the range of intuition, subjectivity, and unpredictability in her own work. In both cases the volunteer introduced an element of uncertainty. Neither her livelihood nor social status depended upon conformity to agency policy or to the standards and procedures of professional casework. Volunteer service conflicted with the administrator's desire for rational, efficient organization and the social worker's identification with the agency as a vehicle for professional achievement.[11]

Bureaucratic organization, as described by Max Weber, exerted pressures for efficiency through the medium of specialized expertise, administrative hierarchy, organizational procedure and regulation, and depersonalization. Between the spontaneous will to serve and those in need intervened agency standards, channels of communication and authority, rules, and a tendency toward elimination from official business of "love, hatred, and all purely personal, irrational and emotional elements which escape calculation." [12] These characteristic features of bureaucracy, although dysfunctional if carried to extremes, influenced social agency structure in the three decades after 1900.

In one important sense the triumph of bureaucracy was complete by the 1920's. The mutual interest of staff and administration in upholding standards through selective hiring had its counterpart in the adoption of the principle of selective voluntarism. By careful screening, training, indoctrination, and supervision, the agency used volunteers for certain specified tasks without compromising its efficiency and administrative integrity. Selective voluntarism sanctioned compliance with the potent rhetoric of citizen responsibility in a democratic society without seriously threatening professional hegemony. It was professional social work's solution to the dilemma of volunteer service in an era of formal organization. Helen P. Kempton, associate director of the American Association for Organizing Family Social Work, explained that the volunteer "cannot be enrolled by the mass method any more than can the paid social worker, or the teacher, or the diplomat; the matter of his choosing is a highly selective process, depending upon his personal qualifications; and his value to the agency enrolling him will be determined largely by the nature and extent of his training." [13] Volunteers had to be "conditionally accepted and wisely utilized." Those who failed to satisfy agency standards could anticipate a diplomatic but firm dismissal.[14]

The consequences of bureaucratization were illustrated in the changing role of the board of directors as well as in the attitude of the paid worker toward her volunteer superiors. The board member of the nineteenth-century charity organization society was no remote figure who met from time to time with other directors to ponder broad questions of policy. He participated actively in the administration and work of the society. The line between executive and board authority, between administrative and treatment responsibility, was blurred. In 1889, for example, fifteen of the eighteen board members of the Boston Associated Charities served as members of district conferences and as friendly visitors.[15] The proportion was similar in Baltimore but changed in the first decade of the twentieth century owing, in part, to the sour skepticism of the paid worker: "Many a new social worker felt when he sat at his first board meeting that the well-to-do businessmen and society women who faced him belonged to a different world from the one in which he planned to function with fine determination to lessen social maladjustments." [16] It became difficult to maintain the cooperative ideal when the paid worker and executive in the early twentieth century began to view the social agency as their vehicle for creative professional careers. One of Zilpha Smith's successors at the Boston Family Welfare Society claimed that agency directors had no mandate to trespass upon executive functions. Being responsible for results, the executive "should have a free hand in regard to organization, method, staff appointments, and even as to salaries, within the limits of the plans and policies determined by the directors." Should the director decide to participate in the agency's work, he thereby automatically subjected himself to the "administrative authority of the executive." [17] It was unlikely that the executive would encourage such personal service. Francis H. McLean of the Russell Sage Foundation suggested that the board observe casework operations from a respectful distance: "In the actual case work of the society a board will be extremely chary of interference." Unless the staff requested its advice, the board should refrain from participation.[18] Having been stripped of the responsibilities assumed by a paid administrative and service staff, how did the board then account for its stewardship? Obviously, by securing "a paid staff that is competent to render the services necessary." [19]

Social workers managed to impress upon board members the fact that wealth, social standing, and good intentions were not substitutes for training and skill.[20] The acceptance of this point of view was essential to the paid worker's professional aspirations. To some degree, her unrelenting emphasis upon efficiency represented an effort to win board support for her claims to technical competence and leadership prerogatives. No board member, as a trustee of other people's money, could dispute the desirability of efficiency as an agency goal, and the word served as a potent weapon in defense of professionalization.

The board member of the 1920's was less anxious than his predecessor of the nineteenth century to meet and serve agency clients personally, or to sacrifice the time to participate in district committees, case conferences, and similar administrative affairs. Now that evangelical zeal and the mystique of personal service had been replaced by a bureaucratic machinery geared to efficiency, philanthropy remained an opportunity to promote business and social contacts and fulfill expected social obligations without the burdens of intimate participation. Those board members who wished to perpetuate the older cooperative tradition were hard-pressed to justify themselves in any logical or functional terms. Once having accepted at face value the paid worker's contention that efficiency was a prime agency goal and specialized training a prerequisite to efficient agency operation, the volunteer board member found it difficult to establish a sound basis for participation in the work of the paid staff. Nothing was solved for the board member who argued that the "emphasis must be laid, not on the professional and the volunteer, but on proper training for *both*," for he could not hope to com-

pete on these terms.[21] The real issue that emerged was not how to divide responsibility for the same services between paid staff and volunteer board, but what essential contribution the board could make (apart from broad policy determination) which did not interfere with the activities of the staff. From this perspective, the interest of both board member and professional in problems of interpretation and liaison assumed considerable significance.

As an interpreter, the board member performed a valuable and vital service without compromising administrative and professional integrity. The board provided an important "link between the highly specialized activity social work has developed into and the great mass of citizens upon whom it depends for support and for whose assistance and benefit it exists." [22] Social work confronted two particularly acute problems of interpretation. There was the persistent challenge of convincing the public that social workers performed a vital task requiring professional skill and training. Some correlation had to exist between what the public demanded and what social workers aspired to do if the profession was to gain confidence, support, and respect. The public had to understand the distinction between casework and charity, between social work as a profession offering skilled services of universal application and social work as a task requiring no particular ingenuity, absorbed in the relief of destitution. This problem of interpretation was immeasurably complicated by the fact that those who derived the least direct benefit from social work and were least likely to request professional services as clients were the ones who had to support and finance the professional superstructure. Under the circumstances, the professional social worker, although opposed to board interference in agency operations, acknowledged its indispensable public relations function. The public needed a "stepping stone to the intricacies of social work," while social work needed a link to the community money and power structure.[23]

The changing function and relationship of the board member to the paid staff pointed to a more general phenomenon—the bureaucratization of voluntarism or the creation of a volunteer subculture with its own hierarchy, specialization, and organization. Social agencies not only found the board member useful as a liaison, but as an advisor or consultant who possessed special legal, financial, literary, or other talents. These could be used in the allotment of board assignments without compromising administrative integrity or exposing clients to "nonprofessionals." The efficiency ethos which permeated professional social work and contributed to the volunteer's acquiescence in agency discipline also led to a sharp distinction between the board member (administrative volunteer) and the service volunteer, who performed a variety of tasks for the agency: escort, case aide, tutor, seamstress, recreation and clerical assistant, fund-raiser. The service volunteer was useful to the agency in performing countless chores which otherwise would have required paid help, including discarded functions of the professional staff. Volunteer specialization and hierarchy were paralleled by formal organization designed to help relate agency needs and volunteer services. An Association of Junior Leagues of America was established in 1921 and a National Committee on Volunteers in Social Work in 1933.

The imperatives of formal organization confronted social work administrators with knotty problems of value and priority.[24] Given the agency's and profession's dependence upon public support and understanding, was it worth sacrificing some measure of efficiency in the short-term, technical sense in favor of widespread volunteer participation? Would personal service dramatize and personalize social work for the ordinary citizen, preventing it from becoming an anonymous bureaucratic machinery which an anonymous public was asked to support on faith? Could the volunteer be used to alert the agency to community needs and opinion, enabling it in the long run to function more efficiently? The principle of selective voluntarism did not satisfactorily resolve these dilemmas nor define the volunteer's role in an era of formal organization. From the viewpoint of those who regarded volunteer service as a citizen and agency responsibility, selective voluntarism was an evasion if it limited participation to a small board of directors at the top and a large number of individuals performing trivial, routine tasks at the bottom. One social work executive admitted that "intelligent volunteers are frequently heard to complain because they are given too little scope for independent action and because they feel that too often they have been assigned routine jobs." [25] A volunteer resented the fact that, although volunteers had founded social work, they were now "regarded as a handicap." The professional workers had become the "actual heads of the social agencies" while the volunteer struggled mightily to retain a "precarious foothold." Assigned unimportant work, they became "bored and unreliable." A vicious circle existed, "unreliability breeding an attitude of superiority from professional to volunteer, which in turn only increased the very quality which begot it." [26]

The theory of supervision as it emerged in the late 1920's epitomized the organizational pressure for efficiency—the apotheosis of rational, predictable performance which led to a regimented voluntarism. Supervision theoretically assured that the worker's performance did not fall below agency standards. This responsibility was particularly important in a field which still relied so much upon apprenticeship training. The limited controls exerted by the professional school and association meant that the supervisor had to assume much of the burden for acculturation and training. Through supervision the values, norms, and performance standards of the profession were conveyed to neophytes and reinforced in the case of experienced workers.

A self-conscious awareness of supervision as a kind of casework with psychiatric content emerged in the late 1920's and early 1930's. It was interpreted as a helping process, applied to the worker instead of the client. Just as the caseworker labored to remove the mental or emotional blocks which obstructed the client's social adjustment, the supervisor endeavored to eradicate or reshape personal attitudes and habits which detracted from the worker's professional effectiveness. "If leadership treatment in a family involves the adjustment of human relationships and the modification of attitudes," one supervisor observed, "how then can a visitor perform those functions unless she herself is satisfactorily adjusted, and until her own attitudes are modified to meet her needs?" [27] The caseworker could not legitimately resent supervision if she honestly believed that her own efforts embodied an "art and a philosophy, not merely a trade practiced on the handicapped and helpless." Supervision was a form of relationship therapy, enabling the supervisor to "influence a case worker's attitude, to assist her in revising or establishing a philosophy of life, and to help her attain emotional maturity in her relation to those with whom she lives and works." [28] Using casework methods to assist the worker in overcoming her "personality limitations," the supervisor helped develop an "effective relationship between the visitor and her community, her particular job and her profession." [29]

The supervisor's responsibility was to insure the "performance of the case work job in the most efficient and masterly fashion possible." [30] Among the means to this end was the integration of the agency's service and administrative structure. The supervisor served as a channel of communication between the executive and service staffs, between the shapers of agency policy and those who applied it. Agency efficiency depended, presumably, upon her adroitness in coordinating "case work practice with the ideals and policies of the administration." [31] This coordination was imperative because the formal organization developed needs of its own apart from those of the individuals who staffed it.[32] The social agency provided the worker with opportunities for a creative professional career, but the "laws of organizational behavior" required that the worker align her individual needs with the standards and procedures the agency had formulated to help accomplish its ends with a minimum of friction, confusion, and waste of personnel or resources. The conception of supervision as a helping process akin to casework was coupled with a stress upon the supervisor's singular administrative responsibilities. It was an "inherent part of her job to see that the work of the organization is accomplished, that agreements with the community are carried out, that proper provision is made for the needs of those who come for help." She saw to it that reports came in on time, that proper records were kept, and that "proper accounting" was made of the money entrusted to the agency.[33] The agency did not wish to crush the worker's individuality or creativity, but it could not leave to chance the "efficient working—or mechanics—of the office routine and the actual process of working with the client." [34] Without supervision, there was danger of overlooking the "general principles of case work which should be applicable under any circumstances, certain standards which must be expected of all." [35]

The supervisory function suggests the relevance to social agency structure of impersonality or depersonalization, one of the bureaucratic characteristics outlined by Weber. It did not mean that bureaucracy eliminated personal emotions and feelings, or that irrational influences did not affect the activities of the organization.[36] But bureaucracy tended, in the name of efficiency, to limit the scope of irrational factors in official business: "The more complicated and specialized modern culture becomes, the more its external supporting apparatus demands the personally detached and strictly 'objective' *expert,* in lieu of the master of older social structures, who was moved by personal sympathy and favor, by grace and gratitude." [37] The irrational was unpredictable, unmeasurable, and, ultimately, uncontrollable. The formal organization imposed rational system and order wherever possible and in the social agency the supervisor played a key role in reducing the influence of personal whim, emotion, and impulse. Undoubtedly the tendency of formal organizations to favor conditions which enhanced the possibilities of rational calculation hastened the substitution of paid, trained workers for volunteers. To the degree that voluntarism increased the boundaries of uncertainty and unpredictability in agency operations, it suffered in the transition from cause to function.

In the process of transition, the social agency may have adhered too faithfully in some respects to the Weberian model. Its goals and professional skills differed from those of bureaucracies where efficiency and effectiveness could be quantified with greater precision. Unlike chemistry, law, and engineering, which dealt with uniform events or handled traditional areas of knowledge, social work involved human relations and efficiency may have depended upon substantial deviation from Weber's laws of organizational behavior.[38] Many social workers objected to supervisory controls, claiming that they restricted independence and growth and were an affront to professional dignity.[39] Formal organization encouraged professionalism and coincided with the needs of the subculture, but the paid staff confronted serious problems of adjustment to those same organizational imperatives which constrained voluntarism.

Supervision was only one area of friction between bureaucratization and professionalization. The professional staff desired to eliminate board interference within its professed sphere of competence and responsibility. It sought to minimize the antagonisms between the agency as a bureaucracy with limited goals and the agency as a locus of professional service with "relatively unlimited commitments." A third persistent conflict arose from administrative pressures favoring procedure, routine, and organization loyalty, as opposed to the profession's stress upon creative skill and service as absolute values.[40] The agency-subculture conflicts did not provide an opening wedge for voluntarism. If anything, they limited the social worker's perspective, directing her attention inward toward problems of agency adjustment rather than outward toward the community and volunteer. The pressing issue became how to mold agency policy and structure in order to minimize points of friction with the profession rather than how to maximize volunteer service.[41]

*

The efficiency goal of the social agency was only one manifestation of the transition from cause to function in social work. The establishment of an elaborate social welfare machinery in the late nineteenth and early twentieth centuries created complex problems of interagency adjustment and relation. Charity organization societies had originally made coordination part of their mission, but in becoming service agencies they gradually abandoned this responsibility. One supporter of the New York Charity Organization Society considered this an unfortunate departure and hesitated about sending in his annual subscription because the Society was duplicating the work of relief agencies instead of coordinating their services and preventing abuses.[42]

The proliferation of welfare and reform organizations not

only intensified the need for coordinating machinery but contributed to the cleavage between casework and social reform.
The caseworker could afford the luxury of immersion in
problems of individual adjustment and professional skill partly
because other public and private organizations arose to supply
relief and crusade for better housing, public health, child
welfare, working conditions, and recreational facilities. Even
in the early twentieth century, when the New York Charity
Organization Society crusaded zealously for preventive social
legislation, Frank J. Bruno dismissed the idea that its district
family work should become the basis for institutional change
and social reform. Caseworkers might furnish data for the
determination of reform policy, but neither their mentality
nor their training equipped them for leadership in social legislation.[43]

Social welfare in America after 1910 was strenuously occupied in the effort to transcend specialization and fragmentation and to coordinate the activities of the swarm of casework,
health, recreation, education, reform, and other welfare
agencies. Out of the drive for financial federation which
blossomed around World War I, came a potent, centralized
pressure for efficiency expressed in the community-wide
machinery of social welfare rather than in the individual
agency. The community chest was the ultimate in bureaucratization, in the shift from cause to function. An anonymous
public supported an anonymous machinery to serve anonymous clients. Support was requested, not for indivdual agencies, but for an organized pattern of welfare service integral
to the social structure of an urban-industrial society. Financial
federation did not contest the professional's claim to agency
leadership. Although the chest actually opened new dimen-
sions for voluntarism, particularly in fund-raising, the voluntarism it encouraged was selective, controlled, and compatible
with an efficient, rational, and well-ordered network of wel-

fare services. Just as the agency discouraged an uninhibited, spontaneous voluntarism in the case of individuals, so the chest sought to insure that no agency undermined the efficiency of the community welfare program. From the perspective of financial federation, the functional administrative unit which had succeeded the cause was not the individual agency but the total welfare machinery. Federation demanded conformity to a rather abstract and remote bureaucracy, governed by the calculus of over-all needs and resources.

The chest was at first only one expression of a much broader and visionary pursuit of social harmony based on principles of social organization capable of overpowering the centrifugal forces of modern life. Although financial federation and other schemes to coordinate the activities of social agencies eventually emerged as the dominant theme in community organization, the original exponents of this new process in social work had cherished hopes of a rejuvenated democracy. Arrangements to improve the efficiency of social welfare machinery were subordinate to the wider objectives of primary group association in neighborhood life, widespread citizen participation in civic affairs, and the shaping of a community loyalty which transcended allegiance to special interest factions. From the viewpoint of early prophets of community organization like Mary P. Follett, Joseph K. Hart, and Eduard C. Lindeman, the future of democracy depended upon the ordinary citizen's ability to regain control of his own destiny through intensive civic association. Only in a creative group life could he realize his own potential as a human being and a citizen and find the strength to resist the external manipulating forces which relegated him to the role of passive observer. Through cooperation with others the citizen minimized the demoralizing effects of community fragmentation. The expert and specialist assisted in the formulation and implementation of community goals, but did not dominate or dictate. The reconciliation of democracy and autonomy with the specialization or expertise indispensable to a complex, industrial society was the fundamental challenge to community organization. In substituting the bureaucratic goal of efficiency for the democratic goal of self-determination and civic participation, financial federation diverged from the original (and perhaps Utopian) ideals.

The neighborhood work of the settlements and charity organization societies represented early experiments in community organization; and settlement workers were prominently identified with a self-conscious and articulate effort to transform the public school into a neighborhood center. Disturbed over the class, ethnic, and cultural atomization of the urban community, they searched for some effective galvanizer of primary group association and saw in the public school a potential urban substitute for the small town church and town hall. If used intelligently, the public school would help transform strangers into neighbors. Interest in the welfare of their children provided a natural bond among residents who would gather for recreational and social occasions as well as discussion of public issues. Wider use of the school plant was stimulated by the ambitious program of the Rochester, New York, school board, which also pioneered in the development of visiting teaching. The board in 1907 appropriated $5000 to a School Extension Committee representing eleven civic and social organizations, and appointed Edward J. Ward, a leader in the community center movement, as its civic secretary. By 1911, when the first National Conference on Civic and Neighborhood Center Development convened, 248 school buildings in 48 cities had opened their doors to neighborhood activity. The Conference eventually led to the organization of a National Community Center Association.

The exponents of the movement hoped that the socialized

school would serve as a magnet to attract citizens whose fragmentation into special interest and occupational groups had obscured their common civic loyalty and responsibility. The school center was a valuable "means of transforming mere residents in a given locality into neighbors." [44] Although the number of socialized schools increased in the 1920's, the movement, conceived as a quest for primary group association, never succeeded. The socialized school did not materialize as one of the "powerful influences of neighborhood life." [45]

Neither did the "Social Unit" plan, the most ambitious and widely advertised scheme of community organization to appear before the 1920's, become a model for neighborhood democracy. The Social Unit was an heroic effort to achieve community organization through the establishment of an organic relation between citizen and specialist. Mr. and Mrs. Wilbur Phillips, who had worked with the Infant's Milk Depot in New York City and with the Milwaukee Child Welfare Commission, originated the Social Unit plan. On the basis of their experience, particularly the child welfare station and baby clinics at Milwaukee, they developed a program which illustrated community organization ideals before absorption of the movement in problems of coordination and rationalization of the welfare machinery.

At a 1915 meeting in Washington attended by medical and social workers Mr. and Mrs. Phillips gained support for their idea; in the following year a National Social Unit Organization was established with Gifford Pinchot as president and the Phillipses as executive secretaries. The Organization selected the Mohawk-Brighton District of Cincinnati for a three-year experiment to end on July 1, 1920. Mohawk-Brighton was a middle-class residential area of about 15,000 population, many of German extraction. The district was split up into thirty-one blocks, each containing about five hundred people. With these blocks as nuclear cells, the sponsors prepared to test their theory that a democratic and effective form of community organization which stimulated people to define and meet their own needs had to divide the citizens into small primary units, organize the occupational specialists, and insure an "organic and co-ordinate working relationship between the representatives of groups having special knowledge or skill for service to the community and the representatives of the residents." [46]

Block residents over eighteen years of age elected seven persons to serve as a block council which selected a block worker as executive. The block workers together formed the Citizens' Council of the Social Unit. The committee of eight local women appointed in Milwaukee to arouse interest in the preventive health work of the child welfare station was the seed from which the block idea evolved. Each occupational group in the Mohawk-Brighton District also elected a council, although the occupational groups were small enough to serve as *de facto* councils. The executives elected by the occupational groups formed the Occupational Council of the Social Unit. In Milwaukee the occupational group was foreshadowed in the election of physicians by their colleagues to staff the baby clinics. The General Council of the Social Unit was composed of the Citizens' and Occupational councils.

In the three years of its existence, the Social Unit concentrated upon public health services, including an infant welfare station with nursing supervision at home and medical examination, prenatal and postpartum medical and nursing supervision of mothers, medical and nursing services for the preschool children, nursing supervision for tuberculous and pretuberculous patients, and medical examination of adults. No service was initiated without prior discussion precipitated by the block workers who explained each proposal and the intended results. As an instrument of community education, the Social Unit experiment was a reasonable success.

Agency and Community

The Social Unit's achievements in promoting citizen interest in public health did not necessarily recommend it as a scheme of organization which could survive the shock of sharp political and economic controversy or racial, religious, and cultural differences. Public health was relatively noncontroversial, affording opportunity for cooperation in a single sphere without commitment to primary group association. The three-year experiment exposed other weaknesses in the Social Unit plan. For the most part, block councils did not function effectively. They assumed little responsibility for directing the block workers and carrying out district policies. The block workers assumed an inordinate burden of executive responsibilities, which deflected their attention from the legislative work of the Citizens' Council. All of the block workers and most members of the block council were women, another limitation which suggested that any scheme of neighborhood organization was handicapped from the outset by the functional decline of the neighborhood. Work took the men outside the neighborhood for most of the day, while modern transportation facilities enabled residents to satisfy many recreational and social needs beyond the immediate neighborhood. The comparatively successful integration of physicians, nurses, and social workers into occupational groups was not paralleled in the case of clergymen and teachers. The Protestant Minister's Council played no active role and the Catholic hierarchy, though not overtly hostile, lent no organized support. The Social Unit failed to influence the public school curriculum in any way.

The Social Unit experiment illustrated community organization ideals in the morning years, when its exponents believed literally in the possibility of a social harmony transcending the fragmentation of American urban life. The Social Unit reflected a quest for unity linking citizen with specialist, neighbor with neighbor, special interest group with community-wide interest. It stressed, not what the social agency and social technician could achieve for the citizen, but the joint responsibility of citizen and specialist in discerning local needs and meeting them through consultation and cooperation. Not efficiency but cooperative democracy was the goal.

The First World War accelerated the search for cooperative democracy through community organization. Directed toward a destructive end, the patriotic fervor in countless American communities forged a unity, spirit of sacrifice, and single-minded devotion to a common cause rarely attained in American life. Americans ostensibly had demonstrated their capacity for cooperation and the wonders it could work. Anything seemed possible, including a group consciousness and devotion to the "community good" powerful enough to subvert the "forms of pseudo- or partial community organization, loyalty to which can and does eclipse loyalty to the community as a whole." [47] Although the wartime pressure for civic unity, expressed in part through the widespread adoption of community councils and war chests, hastened the spread of federation in social work, it also nurtured the nuclear idea of community organization as a crusade for cooperative democracy. The latter vision flourished between 1918 and 1922, when the first general accounts of the theory and practice of community organization appeared.

The New State by Mary P. Follett, a Boston social worker, was one of the earliest and most comprehensive outlines of community organization theory. Focusing upon the creative power of group life, Miss Follett argued that the "true man" discovered his identity and released his potentialities only by means of a satisfactory group relation. The neighborhood represented the best geographic setting for group organization; there people learned the "technique of association" and created a new political unit to substitute for party government. In contrast to the external manipulations of party politics, the neighborhood organization fostered "real unity" in place of the "pseudo unity of party." Organized into their neighborhood group, the people expressed their basic needs, desires, and aspirations. These, rather than the ambitions of politicians, deserved recognition as the "substance of politics," and the measure of public opinion.[48]

Miss Follett did not suggest that it was possible or desirable to obliterate other forms of association such as trade unions, churches, and fraternal societies. As the embodiment of the general will the neighborhood group coordinated the activities of the others and translated their efforts into generalized values and programs. The neighborhood group was a foundation for a new cooperative democracy in which the false distinction between private and civic life disappeared. Work, water, food, and child-rearing—all daily life—was politics; no artificial line separated the home from the city. The educational system faced no greater responsibility than to train children in group consciousness, preparing them for citizenship in cooperative democracy.[49]

In the eyes of Eduard C. Lindeman, the conflict between democracy and party politics was only one instance of a more fundamental tension between democracy and "specialism." He described the Community Movement as a reaction against centralized control, "an attempt on the part of the people who live in a small, compact, local group to assume their own responsibilities and to guide their own destinies." Scientific technology encouraged political, economic, and administrative centralization, and gave birth to "technologists or specialists" whose monopoly of knowledge made them indispensable to progress, but who were also obstacles to any "conscious effort on the part of a community to control its affairs democratically." The fundamental task of community organization was to reconcile the "democratic process" with "specialists, organizations, agencies and institutions by means of recognized inter-relations."[50]

The emergence of financial federation in the 1920's as the leading expression of community organization led to an important shift in emphasis. Community organization by 1929 was "largely dominated by and applied to social-work agencies." Its energies were directed toward the correlation of the "activities of these agencies in order to enhance their efficiency." [51] Federation employed the rhetoric of the early community organization movement, but its intensive concern with the machinery and financing of social welfare diverted attention from cooperative democracy and the creative group life of the ordinary citizen to problems of agency administration and service. It substituted the bureaucratic goal of efficiency through expert leadership for what had been a quest for democratic self-determination through joint efforts of citizen and specialist. Community organization had barely emerged as a cause before it had become a function absorbed into the administrative structure of social work.

*

Businessmen and large donors who were expected to support the community welfare machinery played a major role in promoting financial federation and encouraging centralized coordination. As early as 1900, chambers of commerce and similar organizations slipped into the vacuum created by the failure of charity organization societies to fulfill their original purpose. In 1900 the Cleveland Chamber of Commerce organized a Committee on Benevolent Associations, and two years later San Francisco and Seattle established Charities Endorsement committees. Worcester, Massachusetts, and Lincoln, Nebraska, followed in 1907 and 1909, and by 1910 similar agencies existed in Buffalo, Chicago, Minneapolis, and St. Louis.[52]

Howard Strong of the Cleveland Chamber of Commerce justified the endorsement work as a necessary public responsibility rather than an effort of businessmen to control and dominate the welfare machinery. "The Chamber has in its relation to the charity of the city, assumed as a fundamental principle, that the charity which receives its support from the public is, in a sense, a public institution, and that the public has a right, and a responsibility to know its methods and to demand its conformity with an accepted standard of efficiency." Invariably, the endorsement committees stressed the individual agency's obligation to limit its autonomy in favor of a constructive, community-wide program or equilibrium of needs and resources. The agency was one administrative unit in a broader network of services, whose effectiveness depended upon a cooperative effort to raise standards, prevent duplication, and eliminate waste. As prerequisites to receiving its endorsement card, the Cleveland Chamber of Commerce stipulated that any agency must, first, fill a need great enough to warrant support of a separate institution and, second, "agree to co-operate with other charitable institutions in promoting efficiency and economy of administration in the charities of the city as a whole, and in preventing duplication of effort." [53]

These attempts to promote efficiency by endorsement were not unwarranted intrusions by obtuse businessmen and givers seeking false economies. The confusion and inefficiency resulting from a multitude of local and national agencies competing for funds, duplicating services, and failing to coordinate their efforts were real enough. Although social workers did not agree that a commercial organization like a chamber of commerce should serve as an instrument of community organization, they did not deny that there was need for effective coordination or restraints upon absolute agency autonomy and supported efforts to establish councils of social agencies.[54]

Like the chamber of commerce endorsement committee, the council of social agencies arose in response to the need for rationalizing the community-wide structure of welfare services. The interrelatedness of social work summed up the underlying philosophy of the councils. Each individual agency was the concern of all others because "poor methods, poor standards, poor ideals mean poor work, and nothing gets in the way of an efficient social agency so quickly as the poor work of another agency." [55] Operating through the Charity Organization Department of the Russell Sage Foundation and later the American Association for Organizing Family Social Work, Francis H. McLean assisted in the formation of many of the early councils, which he termed "functional" in contrast to financial federation. Eight were in existence by 1917: Milwaukee, Wisconsin; Rochester, New York; Columbus, Ohio; St. Louis, Missouri; Chicago, Illinois; Minneapolis, Minnesota; Springfield, Illinois; and Columbia, South Carolina.[56]

McLean preferred the functional, noncontractual council of social agencies to the potentially coercive financial federation as an instrument of welfare planning and agency coordination. Financial federation nonetheless grew rapidly after World War I. Although some cities possessed a council but no community chest, or a chest and no council, the typical federated city included both in some combination. Financial federation was the clearest and most explicit expression of the shift in community organization from cooperative democracy to bureaucratic efficiency. Donors, volunteers, and professionals disagreed over its implications. Critics accused the chest of being a menace to the survival of private, voluntary welfare or a conspiracy of businessmen to save money and bother; defenders proclaimed it as the savior of private welfare and an expression of the businessman's sense of community responsibility. Often ignored in the emotion-laden controversy were the structural changes in social welfare which gave rise to the chest and enabled it to flourish despite opposition.

Chapter VII

Federation and the
Bureaucratic Imperative

AFTER a survey of the fourteen financial federations in existence in 1916, a special committee of the American Association for Organizing Charity (AAOC) declared itself "very positively" opposed to further adoption of the plan.[1] The war smothered the committee's plea for restraint and led to a hothouse growth of financial federation in the 1920's. As a technique of community organization the chest was more inclusive than the social service exchange or charities endorsement committee. The councils of social agencies, on the other hand, were described as "hollow organizations" which lacked the financial resources and power necessary to develop a sound community-wide welfare program.[2]

Financial federation captured the imagination of businessmen by promising efficient coordination and organization of the community welfare machinery, immunity from multiple solicitation, economical collection and distribution of funds, and the development of a broad base of support which would relieve the pressure on the small circle of large givers. The corporation, increasingly regarded as a source of gifts, appreciated the conveniences of federated finance.

Much of the opposition to chests stemmed from executives

and board members of "big, individualistic agencies which wanted to keep all their old attributes and privileges, without the concessions necessary to cooperative finance and planning." [3] Their attitude toward the chest was ambiguous. They feared and resented a potential threat to autonomy, but also welcomed liberation from the time-consuming, often frustrating, burdens of fund-raising. On balance, the allure of financial security outweighed the fear of centralized control and the reluctance to sacrifice some autonomy.

Financial federation, which received the support of social work figures like William J. Norton, Elwood Street, C. M. Bookman, Sherman Kingsley, Allen T. Burns, Raymond Clapp, and Edward T. Devine, was not a scheme arbitrarily imposed by businessmen. The chest was the outgrowth of an agency-centered machinery of social welfare which required coordination and a stable source of income, and also of an industrial, corporate economy with a vast economic surplus to provide the funds if systematically exploited. Federation provided a formal link between the two. It sought maximum support for an efficient, constructive, community-wide welfare program; and it attempted to rationalize giving habits to insure the stable income needed for skilled personnel, administration, and coordination. Financial federation increased the influence of bureaucratic efficiency goals in American social welfare. It provided new opportunities for volunteers, but in a regimented, hierarchical, citizen-army of fund-raisers dedicated to supporting the professional machinery. The chest widened the distance not only between volunteer and client but between volunteer and social agency, and obscured the trend toward professional hegemony within the agency.

*

The joint fund-raising appeal and the "whirlwind" campaign were perfected but not invented in the twentieth century. In Liverpool, England, a number of contributors formed a central committee in the 1870's which prepared a yearly pledge sheet listing endorsed charities willing to transmit their appeal through a single office. In New York City in 1879 several hospitals joined in a "Hospital Saturday and Sunday Association" and in Denver, Colorado, in 1887, a charity organization society assumed some fund-raising responsibilities. Two English clergymen familiar with the Liverpool experiment participated in the formation of the Denver Society, which raised some $21,700 for ten agencies in its first campaign. The Jews of Boston and Cincinnati established federations in the middle 1890's, and by 1915 the movement had spread to approximately forty cities.[4]

The short-term, intensive campaign utilizing large numbers of volunteers also appeared in the nineteenth century, and was associated with Charles S. Ward and Lyman L. Pierce of the YMCA. Secretary of the Omaha, Nebraska, "Y" in the early 1890's, Pierce enlisted a hundred men, each responsible for acquiring a new member a month until a total of 1500 was reached. Divided into twenty teams, the recruiters attended regular meetings to report progress and plot strategy. Charles Ward's plan for the Grand Rapids, Michigan, "Y" in 1897 involved an intensive one-month soliciting drive by the Association directors. Shortly thereafter, Ward moved to New York as financial secretary of the International Committee of the YMCA, and was dispatched to various cities to explain his program. Pierce and Ward cooperated for the first time in 1905. Having assumed the post of secretary of the Washington, D.C., YMCA, Pierce decided to embark upon an ambitious $300,000 building campaign. The International Committee sent Ward to assist him in an unprecedented one-week campaign involving numerous volunteers.[5]

Financial federations, virtually nonexistent before 1913 except for Denver and the Jewish philanthropies, made some use of the whirlwind campaign although opinion of its value was divided. Federations had appeared in Elmira, New York, in 1910 and in San Antonio, Texas, in 1912. Thereafter the idea spread more rapidly: Cleveland, Ohio, in 1913; Dayton, Ohio; Richmond, Indiana; South Bend, Indiana; New Orleans, Louisiana; Salt Lake City, Utah; and Birmingham, Alabama, in 1914; Cincinnati, Ohio; Dallas, Texas; Oshkosh, Wisconsin; Erie, Pennsylvania; and Baltimore, Maryland, in 1915; St. Joseph, Missouri; Grand Rapids, Michigan; Milwaukee, Wisconsin; Springfield, Massachusetts; and Houston, Texas in 1916. The San Antonio, New Orleans, Salt Lake City, Birmingham, and Houston federations were short-lived, while that in Springfield barely functioned.

The highly publicized and influential Cleveland Federation was the first modern community chest and marked the real beginning of the movement in the United States. A Committee on Benevolent Associations of the Cleveland Chamber of Commerce launched the campaign which resulted eventually in the establishment of the Federation for Charity and Philanthropy. Martin A. Marks, a Jewish businessman and civic leader, was chairman of the Committee and "instigator of the movement." [6] Disturbed by reports from agencies that fundraising was becoming difficult, and by complaints from givers that the number and urgency of appeals were becoming unmanageable, the committee decided to unearth the facts. It discovered that in 1907 only 13 people contributed 35 percent and 74 persons, 51.5 percent of the funds raised by Cleveland's charities. A follow-up investigation in 1909 revealed that even fewer persons were contributing a larger percentage of the welfare budget: 6 donors were responsible for 42 percent, and 54 for 55 percent; only 253 individuals contributed nearly 75 percent of all the funds. In a city whose population exceeded 600,000, the charities relied upon 5,386 persons for donations of $5.00 or more. Between 1907 and 1909 the amount contributed had increased by 22 percent, although the number of contributors had declined by 11 percent.[7]

Financial federationists often maintained that a disproportionately small number of donors contributed the lion's share of operating expenses. In Erie, Pennsylvania, 2,190 individuals or firms contributed to the support of twelve philanthropies: 75 percent of the contributors gave to only one organization; 4 percent gave 54 percent of the funds; and 10 percent were responsible for 75 percent of the money.[8] Agencies were forced into cutthroat competition so that the "growth of charitable organizations was much more proportionate to their financial canvass and its effectiveness than to the intrinsic worth of the various works."[9] Some social workers like Sherman Kingsley, second secretary of the Cleveland Federation, found the competition oppressive and wasteful. Referring to his days with the Chicago Relief and Aid Society and its relation with the Chicago Bureau of Charities, Kingsley deplored the rivalry and bitterness which prevailed. A frantic competition for contributions was conducted with little reference to the real needs of the community.[10]

A rationalized fund-raising system was not viewed by leading federationists as an end in itself, but as a means of achieving an efficient balance of welfare needs and resources. The chest in its formative years assumed a broad mandate for coordination, research, and welfare planning. This expansive interpretation of its function lent a distinctive flavor to the early federation movement. The creators of Cleveland's Federation did not justify it exclusively in terms of the need to broaden the circle of givers and eliminate the waste inherent in competitive solicitation. It was conceived as an organization which concentrated the entire resources of the community upon the "challenge of the city of today," stimulating not only more gifts and givers, but the "securing of larger results . . . through the exercise of greater economy and efficiency with the help of co-operative effort and co-ordi-nated administration." The Federation was fundamentally an educational endeavor, "a movement which has for its purpose the interpretation of social facts and social forces to the community in such a way as to secure the community's sup-port and then to unify and to co-ordinate this general support in the way to make it most effective in solving what is after all the unified community problem of human welfare." Pre-sumably, it would establish the charitable enterprises of Cleveland on a "solid systematic and scientific basis." [11]

Much criticism was inspired by fears that federation would depersonalize the individual agencies, leaving an anonymous, uninspired relation between the citizenry and the welfare machinery. "Centralization of power in the hands of a few," warned the general secretary of the Boston Associated Chari-ties, "may mean the diminution of interest on the part of the many." In its critical report of 1917, the committee of the AAOC asserted that immunity, lump-sum and undesignated giving, and the whirlwind campaign, even if responsible for a temporary increase in contributions, ultimately failed to "build up as stable a constituency as most organizations in non-federation cities now have." [12] Once the novelty of federation had worn off, contributions and interest would decline. Federationists countered with the arguments that publicity and education would maintain a high level of in-terest while the policy of allowing designated giving guaran-teed a personal relationship between donor and agency.

The prime issue in this controversy was not whether inter-est would increase or decrease as a consequence of federation, but whether philanthropic leadership and direction should come from a central organization or from the individual agencies. From the federationist viewpoint, the transition from cause to function in social welfare and the inability of agencies effectively to siphon off the wealth available for support of philanthropy necessitated a large measure of central control. The financial federation was "an effort to widen the channel for a greater flow of voluntary contributions from the economic surplus by means of modern efficiency and modern organization, in order that we may purchase more quickly better social conditions and a better social order." Effective federation implied restraints upon agency autonomy in favor of a community-wide perspective in social work: "This license to establish agencies at will," a social worker charged, "created a wide diffusion of administrative responsibility centering on fragments of the social problem, and not on the social problem, with a control of the separate agencies lodged in themselves and for themselves, instead of in the community and for the community." The "modern world" demanded efficiency, large-scale organization, and centralization.[13] Federationists insisted that social welfare needs and resources be viewed as a unified whole and believed that they were the first to do so.[14]

The businessman, tired of being solicited and badgered by "every social agency in town," experienced intensified pleas for contributions after the outbreak of World War I, and especially after America's entry in 1917.[15] Some three hundred American communities organized war chests to cope with the mounting flood of appeals from national and local agencies, many of them devoted to foreign relief.[16] This unprecedented philanthropic mobilization accustomed the American public to the intensive, federated, short-term campaign, and popularized the chest method. Often sponsored by chambers of commerce, boards of trade or councils of defense, the war chests solicited in a period of full employment and high wages, and in a climate of war-inspired patriotism they had little difficulty in reaching their quotas. Returns from 43 cities with an aggregate population of 7,068,750 persons showed that 2,273,216 persons, or 32 percent contributed an average sum of $30.40. The success of the war chests induced five state councils of defense to recommend state-wide adoption of the plan.[17]

The war chests confirmed the federationist argument that a central organization specializing in fund-raising could amass more money with less annoyance to givers than a multiplicity of independent drives converging upon a limited constituency. In contrast to the sporadic, *ad hoc* efforts of single agencies, the war chests established an elaborate, systematic canvassing machinery designed to reach every potential contributor. An executive committee directed the campaign or delegated this function to a special committee. Budget, publicity, supply, statistics, and records committees were supplemented by the important soliciting divisions which canvassed trade and occupational groups. The aggressive chest drives led in some instances to coercion. One kind stemmed from the competition for pledges between departments of a factory or between factories in a community. It took a courageous man to refuse to subscribe in view of the social pressure and stigma of disloyalty to the war effort. Some cities maintained investigation departments with paid employees to follow up delinquent pledges, and in Albany a "Loyal Legion" pursued slackers. In many cities pledges were deducted from the pay envelopes of industrial and public utility employees. To insure that labor turnover and mobility did not obstruct chest collections, factories in Youngstown, Ohio, deducted the unpaid pledge remainder from the departing employee's paycheck, and in Detroit factories were asked to underwrite employee subscriptions.[18]

Although federationists were delighted with the achievements of the war chests, they conceded that the chests had serious flaws. Some displayed poor judgment in their appropriations, like the city whose chest had benefited appreciably from labor contributions only to designate a strike-breaking "home guard" as its first beneficiary. Another fault was the limited agency control over chest policy when a federation ideally represented a cooperative effort of contributors and agencies. Most important, from the perspective of efficient, scientific fund-raising and community organization, was the chests' failure to adopt sound budgeting procedures. Although all local federations recognized budgeting as essential to their success, the pressure of war needs resulted in the adoption of community quotas and an allotment of funds based upon guesswork.[19]

The local war chests distributed much of their income to national agencies occupied with relief at home and abroad and with recreation and morale in army camps. The campaigns of national agencies to raise enormous sums of money played a significant role in popularizing the whirlwind technique. The first of the great national drives took place in the spring of 1917, when the YMCA sought $3,500,000 and raised more than $5,000,000. The Red Cross followed in June 1917, seeking, and exceeding, the incredible sum of $100 million. Both Ward and Pierce assisted Henry P. Davison in plotting this campaign. The YMCA entered the field again in the fall of 1917, exceeding its quota of $35,000,000 by nearly $20,000,000. In the spring of 1918 the Red Cross again requested $100 million, and raised $170 million.

The last national drive, and a federated one, took place in 1918. President Wilson in September requested Harry E. Fosdick, Chairman of the Commission on Training Camp Activities, to arrange a united appeal for the seven agencies recognized by the War Department as instrumentalities through which servicemen were "assisted in many essential matters of recreation and morale." The agencies (YMCA, YWCA, National Catholic War Council, Jewish Welfare Board, War Camp Community Service, American Library Association, and Salvation Army) agreed upon a joint campaign during the week beginning November 11, and established a quota of $170,500,000. The United War Work Campaign raised $203,000,000, described by Director General John R. Mott as the "largest sum ever provided through voluntary offerings for an altruistic cause" in the history of mankind.[20]

The United War Work Campaign announced its intention "to see that every man, woman and child in America is given an opportunity to subscribe to this fund." An accomplishment of this magnitude depended upon a "thoroughness of organization from the largest city down to a school district in the remotest part of a country," reaching every person "irrespective of race or creed."[21] The Campaign's central organization included a national chairman, director general, united committee, and executive cabinet, supported by a series of special divisions: field organization, special groups, publicity, finance, industries, rural, victory boys, victory girls, speakers, students, military and naval camps, Negroes, Americans abroad, and insular possessions. Local organizations established similar divisions. The United War Work Campaign not only exceeded its goal, but did so in the midst of a devastating influenza epidemic and after the Armistice was declared.

*

The Red Cross and the groups affiliated with the United War Work Campaign were just a few of the national agencies with which the war chests and their successors had to contend. The number of national agencies had increased rapidly after 1900, and the outbreak of war in 1914 provided additional stimulus to their growth. It was apparent by 1918 that some satisfactory relation had to be established between local federations and national agencies, if the former were to rationalize giving and develop an efficient, coordinated network of welfare services.

Federation

The need for some means of detecting and excluding disreputable agencies induced a number of chests to sponsor the National Investigation Bureau (later National Information Bureau) in 1918 to collect data and provide a service comparable to that of the chamber of commerce endorsement committees. By 1922 the Bureau had filed information on more than 1800 agencies.[22] Endorsement was a minor problem in comparison to the task of integrating local affiliates of powerful, but reputable national agencies like the Red Cross and YMCA with federation budget and community organization policy; in some cases these affiliates were prevented by national headquarters from adapting their work to the local program. Especially aggravating from the viewpoint of efforts to promote efficiency and eliminate waste was the spectacle of national agencies competing for funds and providing duplicate services. The lack of coordination, the failure to define fields of service clearly, the occasional misuse of funds, "heavy overhead charges," and waste persisted.[23]

In the early 1920's, the National Information Bureau appointed a committee, including Porter Lee and Walter Pettit, to examine the work of forty-six national agencies in fourteen American cities. Only twelve of these had been in existence before 1900, and of the remaining thirty-four, thirteen had been organized in 1917 or afterward. The committee reported a fairly widespread local belief that there was an excess of national agencies and that "representatives of national organizations tend to be interested only in their own local agencies rather than in the relation of these local agencies to the community as a whole." In several cities local affiliates of one national agency were forbidden to cooperate with those of another.[24]

An uneasy truce punctuated by open declarations of war characterized the relation between federations and national health and welfare agencies. Manifestos defended the national agencies as champions of the traditional American heritage of voluntarism or accused them of a selfish individualism. Other statements affirmed the right of federations to establish community welfare policy or condemned them as charitable monopolies seeking to squelch voluntarism. Insofar as the debate focused upon emotional, value judgments about voluntarism, it contributed little to an understanding of American welfare. Multimillion-dollar national agencies with hundreds of thousands of contributors and perhaps professional staffs did not precisely fit into the volunteer tradition of village neighborliness. Voluntarism was more fundamentally affected by the imperatives of formal organization and professionalization than by chest policy. The pertinent question was not whether the chest nurtured or obstructed voluntarism but whether it served its avowed purpose.

Expressed frequently in terms of a communal mystique, no doctrine was more typical of financial federation than the need for coordination, cooperation, and over-all administrative efficiency. Adopting the idealistic rhetoric of the early community organization movement, chests referred often to the war experience in their efforts to arouse a militant civic patriotism transcending race, class, and religion. "During and immediately after the war," explained C. M. Bookman of Cincinnati, "citizens in all walks of life were willing to accept more communal responsibility. . . . War brought us together with a unity of purpose and of action capable of doing anything. . . . One method of retaining this interest in process of demonstration is called the Federation Plan or community chest plan." The soap manufacturer William C. Proctor described the chest as the agent of brotherhood which embodied the "great impulse" of the war period. The contribution of the war chests to civic solidarity outweighed their financial achievements. "People laid aside lesser considerations and worked together for the greater things." Referring to a forthcoming chest campaign, a St. Louis businessman and civic leader guaranteed success, if the "spirit of our people is aroused as it was during the World War." [25]

Chest influence depended, in good measure, upon acceptance of the doctrine that a city's welfare program should be an organic whole. It was necessary, urged one chest executive, to think "in terms of the total available resources, financial and otherwise, in relation to the total ascertained needs." Sooner or later, social work would be "tested by its capacity to integrate itself into a community program on the basis of generally accepted professional practice, not upon the excellence of any special technique." [26] A major assumption underlying federation's characteristic apotheosis of community was that the era of pioneering had given way to one of organization, consolidation, and administration similar to that in other spheres of American life. Social work, observed a sociologist sympathetic to federation, would always be experimental and pioneering. "But the past half century of social-work development in American cities has demonstrated a number of things that need not be demonstrated over again." Social work had been accepted as a "fundamental part of the life of the community" and could no longer progress in a "spontaneous, irregular and unplanned" fashion.[27]

In a variation of the ubiquitous community theme, federation allied itself with democracy. Federationists argued that social work too often withdrew into an institutional exclusiveness. "My lady of leisure, my gentleman of wealth, and my worker with a call to service" persisted in "regarding separate agencies as their own property" and resented the "public's right to ask questions." In contrast to private agency directors and executives, federation boards presumably had no choice but to "listen to *vox populi*." [28] Federationists encouraged the belief that the community's entire welfare machinery was a quasi-public trust rather than private property and subject to supervision and control by the central federation. Social welfare was a communal administrative responsibility rather than a private humanitarian crusade, let alone an opportunity for any person to exercise the benevolent instinct in any manner whatever. In the event of a conflict of loyalties, "the larger loyalty, the one which subordinates the particular institution or agency to the central idea of a high standard of life in the community as a whole, must prevail." [29]

Humanitarians of an earlier generation, like Joseph Lee of Massachusetts, were depressed rather than inspired by the "passing of control of the destiny of social work from the few choice spirits who created and lovingly fostered it to the great and merciless democracy." [30] As one chest executive observed, "we are facing here the age-long and inevitable conflict which exists in any society between the urge for individual independence and initiative on the one hand, and the need for social control on the other." [31] Lee refused to admit that the chest was a logical response to the development of agency-centered, professional social work and the problems of administration and financing it created. In his estimation the chest was a device which enabled the businessmen who raised the money to concentrate "dictatorial power" in their own hands; and as a consequence the chest exhibited an "inevitable hostility to new things." The essence of private, voluntary social work, Lee believed, was its pioneering quality, implying the right to experiment and even make mistakes. The best the chest could offer, given its pressure toward standardization and repugnance toward "new and untried things," was a bland mediocrity.[32] Stockton Raymond of Boston agreed that the chest, exerting its power to "suppress new activities," was ultimately pernicious because "hitherto, one of the most precious possessions of the social agency in an American city has been its power of individual initiative." [33] Apparently the chest was for or against "democracy," a stimulus or a drag to "voluntarism," depending on whether one interpreted welfare from the viewpoint of agency initiative and autonomy or the rational community calculus of needs and resources.

Since the chest was a federation which depended upon the cooperation of affiliated agencies, whose representatives shared in administration and policy formulation, critics exaggerated its powers of coercion. Federation enthusiasts, however, exaggerated the ability of chests to develop a unified but flexible welfare program based upon a galvanized community ethic. One thing was certain—with varying degrees of success community chests exerted a pressure toward rationalization of the professional welfare machinery which had emerged in the twentieth century. They labored persistently, if often fruitlessly, to define the roles of professional, agency, and volunteer in a complex network of specialized services and organizations.

As a consequence of its emphasis upon economy, efficiency, and uniform service standards, federation endorsed the professional worker's contention that philanthropic leadership and client care were the prerogatives of the trained and skilled. No conflict, in this respect, existed between the chest and the professional subculture.[34] In focusing upon the welfare machinery and equating efficiency with professionalism, the chests proceeded to undermine their own ideal of welfare as an expression of civic unity drawing upon the services of all for the benefit of all. By extending the social agency's constituency to a vast, anonymous contributing public, and releasing it from excessive dependence on a few large contributors who might insist on a voice in policy formation or the right to participate in the agency's work, federation furthered the growth of professional welfare.

Community chests were identified with a variety of measures to improve professional service standards and administration. Even the prewar chests engaged in "community tasks" as distinct from fund-raising.[35] The Cleveland Federation sponsored conferences to standardize and coordinate welfare activities. The introduction of mental testing in the work of some organizations which served unwed mothers and the use of Federal Children's Bureau report forms were among the positive accomplishments of a conference on illegitimacy. A conference on the handicapped resulted in a survey of cripples in order to provide a factual basis for future work with this group of dependents. The Federation participated in the formation of a Hospital Council, and prepared an analysis of expenditures for all hospitals, orphanages, and fresh air camps. It studied the accounting methods of affiliated agencies, and refused to distribute money from its discretionary funds to those which had unsatisfactory accounting procedures. In addition, the Federation encouraged the use of the confidential exchange maintained by the Associated Charities.

The lack of trained personnel and the faulty organization of welfare services in outlying counties attracted the attention of the Baltimore Federation. It employed an experienced social worker to survey conditions throughout the state. His efforts resulted eventually in the establishment of a Social Service Association in Prince George's County under the leadership of a former district secretary of the Baltimore Federated Charities. In cooperation with Johns Hopkins, the Federation instituted a training course for county attendance and probation officers. It encouraged research to provide a realistic foundation for planning, administration, and coordination, including studies by the bureau of state and municipal research on the district work of the city's charitable agencies, and on the activities of casework agencies. In Cincinnati, the Federation employed an accountant to assist affiliated organizations with bookkeeping, and appointed a committee on standards for relief. With the Federation's approval, the Anti-Tuberculosis League turned over its relief work to the Associated Charities. The Federation established a permanent committee on planning and authorized a city-wide survey of the status of the Negro.

Fact-finding, standardization of records, improved bookkeeping and accounting procedures were noncontroversial, offering little threat to autonomy or voluntarism. Federationists, however, insisted that inefficient agencies or those which unnecessarily duplicated the work of others should be eliminated, and, conversely, that no group of citizens possessed the right to establish a new agency unless it served an essential need and contributed to a balanced community welfare program. Agencies were obliged to refrain from arbitrary expansions or contractions of their services. "The recognition of the common objectives," explained an official of the Cincinnati Federation, "negatives the possibility of an effective independent action." The secretary of the Cleveland Associated Charities warned that "any social organization that is unwilling to see its problems as an element of the whole, unwilling to give and to get with the others, better get on that sane, sound basis as soon as a sound and equitably managed federation can become a part of its community." According to Norton, director of the Cincinnati Federation, the "day of unrestrained initiative" was passing in social work, now that fields were "largely occupied" and a body of "scientific facts and principles" existed. The need for professional standards and administrative efficiency justified the same federation restraints upon "voluntarism" as those imposed by the individual agency in its specialized field.[36]

Federation's success or failure in developing a community program hinged, in large measure, upon the power and intelligence of the budget committee. Through its budgeting procedure, theoretically, the chest gained insight into the needs and resources of a community and exerted an influence over constituent agencies more potent than moral suasion. The

Cincinnati Federation was among the first to work out satisfactory "budgetary control." [37] It required each affiliated agency to submit monthly and annual reports on standardized forms. A public accountant examined these against the agency books. The funds allotted to each organization were determined by the budget committee after consultation with agency executives and board members and after examination of the agency's operations. Presumably, the precise sum authorized by the budget committee represented a compromise between the agency's needs, the most urgent welfare needs of the community, and the amount which the committee thought it possible to raise.

Selection of the budget committee varied from place to place, as did the general organization of the chests. In the early 1920's the Rochester Chest was a federation of contributors, and the president selected the six members of the budget committee. The Philadelphia Chest was also a federation of contributors, and the board of trustees appointed the budget committee. The Louisville Welfare League was a federation of agencies with some contributor representation, and the president of the League appointed the budget committee of seven. In Cleveland, an elaborate, interlocking chest-council organization prevailed; the Welfare Fund and Welfare Federation possessed separate offices and staffs, but the same executive staff directed both groups; the budget committee was composed of one representative from each affiliated agency. In Cincinnati, the once separate chest and council had merged, and the Community Chest and Council of Social Agencies consisted of both contributors and social agencies; four members of the budget committee were selected by the chairman of the board and another five by the agencies.[38]

It was apparent to federationists and critics alike that budgetary control was the keystone of the community chest. The broad perspective associated with central budgeting resulted, hopefully, in the establishment of priority scales and the funneling of limited funds where most needed. "Because budget committees have had to sit down before the whole welfare program and its financing, or at least before the financing program of a considerable group of agencies, and because the amount of money available is always less than the amount of money needed, budget committees have been forced to reckon with the problem of relative urgencies." A direct relation existed between budgeting and higher professional standards because the "very association that is created by comparative studies of costs and services, the overlappings that are discovered, the close association of people working in the same field . . . all tend to spur on social works and social-workers to attain higher standards in the fields in which they operated." The "budgetary principle" was essential, and "the movement could not succeed in the long run without it." [39]

The danger always existed that opposition to controls by affiliated agencies would transform budgeting from social planning into a logrolling operation that merely balanced conflicting claims. The path of least resistance for any budget committee was to subordinate comprehensive, effective social planning and the coercion and unpleasantness it implied to more limited financial objectives. Federated groups claimed reasonable success in reducing fund-raising competition, but confronted difficulties in controlling the expenditure of funds because of the influence of constituent agencies in shaping or resisting chest policy.[40] The experience of the Washington, D.C., chest, for one, suggests that on the level of social organization and planning federation has suffered historically from a deficiency rather than an excess of power. Financial troubles which threatened the survival of several organizations in the late 1920's created a pro-federation sentiment among Washington social agencies.[41] A chest was established which explicitly assumed the responsibility for "judicious expenditure of all moneys collected." Unfortunately, from the budget committee's point of view, the chest was not achieving its constructive social goals. The committee was handicapped by general confusion as to whether the chest was a financial contrivance and servant of the agencies or a community leader with authority to supervise agency activities. Although the committee did not doubt that its work involved community planning as well as fund-raising, it lacked any clear understanding of the extent of its responsibilities or authority over agency policy. What use was it if "busy men and women spend hours in discussion as to how to expend the funds collected in a way that will best take care of the needs of the city," if the agencies ignored the committee's recommendations?[42]

*

The federation movement, struggling to coordinate and rationalize the community welfare machinery, confronted equally arduous tasks of interpretation and financing. The chest became a public relations arm of professional social work, seeking to convince the average citizen that support of welfare was a fundamental civic obligation. Critics of federation lacked perspective when they argued that the annual contribution was akin to a tax which sterilized giving by eliminating any sense of personal identification between giver and ultimate recipient. Federation attempted to make giving systematic and sufficient; it did not create the welfare machinery with its insatiable appetite for funds. What sterility existed in the relation between contributor and social work was a product not of federation, but of professionalism and the transition from cause to function.

In the early twentieth century the anatomy of contemporary private social work took shape: a compound of national health and welfare agencies and, in the larger cities, a host of specialized agencies involved in casework, group work, community organization, and social reform. Caseworkers moved into new settings such as the hospital and public school and sparked a drive for professional status, rooted in scientific knowledge and skill acquired through training and experience. A professional subculture sought to nurture a group consciousness and channel career opportunities. These widened the chasm between paid workers and volunteer or, more generally, between agency-centered, professional social work and average citizen. Federation developed a self-conscious publicity and public relations program not only to stimulate contributions but to interpret and to sell the new structure of social welfare to the public.

Business advertising provided the only model for an effective public relations campaign; welfare was a product to be marketed. If merchants and manufacturers could "get returns on thousands of millions of dollars expended each year in practical publicity," so could social work. The returns to the community would not be measured in dollars and dividends, but in health, happiness, and better lives. The best "social advertising" approximated the "best types of commercial advertising." [43] The challenge was to adapt techniques developed by business in order to compete with business for the consumer's dollar. In its publicity efforts, federation followed that "analogy with business methods which calls for publicity and appeals based on the same principles as successful advertising and sales." [44]

Although the Cincinnati and Baltimore federations employed publicity agents, the Cleveland Federation was perhaps the first to introduce systematic public relations into its scheme of operations. Much of the credit belonged to Charles Whiting Williams, its executive and a skilled publicist who knew how to stimulate interest in the work of the Federation and its affiliated agencies.[45] The Federation used every possible medium, including newspapers, window and bulletin board posters, stereopticon slides, bulletins, yearbooks, exhibits, and a speakers' bureau. Cleveland's emphasis upon publicity and education had a "profound influence" upon the federation movement.[46]

Critics did not deny the importance of publicity but argued that the federation variety performed a disservice to social work in the long run. In basing its publicity upon a rather abstract concept of civic responsibility, federation once again depersonalized the individual agencies. Ultimately this "lessened contact between givers and the objects of their gifts" would diminish interest and social intelligence with "unfortunate results on every side."[47] Coupled with this criticism was the somewhat contradictory assertion that federation's whirlwind campaign and broad, inclusive appeal put a premium upon emotionalism at the expense of intelligent, informative publicity. The AAOC committee offered some examples of the sentimental appeal at variance with the "constructive ideals" of the federation itself and of preventive social work in general. One federation had implied that the Associated Charities had relieved and rehabilitated the families under its care for five dollars per family, a gross exaggeration and misuse of the word rehabilitate. Another issued a leaflet whose cover cartoon pictured "Old Man Grump" with a basket on his arm and money in his hand, remarking that "Huh! I guess it won't hurt some of us to think about the other fellow a little." Another selected as its campaign slogan, "Let us Save the Kiddies and their Mothers." Still another, disregarding the confidential relation between agency and client, printed store-window posters with a picture of a couple "snatched from almost certain ruin and death by the Associated Charities." The poster of another federation pictured a five-year-old asleep in the street, and in the text referred to the "cry of the hungry for bread" and the "orphan unguarded from the cold." This federation urged all to "share their bounty with the poor." The appeal letter of one federation beseeched the recipient to imagine his children "left penniless and orphaned . . . manly little Joe, with his cherubic face, his tousled curls, and his effort to walk and talk like father—dainty Bessie, fragile and delicate, your heart's treasure, whose golden head is always nestling against you." [48]

It would not be difficult to find intelligent specimens of federation publicity and, conversely, similar sob story appeals issued by individual agencies. Federation did not monopolize the simple-minded slogan; it reflected in acute form a common uncertainty about the purpose and substance of social work publicity. Social workers in theory wanted an "informed constituency" enlightened by appeals to reason and intelligence; therefore they wished the federations to emphasize a "conception of the whole community and . . . use of the scientific method in developing the life of that community." [49] But how intellectual could publicity directed to a vast, anonymous public be in an era of agency-centered, professional social work? A sophisticated program emphasizing preventive and constructive ideals lacked the capacity to stimulate more than passive or indifferent loyalty. "We are so afraid of being caught in sentimentalizing that we crush out of our public and private speech all natural sentiment," explained one social worker. "We tend to present the methods, the technique, and the tools of our work and leave out all that we hope to build with them. We are so concerned for recognition of the scientific aspects of our work that we present it as though it were inhuman." [50] Once the agency expanded its appeal beyond a limited, select membership, it confronted knotty problems of interpretation, involving the relative proportion of emotionalism and sloganeering, on the one hand, reason and constructive argument, on the other. The character of social work publicity in the twentieth century was not attributable to federation but to the nature of the public or "market."

Federations and social agencies in the 1920's launched a search for effective techniques of presentation. This development paralleled the emergence of public relations as a distinct occupation and another aspiring "profession." [51] Concentration upon technique permitted the philanthropic publicist to seek necessary public support and funds even though fundamental questions of purpose and content were unresolved. The important thing was unremitting publicity "couched in terms that will be understood by the common people." [52]

Unlike the businessman who offered a tangible article to the consumer, the social worker sold a faith in her ability to perform a service important to the entire community. Systematic publicity cultivated this faith, and increased contributions. Yet no amount of publicity could compensate for faulty organization of the fund-raising mechanism which, geared to a mass giving public, was the ultimate key to philanthropic finance. Federation emerged not only to rationalize the community welfare machinery but also to supply it with a stable income through rationalization of giving habits.

As early as 1905, William H. Allen, general agent of the New York Association for Improving the Condition of the Poor, issued a plea for a "systematic method of raising funds." He insisted that altruistic motives were governed not by caprice but by "laws which can be analyzed, understood and cultivated, as well as those of pedagogics and criminology." [53] After Allen became director of the Bureau of Municipal Research in New York, he launched a pioneer investigation of "efficient appealing and giving" based upon analysis of 6000 supplicant letters addressed to Mrs. Harriman, a New York philanthropist. Coming from American and foreign individuals and institutions, these appeals totaled some $267 million. Allen concluded that no correlation existed between community needs and community resources: givers had no way of knowing the most urgent requirements of their community; even the simpler forms of philanthropy were not comprehensively organized and, as a general rule, helpfulness lagged behind "easily remedial necessity"; existing agencies had more assurance of an audience with the rich than "new activities representing urgent needs"; giving habits were better adapted to the past than to the present or anticipated future. There could be no further delay in discovering the laws of a business which channeled millions of dollars a year from definite to indefinite "forms of productive investment." Progress in philanthropy depended upon conquest of "vagrant giving." [54]

In subsequent years social workers, businessmen, and economists joined federationists in an effort to define the elements of "responsible giving" by establishing criteria to measure desirable amounts and objects of donations. Giving was described as an investment requiring as much thought and care as any commercial venture. The ultimate test for the conscientious "citizen stockholder" was advancement of the "common welfare" which meant, for all practical purposes, support only of efficient agencies providing necessary services. "It is the duty of every giver," a chest executive insisted, "to require such efficiency as the condition of his gift; for without it, the fullest effectiveness of the gift cannot be realized." [55] The belief that intelligence, not caprice or emotion, should govern altruism hastened the acceptance of federation. The united appeal promised to eliminate the waste inherent in multiple drives and to increase the effectiveness of gifts through a balanced, efficient community welfare program. Most important, federation promised to increase the total support available. It assured a satisfactory flow of funds for the community welfare structure as a whole; it not only secured more money from more people with less annoyance than any alternative scheme, but, equally important, tended to "dissipate the institutionalism of the social agencies and to increase the public fund of intelligent interest in them as an element in the social economy of the community." [56]

Federation did broaden the giving base, as its supporters

desired, but it did not radically modify a situation in which a minority of donors accounted for a majority of funds contributed. It succeeded, not in easing the burden of the large giver, but in regimenting him by providing a convenient central channel through which to funnel his contributions. Federation guaranteed that those vital contributions would support a community-wide machinery of welfare rather than a few fortunate agencies. The chest also labored to enrich the philanthropic coffers with corporation booty. The corporate giver had become vital to chest campaigns by the end of the 1920's, despite the absence of generous tax-exemption laws, and the federation movement generally assumed an important mediating role between professional social work and the business corporation.

The fact-finding committee of the AAOC had not been impressed by the financial achievements of the prewar federations. It admitted that the initial year of federation usually resulted in a gain, but added that "financial success is much less surely shown" in later years. Any gains were negated by immunity, undesignated giving, and the whirlwind campaign, all of which undermined the growth of a stable constituency.[57] By the pragmatic test of success, federations more clearly justified their existence in the 1920's. Beginning with 39 campaigns in 1920, the number steadily increased for each succeeding year until it reached 353 in 1930. In round numbers, the amount raised in 1920 was $19,000,000; in 1930 it was $75,000,000. In 1922, the chests raised 87.8 percent of their quota; in other years they never dropped below 92.9 percent.[58]

Since large donors counted decisively in these campaigns, the chest duplicated the pre-or nonfederation pattern of giving. Boston, for example, was nonfederated in the 1920's. A survey by the Chamber of Commerce of contributions to 133 agencies in 1923–24 disclosed that approximately 43,800 persons donated more than $2,600,000. Only 478 persons, or 1 percent of the total, contributed $1,309,946, or 50 percent of all the money raised. The 3,822 persons who donated $100 or more accounted for 82.6 percent of the amount.[59] Breakdowns of chest contributions made by the American Association for Community Organization revealed a similar dependence upon the large giver. After a survey of 60 community funds in 1923 the AACO concluded that the "enormous sum of money needed to carry on welfare work in our American communities is supplied by the few rather than the many" (Table I).

TABLE I. Number of contributors responsible for certain percentages of the total raised in selected chest cities in 1923.

City	Number of Contributors	Percentage of total
Philadelphia, Pennsylvania	440	46.4
Detroit, Michigan	341	57.5
Cleveland, Ohio	571	50.3
St. Louis, Missouri	463	52.7
Baltimore, Maryland	140	42.0
Buffalo, New York	385	50.5
Milwaukee, Wisconsin	294	43.3
Minneapolis, Minnesota	300	57.4
Nashville, Tennessee	225	53.0
Scranton, Pennsylvania	274	52.2
Youngstown, Ohio	58	57.1

SOURCE: American Association for Community Organization, *Bulletin* No. 20, September 17, 1923, p. 10.

A similar survey of contributions to 72 chests in 1924 revealed that, although they relied somewhat less than the Boston agencies upon contributions of $100 or more, particularly in the smaller chest cities, such donations constituted a majority of the money raised; and, in addition, that contributions of $1,000 or more were absolutely vital. The chest cities included in the 1924 survey which had a population in excess of 200,000 or raised more than $350,000 depended upon contributions of more than $100 for 69.5 percent of the total; contributions of $1,000 or more accounted for 42.2 percent of the total. Cities with a population ranging from 60,000 to 200,000 or raising between $150,000 and $350,000, acquired 61.2 percent of their total from contributors of more than $100; contributions of $1,000 or more accounted for 24.8 percent of the total. In chest cities with less than 60,000 population, or raising less than $150,000, contributions of more than $100 were responsible for 57.2 percent of the total; donations of $1,000 or more accounted for 18.9 percent of the money raised.[60]

Federation critics who described the chest contribution as an annual tax which separated the giver from the object of his benevolence and aroused little personal enthusiasm or gratification did not fully appreciate the potency of systematic organization as a substitute for personal identification with a cause. The carefully planned, intensive chest campaign reached every possible contributor and wrested every possible penny from the large individual or corporate giver, supplementing this with whatever could be procured from salaried employees. The fund-raising cavalcade used a series of deliberate, calculated measures, beginning with the selection of a professional manager and a volunteer general chairman, preferably a distinguished citizen with widespread community influence. Following the appointment of division chairmen and the establishment of general policy by a campaign committee, the manager administered the campaign, utilizing the influence of the general chairman when needed. From the top leaders the chain of command descended to district chairmen, captains, and teamworkers. This elaborate organization, supplemented by publicity, rallies, and quotas, and careful preparation and allotment of prospect cards, was based upon "an advance comprehensive survey and study of the geographical aspects of the territory to be canvassed, a knowledge of prevailing economic conditions and the assembling of information upon which to base an estimate of the number of prospective givers and the aggregate value of prospects." [61]

A Rochester campaign, for instance, included numerous soliciting and nonsoliciting divisions, involving more than five thousand workers: a special committee, individual subscriber division, industrial employee division, trades employee division, utility employee division, public employee division, and speakers, publicity, complaint and appeal, and auditing divisions. The special committee of influential citizens to secure gifts from the rich was characteristic of chest campaign organization, as was the mobilization of employee groups. In Denver in 1923 a Big Gifts Committee composed of twenty-five business and professional leaders was supplemented by an Industrial Division which canvassed 750 business firms with ten or more employees. Chest teams assigned to different firms or plants cooperated with management in organizing the campaign committees responsible for solicitation. In Harrisburg, Pennsylvania, a Prospect Committee composed mostly of bankers compiled lists and ratings. Special committees were organized before the campaign in Scranton, Pennsylvania, and Grand Rapids, Michigan, to secure pledges from large givers. In South Bend, Indiana, civic leaders met two weeks before the campaign to divide prospect cards of large givers among themselves. Each business firm in Akron, Ohio, established a campaign committee and subscriptions were collected from employees or deducted from paychecks.[62]

The chest could not have survived without the cooperation and support of businessmen, who contributed large sums, persuaded others to give, and permitted chests to reach into their establishments in pursuit of employee donations. In some places the competitive, newsworthy chest campaign eventually superseded church work as an "adjunct" to the business career.[63] The chest, which offered the businessman an excellent opportunity to display his administrative prowess and advertise his firm, gradually forged an alliance between organized philanthropy and the organized business system, as a consequence of which philanthropy siphoned off a measure of surplus corporate wealth.

The YMCA in the late nineteenth and early twentieth centuries established a significant precedent for corporate philanthropy when it induced employers and firms to support railroad and industrial "Y's." The aggressive "Y" building campaigns after 1904 benefited from donations by corporations which often contributed to current operating budgets as well.[64] The war chests and national war drives of 1917–18 elicited the most decisive affirmation of corporate responsibility for social welfare. Most war chests requested corporations to subscribe, and many assigned quotas.[65] Corporations contributed to all five national drives, partly on their own initiative and partly under pressure from the campaign organizations. The United War Work Campaign established a central industries division and advised local affiliates to create similar divisions in order to canvass business firms and their employees.[66]

The spectacle of widespread corporation giving during the war launched a search for norms of corporate solicitation and response in the 1920's. By the close of the decade, federations had become dependent upon corporate generosity. Corporation contributions to 129 chests, which in 1929 raised over 80 percent of the national total, came to $12,954,769, or 22 percent, having increased from $2,535,819 in 1920. The overwhelming percentage of corporation contributions came from manufacturing and retail and wholesale trade (including chain store) enterprises.[67] In many communities, corporation gifts accounted for 25 percent or more of chest income (Table II).[68] With the exception of the YMCA and the disaster appeals of the Red Cross, nonfederated local or national agencies did not benefit appreciably from corporation contributions.

TABLE II. Corporation contributions to selected chest cities,
by percentage, in 1929.

City	Percentage
Milwaukee, Wisconsin	29.0
New Orleans, Louisiana	27.8
Cincinnati, Ohio	26.5
Kansas City, Missouri	29.6
Seattle, Washington	48.8
Indianapolis, Indiana	42.1
Toledo, Ohio	27.8
Columbus, Ohio	36.6
Denver, Colorado	25.5
Portland, Oregon	29.7
Atlanta, Georgia	25.4
St. Paul, Minnesota	38.0
Omaha, Nebraska	25.7
Memphis, Tennessee	35.5
Grand Rapids, Michigan	41.4
Salt Lake City, Utah	39.5
Tacoma, Washington	40.6

SOURCE: Williams and Croxton, *Corporation Contributions*, pp. 104–107.

The American Association for Community Organization (which became the Association of Community Chests and Councils in 1927) devoted considerable attention to the establishment of a satisfactory relation between organized philanthropy and the corporate business system. Of particular concern to the Association and the regional conferences it sponsored was the formulation of policy regarding the philanthropic obligations of local affiliates of national corporations. "The absence of any general policy, taken in conjunction with the increasing number of community chest appeals," was a source of irritation and uncertainty. Although local chests exhibited a widespread interest in corporate contributions, few possessed any "definite policy or working principle on which they expect to get contributions from non-local concerns." [69]

In 1929, J. Herbert Case, president of the ACCC, described corporation giving as the "outstanding chest problem with which we are wrestling." [70] Federation leaders had not worked out any formula for solicitation but they had established a rationale for philanthropy as corporation policy, and for the chest as the most efficient medium for giving. Through the chest the corporation could discharge a general responsibility for the health and welfare of the community in which it did business and a particular responsibility toward its employees. The same conditions which made a community desirable for business also created problems of dependency, delinquency, health, and use of leisure time. Therefore, a corporation which reaped the "benefits from a given set of circumstances should also help carry its share of the burden caused by the problems which these same favorable circumstances" created.[71] Philanthropy also paid off in terms of healthier, happier, and more productive workers, as well as a community good-will which increased profits in the long run.

Support of philanthropy not only increased profits but reduced taxes. If anything, federationists exceeded the zeal of businessmen in demanding tax exemption for charitable gifts. A subcommittee on corporations and chests, established by a Citizens Conference on Community Welfare in 1928, agreed that "necessary federal legislation should be promptly secured whereby corporations should be permitted to consider as expenses their payments to specified social welfare activities." [72] Philanthropy possessed a second tax advantage. An efficient private welfare machinery cost less than the taxes needed to support public welfare programs. During the New Deal period the chairman of the General Motors Finance Committee explained to Allen Burns of the ACCC that the stability of our political institutions was menaced by government paternalism and the potential political power of those who preferred relief to work.[73]

*

The *American Mercury* brought to the attention of its readers in 1928 the "Big Wind" sweeping across philanthropy: "Where money-getters on the prowl once devoted themselves almost solely to the Big Money Boys, they now seek to be democrats, giving everybody, high or low, a fair chance to do his bit for the Worthy Cause. Instead of chasing after fat checks of six figures, they snatch up whatever is offered— dimes and nickels, and even pennies. And what was once a simple art, practiced exclusively by amateurs, is now in the hands of Science and Organization. It has become, indeed, a Great Profession, with trained specialists who, for a fee and expenses, stand ready day or night to raise funds for any Great Cause." [74]

The professional fund-raising firm, like federation, the whirlwind campaign, and corporation giving, was nurtured by World War I. Many of the founders and staff members of professional fund-raising corporations in the 1920's, such as Tamblyn and Brown, John Price Jones, and Marts and Lundy, participated in the war drives or were influenced by their success in adopting fund-raising as a "professional" career. Charles S. Ward, whose fund-raising techniques had enriched YMCA treasuries, helped out with the national war drives, and in 1919 he formed a firm which included Arnaud C. Marts as a junior partner. Marts and George Lundy established their own firm in 1926. George O. Tamblyn had participated in some sixty chest campaigns and Red Cross drives during the war. By 1920 the John Price Jones Corporation was developing the techniques of campaign organization and mass solicitation by volunteer armies applied so profitably during the war period. Like the federations, the professional fund-raisers encouraged a disciplined, controlled voluntarism most beneficial to the institutions and organizations which monopolized the humanitarian impulse in modern times.

The community chests could learn much about campaign technique from the fund-raisers who, undistracted by responsibilities for community organization, devoted full time to their task. A brief account of some activities of the John Price Jones Corporation (JPJC) will illustrate the manner in which fund-raising had passed from the hands of benevolent amateurs to high-powered professionals who left nothing to chance. In developing a campaign on behalf of the United Unitarian Fund Committee in 1920, the JPJC prepared a typically elaborate, comprehensive, systematic plan of operations long in advance of actual solicitation. The plan included a general survey of the problem, a general outline of the entire campaign organization, an analysis of necessary preliminaries to organization, the scheme of campaign operation, and publicity devices. The JPJC advised that, in a religious campaign of this sort, random solicitation was wasteful; it recommended instead a careful tabulation of every member of the American Unitarian Association according to financial standing, church interest, and general philanthropy. The preparation of a prospect list was indispensable in the case of wealthy members who had to be solicited personally in advance and upon whose generosity the entire campaign revolved.[75] A subsequent Unitarian campaign suggested that churches and other nonprofit organizations were becoming dependent upon professional fund-raising assistance in the 1920's. A number of board members of the National Unitarian Association had begrudged the fee paid to the JPJC in the first campaign, and decided in 1925 to dispense with expert advice. With some measure of ill-concealed satisfaction, a JPJC executive reported that the effort had "entirely broken down and the project is a failure."[76]

The JPJC, after many years of experience in raising funds for churches, schools, and some charitable agencies, concluded that success invariably hinged upon a "carefully conceived plan" which "lays down a course of action to be followed, sets forth the goal to be achieved, and by mathematical calculation, based on averages in past efforts, estimates the probable limits of the effort." For fund-raising purposes, any social program had to be pared to the "limits of immediate practicability." [77] Echoing the sentiments of federation fund-raisers, the professional argued that campaign goals could not be realistically formulated on the basis of objective social or agency needs, but upon the "amount of money that the community gives according to its financial strength, even though that program may not be the ideal program." [78] The scientific campaign plan implied a limited goal attained through calculated publicity and organization—"well-defined, concrete, logical appeals, supported by straightforward, modern, business methods." [79]

Neither community chest nor professional fund-raiser, both dedicated to the diversion of "surplus wealth into uses economically and socially sound," could succeed without volunteer assistance.[80] In connection with its Unitarian campaign, the JPJC anticipated the recruitment of 10,000 or more volunteers. The "most powerful workers" and "best salesmen," however, were reserved for direct solicitation of large givers.[81] The professional campaign staff remained in the shadows, directing operations but delegating to volunteers the responsibility for eliciting contributions from friends, business associates, and strangers. Random solicitation was to be avoided; volunteers did not arbitrarily ask whatever they wished from whomever they decided to see. The volunteer, according to a chest executive, found "his work mapped out for him in such a way that he has only to exercise ordinary diligence and persistency to obtain results. He is assigned a definite task and soon realizes that if he follows instructions he has an equal chance to make a creditable showing. He immediately senses that he is a responsible unit in a well-organized, smooth-working machine. In a word, he recognizes the power and responsibilities of well-directed, aggressive organized effort, and enjoys his share in it." [82]

The community chest and professional fund-raising firm epitomized the changing function and status of the volunteer in an era of professional social work. Just as the individual agency discouraged a spontaneous, unregulated voluntarism, federation worked toward a controlled voluntarism best suited to its function—rationalization of the welfare machinery and an increase in the economic surplus diverted to its support.

Federation reflected with unusual clarity a more general tendency to adjust and harness volunteer service to a bureaucratic, professionalized welfare machinery. The adjustment frequently took the form of a marginal voluntarism, remote from the day-to-day administrative and treatment work of social agencies. Federation reinforced this tendency in its wholesale diversion of volunteer energies into fund-raising tasks detached from the work of any particular agency or the clients it assisted. It provided the professional subculture and the social agency with a measure of autonomy far removed from the "democratization" and community controls espoused by Norton, Street, Bookman, and other founding fathers. A recent report on welfare agencies contends that chest and united funds "have become more concerned in too many cases with serving the vested interests of the member agencies. It is not uncommon for the board of directors of a united fund or community chest to be composed predominantly of trustees of constituent agencies. As such, these boards may be no longer representative of the community but of particular health and welfare interests." [83] To the extent that this generalization is correct, federation nurtured a voluntarism which emphasized, not responsible agency participation and partnership with professionals, but financial and moral support of an existing welfare machinery. The partnership concept typical of the charity organization societies in the nineteenth century was radically modified in the twentieth, when all the institutional pressures worked toward a controlled, frequently marginal, voluntarism.

Conclusion

Specialization and the idealization of expertise, the growth of an occupational subculture, and bureaucratization were instrumental in shaping the character of twentieth-century social work. These typical features of an urban-industrial society have affected not only the professions but most spheres of life, and their controlling influence will undoubtedly remain potent. For this reason sentimental regrets over the decline of voluntarism in social work are futile. It would be more useful to understand voluntarism and its alleged decline in functional rather than normative terms, avoiding idealized visions of democratic pluralism and citizen participation. In the determination of social roles one must consider the realities of prior obligation to job and family as well as the constraints imposed by specialization and bureaucratization.

Certainly romantic nostalgia and unrealistic norms of citizen participation should not obscure another consequence of professionalization in social work: the emergence of a therapeutically oriented casework as the nuclear image and skill. Casework rooted in a psychiatric explanation of human behavior was a key, presumably, to a knowledge base and helping technique more "scientific" and hence more professional than "social diagnosis" or social reform which exaggerated environmental and rational factors in behavior and its control.

Yet if social work could claim any distinctive function in an atomized urban society with serious problems of group

Conclusion

communication and mass deprivation, it was not individual therapy but liaison between groups and the stimulation of social legislation and institutional change. Since no other occupational group presumes as does social work a generalized mandate to perform these indispensable functions, the preëminence of the therapeutic role created a vacuum which remains unfilled. Professionalization—the machinery of altruism—was adapted far more successfully to a limited individual and group service process than to the distinctive social work functions of liaison and resource mobilization.

Appendix. Professional Organization and Education since the 1930's

Four professional social work organizations were in existence between 1918 and 1946: the American Association of Medical Social Workers (1918); the National Association of School Social Workers (1919); the American Association of Social Workers (1921); and the American Association of Psychiatric Social Workers (1926). An American Association of Group Workers was organized in 1946, although members had been associated informally since 1936. An Association for the Study of Community Organization was also established in 1946, followed by the Social Work Research Group in 1949. A Temporary Inter-Association Council of Social Work Membership, formed in 1952 to consider the possibility of merger between the various associations, led in 1955 to the establishment of the National Association of Social Workers. Membership in the NASW is based upon graduation from an accredited school of social work.

In 1960 the NASW inaugurated a voluntary licensing or registration system (there had been one for several years in California where a state board prepared examinations). Membership in the "Academy of Certified Social Workers" (ACSW) was open to those who held a master's degree from an accredited school of social work and membership in the NASW, and who possessed two years of experience in an agency under the supervision of a member of the ACSW.

In the field of professional education, significant developments in the 1930's based upon rulings of the American Association of Schools of Social Work included the "minimum curriculum" requirement of 1932, the requirement in 1933 that member schools offer at least one year of graduate study, the 1935 regulation that schools be associated with institutions approved by the Association of American Universities, and the 1939 decision that professional education would be based upon a two-year graduate program leading to a master's degree (although until 1952 the AASSW maintained a membership classification for schools which offered one year of graduate education). The minimum curriculum of 1932 was revised in 1944 when the "basic eight" was substituted. These eight fields consisted of casework, group work, community organization, public welfare, social administration, social research, medical information, and pyschiatric information.

The Professional Altruist

A second accrediting agency—the National Association of Schools of Social Administration—was organized in 1942. It was sponsored by schools which during the depression had established combined undergraduate and graduate training programs to help fill the demand for personnel in the public welfare services. The dissatisfaction resulting from dual accrediting groups led to the formation of a National Council on Social Work Education in 1946. With the help of the Carnegie Foundation, it sponsored a study (Ernest V. Hollis and Alice L. Taylor, *Social Work Education in the United States* [New York, 1951]) of the entire field of social work education which stimulated action leading to the merger of the National Council and the two associations and the formation of the Council on Social Work Education in 1952.

Through its control over accreditation and curriculum policy the CSWE has attempted to influence educational standards. Accreditation by the CSWE's Commission is based upon periodic review of each school, which must offer a two-year "generic" program adopted in 1952, including human growth and behavior, social services, and social work practice as the major areas. The CSWE's most ambitious curriculum project was its thirteen-volume curriculum study published in 1959:

Werner W. Boehm, *Objectives for the Social Work Curriculum of the Future.*

Herbert Bisno, *The Place of the Undergraduate Curriculum in Social Work Education.*

Sue Spencer, *The Administration Method in Social Work Education.*

Harry L. Lurie, *The Community Organization Method in Social Work Education.*

Elliot Studt, *Education for Social Workers in the Correctional Field.*

Ruth M. Butler, *An Orientation to Knowledge of Human Growth and Behavior in Social Work Education.*

Irving Weissman and Mary R. Baker, *Education for Social Workers in the Public Social Services.*

John J. Horwitz, *Education for Social Workers in the Rehabilitation of the Handicapped.*

Samuel Mencher, *The Research Method in Social Work Education.*

Werner W. Boehm, *The Social Casework Method in Social Work Education.*

Marjorie Murphy, *The Social Group Method in Social Work Education.*

Irving Weissman, *Social Welfare Policy and Services in Social Work Education.*

Muriel W. Pumphrey, *The Teaching of Values and Ethics in Social Work Education.*

Bibliographical Note

Notes

Index

Bibliographical Note

MANUSCRIPT SOURCES

The Jeffrey R. Brackett and Zilpha D. Smith scrapbooks, and the Minutes of the Administrative Board of the Boston School for Social Workers—all in the archives of the Simmons College School of Social Work—provide information relating to the origins and development of the Boston School for Social Workers. The Ida Cannon Papers at Massachusetts General Hospital are an important source for the history of medical social work. The voluminous Mary Richmond Papers at the Columbia School of Social Work, as yet uncatalogued, are rich in material pertaining to Miss Richmond's career and the development of social work in general. The archives of the Community Service Society of New York, combining the records of the Charity Organization Society and Association for Improving the Condition of the Poor, are of value in understanding the evolution of two important casework organizations. The archives of the United Community Funds and Councils of America constitute a valuable source of published and unpublished materials dealing with community chests. The archives are strongest for the period after 1930. At the Baker Library at Harvard are the John Price Jones Papers, a huge collection of materials dealing with one of the first professional fund-raising firms.

CHARITY ORGANIZATION

The *Proceedings* of the National Conference of Charities and Correction (NCCC) provide an excellent cross section of opinion on charity organization in the nineteenth century. These should be supplemented by the *Reports* of various leading societies, such as New York, Buffalo, Boston, Philadelphia, Baltimore, and Indianapolis, and the many articles in *Lend-a-Hand* and the *Charities Review*. Useful are the accounts of the work by such leaders as Zilpha Smith, Josephine Shaw Lowell, Oscar C. McCulloch, Robert Treat Paine, Daniel Coit Gilman, John M. Glenn, and S. Humphreys Gurteen. Zilpha D. Smith, *Deserted Wives and Deserting Husbands: A Study of 234 Families Based on the Experience of the District Committees and Agents of the Associated Charities of Boston* (Boston, 1901), deals with a subject of importance to charity organizationists. Margaret E. Rich presents a concise review of Zilpha Smith's life and career in

Bibliographical Note

"Zilpha Drew Smith, 1852–1926," *The Family*, XI (1930), 67–79. Josephine Shaw Lowell, *Public Relief and Private Charity* (New York, 1884), is revealing. William Rhinelander Stewart includes many letters to and from Mrs. Lowell in *The Philanthropic Work of Josephine Shaw Lowell* (New York, 1911). Alexander Johnson evaluated McCulloch's contribution in "Oscar Carlton McCulloch," *The Family*, IV (1923), 79–87. Johnson relates his own story in *Adventures in Social Welfare: Being Reminiscences of Things, Thoughts and Folks During Forty Years of Social Work* (Fort Wayne, Ind., 1923). Representative of the moral assumptions and social objectives of charity organization in the nineteenth century are S. Humphreys Gurteen, *A Handbook of Charity Organization* (Buffalo, 1882), and *Provident Schemes* (Buffalo, 1879).

Among the works which provide insight into attitudes toward relief, poverty, and dependency as well as charity organization in the nineteenth century, the following are helpful: Mary W. Brown, *The Development of Thrift* (New York, 1899); Joseph H. Crooker, *Problems in American Society: Some Social Studies* (Boston, 1889); Daniel C. Gilman, ed., *The Organization of Charities*, Sixth Session of the International Congress of Charities, Correction, and Philanthropy (Chicago, 1893); Charles D. Kellogg, *History of Charity Organization in the United States* (Report of Committee of National Conference of Charities and Correction, 1893); Charity Organization Society of New York, *Hand-Book for Friendly Visitors Among the Poor* (New York, 1883); Mary E. Richmond, *Friendly Visiting Among the Poor: A Handbook for Charity Workers* (New York, 1899); Amos G. Warner, *American Charities: A Study in Philanthropy and Economics* (Boston, 1894); Helen Bosanquet, *Social Work in London, 1869 to 1912: A History of the Charity Organisation Society* (London, 1914).

Frank D. Watson, *The Charity Organization Movement in the United States: A Study in American Philanthropy* (New York, 1922), is useful for factual background, though deficient in other respects. More recent interpretations include Verl S. Lewis, "The Development of the Charity Organization Movement in the United States, 1875–1900: Its Principles and Methods" (unpub. diss., Western Reserve University, 1954); and Robert H. Bremner, " 'Scientific Philanthropy,' 1873–93," *Social Service Review*, XXX (1956), 168–173. Dorothy G. Becker, "The Visitor to New York City Poor, 1843–1920" (unpub. diss., Columbia School of Social Work, 1960), examines the volunteer and paid worker in the New York Charity Organization Society and Association for Improving the Condition of the Poor.

FROM FRIENDLY VISITING TO CASEWORK

Periodicals such as *Charities and the Commons*, and its successor, *The Survey*, touch on all phases of social work in the early twentieth

Bibliographical Note

century. The *Proceedings* of the NCCC (changed in name in 1917 to National Conference of Social Work) are useful. For the evolution of family social work the reports of the respective societies are valuable and should be supplemented by the reports of children's aid agencies. Edward T. Devine, *The Principles of Relief* (New York, 1905), Joanna C. Colcord, *Broken Homes: A Study of Family Desertion and its Social Treatment* (New York, 1919), and Alice W. Solenberger, *One Thousand Homeless Men: A Study of Original Records* (New York, 1911) treat specialized subjects. The interests of Edward T. Devine and Mary E. Richmond traversed the entire range of family social work; Devine is representative of the environmental meliorism of the early twentieth century, while Miss Richmond embodied the quest for a scientific, differential casework based on understanding and adjustment of the social environment. A prolific writer, Devine's publications include, *Misery and its Causes* (New York, 1909), *Social Forces* (New York, 1910), *The Family and Social Work* (New York, 1912), *The Spirit of Social Work* (New York, 1911), *The Normal Life* (New York, 1915), and the retrospective, *When Social Work Was Young* (New York, 1939). A convenient compendium of Mary Richmond material spanning her entire career is, Joanna C. Colcord and Ruth Z. S. Mann, eds., *The Long View: Papers and Addresses* (New York, 1930). Miss Richmond's *The Good Neighbor in the Modern City* (New York, 1907), is minor in influence compared to her *Social Diagnosis* (New York, 1917) and *What is Social Case Work?* (New York, 1922). For a detailed account of her first decade in social work consult Muriel W. Pumphrey, "Mary Richmond and the Rise of Professional Social Work in Baltimore: The Foundations of a Creative Career" (unpub. diss., Columbia School of Social Work, 1956). A brief, generally factual account of the evolution of family social work is Margaret E. Rich, *A Belief in People: A History of Family Social Work* (New York, 1956).

The *Annual Reports* of the Social Service Department of Massachusetts General Hospital, beginning in 1905, provide valuable insight into the activities and goals of early medical social workers. The first general formulation of medical social work principles appears in Ida M. Cannon, *Social Work in Hospitals: A Contribution to Progressive Medicine* (New York, 1913; rev. ed. 1923). Richard Cabot explains social medicine in *Social Service and the Art of Healing* (New York, 1909) and *Social Work: Essays on the Meeting-Ground of Doctor and Social Worker* (Boston, 1919). The issues of *Hospital Social Service*, beginning in 1919, contain much useful information. Ida Cannon discusses the beginnings of medical social work in *On the Social Frontier of Medicine: Pioneering in Medical Social Service* (Cambridge, Mass., 1952).

Bibliographical Note

The following are helpful in tracing the emergence and development of visiting teaching: Harriet M. Johnson, *The Visiting Teacher in New York City* (Public Education Association of New York, 1916); *The Visiting Teacher in the United States: A Survey by the National Association of Visiting Teachers and Home and School Visitors* (Public Education Association of New York, 1921); Mabel B. Ellis, *The Visiting Teacher in Rochester: Report of a Study* (New York, 1925); Julius J. Oppenheimer, *The Visiting Teacher Movement, with Special Reference to Administrative Relationships* (New York, 1925). Interpretations of the movement by some of the early leaders include: Lydia H. Hodge, "Why a Visiting Teacher?" National Education Association, *Addresses and Proceedings*, LV (1917), 223–226; Howard W. Nudd, "The History and Present Status of the Visiting-Teacher Movement," NCSW, *Proceedings* (1923), 422–425; Anna B. Pratt, "The Relation of the Teacher and the Social Worker," American Academy of Political and Social Science, *Annals*, XCVIII (1921), 90–96; and Jane F. Culbert, "Visiting Teachers and Their Activities," NCCC, *Proceedings* (1916), 592–598, "The Public School as a Little Used Social Agency: As a Factor in the Treatment of the Socially Handicapped Child," NCSW, *Proceedings* (1921), 95–98, and "The Visiting Teacher," American Academy of Political and Social Science, *Annals*, XCVIII (1921), 81–89. Changes in educational theory are discussed in Lawrence A. Cremin, *The Transformation of the School: Progressivism in American Education, 1876–1957* (New York, 1961).

The problems created for sectarian charitable organizations by the rise of "scientific" philanthropy are considered in William J. Kerby, *The Social Mission of Charity: A Study of Points of View in Catholic Charities* (New York, 1921).

PSYCHIATRY, CASEWORK, AND DIFFERENTIAL DIAGNOSIS

Histories of psychiatry and related subjects include: Albert Deutsch, *The Mentally Ill in America: A History of Their Care and Treatment from Colonial Times* (2nd ed., rev., New York, 1949); Lawson G. Lowrey and Victoria Sloane, eds., *Orthopsychiatry, 1923–1948* (American Orthopsychiatric Association, 1948); American Psychiatric Association, *One Hundred Years of American Psychiatry* (New York, 1944); Arthur E. Fink, *Causes of Crime: Biological Theories in the United States, 1800–1915* (Philadelphia, 1938). On heredity, see Mark Haller, *Eugenics: Hereditarian Attitudes in American Thought* (New Brunswick, N.J., 1963).

Clifford W. Beers, *A Mind that Found Itself* (New York, 1909), with successive editions, is indispensable for mental hygiene. The development of the National Committee for Mental Hygiene is traced

Bibliographical Note

in Lewellys F. Barker, "The First Ten Years of the National Committee for Mental Hygiene, with Some Comments on its Future," *Mental Hygiene*, II (1918), 557–581, and George K. Pratt, "Twenty Years of the National Committee for Mental Hygiene," *Mental Hygiene*, XIV (1930), 399–428. Nina Ridenour, *Mental Health in the United States: A Fifty-Year History* (Cambridge, Mass., 1961), is a brief, factual account. Stanley P. Davies, *Social Control of the Mentally Deficient* (New York, 1930; rev. ed. 1961), is a standard work. For a flavor of the alarmist period see Henry H. Goddard, *The Kallikak Family: A Study in the Heredity of Feeble-Mindedness* (New York, 1912), and *Mental Deficiency from the Standpoint of Heredity*, Massachusetts Society for Mental Hygiene, Pub. No. 15 (1916).

Alfred Lief, ed., *The Commonsense Psychiatry of Dr. Adolf Meyer: Fifty-Two Selected Papers* (New York, 1948), is valuable on the development of social psychiatry. A major landmark is William Healy, *The Individual Delinquent: A Text-Book of Diagnosis and Prognosis for all Concerned in Understanding Offenders* (Boston, 1915). The origins of the Juvenile Psychopathic Institute of Chicago are discussed in William Healy and Augusta F. Bronner, "The Child Guidance Clinic," in Lowrey and Sloane, *Orthopsychiatry*. John C. Burnham, "Psychiatry, Psychology, and the Progressive Movement," *American Quarterly*, XII (1960), deals with social psychiatry and behaviorism in the context of Progressive ideology.

The relevance of psychiatry to social work is the subject of William Healy's, "The Bearings of Psychology on Social Case Work," NCSW, *Proceedings* (1917), 104–112. Discussions of psychiatric social work by psychiatrists include Bernard Glueck, "Special Preparation of the Psychiatric Social Worker," NCSW, *Proceedings* (1919), 599–606; Abraham Myerson, "The Psychiatric Social Worker," reprint, *Journal of Abnormal Psychology* (1918); C. Macfie Campbell, "The Minimum of Medical Insight Required by Social Workers with Delinquents," *Mental Hygiene*, IV (1920), 513–520. The contributions of psychiatry to social work and the function of psychiatric social work are discussed by Mary Jarrett in "Possibilities in Social Service for Psychopathic Patients," reprint, *Boston Medical and Surgical Journal* (1917), "Psychiatric Social Work," *Mental Hygiene*, II (1918), 283–290, "The Psychiatric Thread Running Through all Social Case Work," NCSW, *Proceedings* (1919), 587–593; "Psychiatric Social Work," NCSW, *Proceedings* (1921), 381–385; "The Place of Psychiatric Social Work," *Hospital Social Service*, IV (1921), 63–66. Training for psychiatric social work, with special reference to the Smith College course, is considered by E. E. Southard, Mary Jarrett, and others in *Mental Hygiene*, II (1918), 582 ff. Jessie Taft, "Qualifi-

Bibliographical Note

cations of the Psychiatric Social Worker," NCSW, *Proceedings* (1919), 593–599, is illuminating. An account of the pioneer experiments in psychiatric social work in New York State appears in M. Elizabeth Dunn, "History of Social Service Work in the New York State Hospitals," reprint, *State Hospital Quarterly* (May 1924).

SOCIAL WORK IN THE 1920'S

The Commonwealth Fund publications, particularly those describing the Program for the Prevention of Delinquency, rank high in importance for this period. The following deal with child guidance clinics and the training of psychiatric social workers: Ralph P. Truitt, et al., *The Child Guidance Clinic and the Community* (New York, 1928); Porter R. Lee and Marion E. Kenworthy, *Mental Hygiene and Social Work* (New York, 1929); Lawson G. Lowrey, ed., *Institute for Child Guidance Studies: Selected Reprints* (New York, 1931); Sarah H. Swift, *Training in Psychiatric Social Work at the Institute for Child Guidance, 1927–1933* (New York, 1934); Lawson G. Lowrey and Geddes Smith, *The Institute for Child Guidance, 1927–1933* (New York, 1933); George S. Stevenson and Geddes Smith, *Child Guidance Clinics: A Quarter Century of Development* (New York, 1934). School social work is the subject of Mary B. Sayles, *The Problem Child in School: Narratives from Case Records of Visiting Teachers* (New York, 1926); Jane F. Culbert, *The Visiting Teacher at Work* (New York, 1929); Clara Bassett, *The School and Mental Health* (New York, 1931). The *Annual Reports* of the Commonwealth Fund after 1922 are also useful.

The growing influence of mental hygiene and psychiatry upon social work theory is reflected in such publications as *The Family* and *Mental Hygiene*. Family agency relief policy from a psychiatric perspective is discussed in Grace F. Marcus, *Some Aspects of Relief in Family Casework: An Evaluation of Practice Based on a Study Made for the Charity Organization Society of New York* (New York, 1929), and Eleanor Neustaedter, "The Integration of Economic and Psychological Factors in Family Case Work," NCSW, *Proceedings* (1930), 198–216. The uncritical acceptance of psychiatry typical of the period is reflected in Edward D. Lynde, "The Place of Psychiatric Social Work in a General Case Work Agency," NCSW, *Proceedings* (1924), 438–442, and Malcolm S. Nichols, "New Emphases in Family Social Work," *The Family*, IX (1928), 188–193. A curious book reflecting the aggressive optimism and missionary zeal of the psychiatric social worker in the 1920's is E. E. Southard and Mary C. Jarrett, *The Kingdom of Evils* (New York, 1922). Grace Marcus argues that the future of casework lies in assimilation of the "subjective point of view" in "The Psychiatric Point of View in Social Work," *Mental*

Bibliographical Note

Hygiene, VII (1923), 755–761. The problems and prospects of psychiatric social work at the end of the decade are discussed in Christine C. Robb, "Changing Goals of Psychiatric Social Work," *American Journal of Orthopsychiatry*, I (1931), 476–486. In sharp contrast to Mary Richmond's *Social Diagnosis* is Virginia P. Robinson, *A Changing Psychology in Social Case Work* (Philadelphia, 1930).

THE PROFESSIONAL SUBCULTURE

The literature dealing with the sociology of the professions and occupations has been sparse until recently. A. M. Carr-Saunders and P. A. Wilson, *The Professions* (Oxford, 1933), contains a wealth of historical data on English professional groups. An early discussion is Emory S. Bogardus, "The Occupational Attitude," *Journal of Applied Sociology*, VIII (1924), 171–177, and more recently, Howard S. Becker and James W. Carper, "The Elements of Identification with an Occupation," *American Sociological Review*, XXI (1956), 341–348, and by the same authors, "The Development of Identification with an Occupation," *American Journal of Sociology*, LXI (1956), 289–298. Everett C. Hughes, *Men and Their Work* (Glencoe, Ill., 1958), is rewarding. Different characteristics of professionalism are analyzed in Morris L. Cogan, "Toward a Definition of Profession," *Harvard Educational Review*, XXIII (1953), 33–50; Ernest Greenwood, "Attributes of a Profession," *Social Work*, II (1957), 45–55; William J. Goode, "Community Within a Community: The Professions," *American Sociological Review*, XXII (1957), 194–200; Harvey L. Smith, "Contingencies of Professional Differentiation," *American Journal of Sociology*, LXIII (1958), 410–414; T. H. Marshall, "The Recent History of Professionalism in Relation to Social Structure and Social Policy," *Canadian Journal of Economics and Political Science*, V (1939), 325–340. An important treatment of the subject is "The Professions and Social Structure," in Talcott Parsons, *Essays in Sociological Theory* (rev. ed., Glencoe, Ill., 1954). General discussions of professional education include Ralph W. Tyler, "Distinctive Attributes of Education for the Professions," *Social Work Journal*, XXXIII (1952), 55–62, 94, and William J. McGlothlin, *Patterns of Professional Education* (New York, 1960). Studies of medical and legal education, useful for comparative purposes in the formative years of social work education, include Abraham Flexner, *Medical Education in the United States and Canada* (New York, 1910), and Alfred Z. Reed, *Training for the Public Profession of the Law: Historical Development and Principal Contemporary Problems of Legal Education in the United States with Some Account of Conditions in England and Canada* (New York, 1921). On education see Myron Lieberman, *Education as a Profession* (Englewood Cliffs, New Jersey, 1956), and Raymond E. Callahan,

Bibliographical Note

Education and the Cult of Efficiency: A Study of the Social Forces that have Shaped the Administration of the Public Schools (Chicago, 1964).

Abraham Flexner argues that social work lacks a definite skill characteristic of a profession in "Is Social Work a Profession?" NCCC, *Proceedings* (1915), 576–590. For a contrary view, see William Hodson, "Is Social Work Professional? A Re-examination of the Question," NCSW, *Proceedings* (1925), 629–636. The occupational status of the social worker is considered in Kate H. Claghorn, *Social Work as a Profession for Men and Women* (pamphlet, 1915); and three publications of the American Association of Social Workers: *Vocational Aspects of Psychiatric Social Work* (New York, 1925); *Vocational Aspects of Family Social Work* (New York, 1925); *Vocational Aspects of Medical Social Work* (New York, 1927). An important general statement of social work prospects published by the American Association of Social Workers is *Social Case Work: Generic and Specific: An Outline. A Report of the Milford Conference* (New York, 1929).

Early pleas for specialized social work training were voiced by: Anna L. Dawes, "The Need of Training Schools for a New Profession," *Lend-a-Hand*, XI (1893), 90–97; Mary E. Richmond, "The Need of a Training School in Applied Philanthropy," NCCC, *Proceedings* (1897), 181–186; and Philip W. Ayres, "Training for Practical Philanthropy," *American Monthly Review of Reviews*, XIX (1899), 205–206. The catalogues and announcements of the early schools reveal the courses offered as well as the professed goals of social work education, and the following publications provide information on the growth and character of social work education at different periods: Edith Abbott, "Education for Social Work," Department of the Interior, Bureau of Education, *Report of the Commissioner of Education for the Year ended June 30, 1915* (Washington, 1915), I, 345–359; Jesse F. Steiner, *Education for Social Work* (Chicago, 1921); James H. Tufts, *Education and Training for Social Work* (New York, 1923); Sydnor H. Walker, *Social Work and the Training of Social Workers* (Chapel Hill, N.C., 1928); James E. Hagerty, *The Training of Social Workers* (New York, 1931). Edith Abbott, *Social Welfare and Professional Education* (2nd ed., rev., Chicago, 1942) contains interpretive essays on social work education in the 1920's. For developments in social work education after the period covered in this study, the successive editions of Esther L. Brown, *Social Work as a Profession* (New York, 1935), contain useful summaries. Ernest V. Hollis and Alice L. Taylor, *Social Work Education: The Report of a Study Made for the National Council on Social Work Education* (New York, 1951), is important. For theoretical statements, see Bertha C. Reynolds,

Bibliographical Note

Learning and Teaching in the Practice of Social Work (New York, 1942); Charlotte Towle, *The Learner in Education for the Professions, as Seen in Education for Social Work* (Chicago, 1954); Rosa Wessel, "The Meaning of Professional Education for Social Work," *Social Service Review*, XXXV (1961), 153–160.

The eagerness for professional association which resulted ultimately in the formation of the American Association of Social Workers is reflected in "A Call to Social Workers," *Survey*, XLV (1920), 169; J. B. Buell, "By Our Own Bootstraps," *The Family*, II (1921), 64–66; Paul L. Benjamin, "Social Workers," *Survey*, XLVI (1921), 181. Histories of the AASW, which focus largely on organizational matters include Frances N. Harrison, *The Growth of a Professional Association* (New York, 1935), and Walter B. Johnson, "History of the American Association of Social Workers" (unpub. diss., Washington University, St. Louis, Mo., 1937). A brief account is Frank J. Bruno, "The First Twenty-Five Years of the AASW," *Compass*, XXVII (1946), 9–12. The *Compass*, official journal of the AASW, provides a useful source of information on the Association's evolution. For professional association in medical and psychiatric social work, consult Mary A. Stites, *History of the American Association of Medical Social Workers* (Washington, 1955), and Lois French, *Psychiatric Social Work* (New York, 1940), Appendix A. Lula J. Elliott, *Social Work Ethics* (New York, 1931), is an early treatment of a subject of concern to any professional group. Some of the events leading to the formation of the National Association of Social Workers in 1955 are recounted in Melvin A. Glasser, "The Story of the Movement for a Single Professional Association," *Social Work Journal*, XXXVI (1955), 115–122.

FORMAL ORGANIZATION AND ADMINISTRATION

For Max Weber's theory of bureaucratic structure, see H. H. Gerth and C. Wright Mills, eds., *From Max Weber: Essays in Sociology* (New York, 1958). A brief, informed survey of the subject, revising Weber at several strategic points, is Peter M. Blau, *Bureaucracy in Modern Society* (New York, 1956). Robert K. Merton, et al., *Reader in Bureaucracy* (Glencoe, Ill., 1952), is a useful compendium. Eugene Litwak, "Models of Bureaucracy Which Permit Conflict," *American Journal of Sociology*, LXVII (1961), 177–184, is important. The relation between "differential expertise" and bureaucracy is discussed in Israel Gerver and Joseph Bensman, "Toward a Sociology of Expertness," *Social Forces*, XXXII (1954), 226–235. Everett C. Hughes, "Institutional Office and the Person," *American Journal of Sociology*, XLIII (1937), 404–413, deals with institutional careers. Executive leadership and formal organization are discussed in Herbert A. Simon,

Bibliographical Note

Administrative Behavior: A Study of Decision-Making Processes in Administrative Organization (2nd ed., New York, 1957), and Chester I. Barnard, *The Functions of the Executive* (Cambridge, Mass., 1938). Still provocative is Henry C. Metcalf and L. Urwick, *Dynamic Administration: The Collected Papers of Mary Parker Follett* (New York, 1940).

"Social Work as Cause and Function," Porter R. Lee's presidential address before the NCSW in 1929, is a perceptive diagnosis of structural changes in social work. Gertrude Vaile, "Some Significant Trends Since Cleveland," NCSW, *Proceedings* (1926), 3-11, also touches on the implications of formal organization. *Better Times*, a journal published in the 1920's, contains considerable discussion of social agency administration and executive responsibility. An early text is Elwood Street, *Social Work Administration* (New York, 1931). Administrative structure has continued to occupy the attention of social workers since the 1920's. A sampling of the literature includes: Pierce Atwater, *Problems of Administration in Social Work* (Minneapolis, 1940); Helen W. Hanchette, et al., *Some Dynamics of Social Agency Administration* (New York, 1947); Ella W. Reed, ed., *Social Welfare Administration* (New York, 1961); Ray E. Johns, *Executive Responsibility: An Analysis of Executive Responsibilities in the Work of Voluntary, Community Social Welfare Organizations* (New York, 1954).

The following discuss the implications of bureaucracy for voluntary association: David L. Sills, *The Volunteers: Means and Ends in a National Organization* (Glencoe, Ill., 1957); Sherwood D. Fox, "Voluntary Association and Social Structure" (unpub. diss., Harvard University, 1952); Bernard Barber, "'Mass Apathy' and Voluntary Social Participation in the United States" (unpub. diss., Harvard University, 1948); Herbert Goldhammer, "Some Factors Affecting Participation in Voluntary Associations" (unpub. diss., University of Chicago, 1942); Harold L. Wilensky and Charles N. Lebeaux, *Industrial Society and Social Welfare: The Impact of Industrialization on the Supply and Organization of Social Welfare Services in the United States* (New York, 1958), esp. ch. X, "Agency Structure and the Social Welfare Policy"; Samuel Mencher, "The Future for Voluntaryism in American Social Welfare," in Alfred J. Kahn, ed., *Issues in American Social Work* (New York, 1959), 219-241, is pertinent. Robert D. Vinter, "The Social Structure of Service," *ibid.*, 242-269, focuses upon the professional staff.

An early discussion of the agency board member is Ada E. Sheffield, *The Charity Director: A Brief Study of his Responsibilities*, Charity Organization Department of the Russell Sage Foundation, Pub. No. 33 (New York, 1913). The subject is discussed frequently during the

Bibliographical Note

1920's in *The Family* (journal of the Family Service Association of America) and is covered in Francis H. McLean, *The Family Society: Joint Responsibilities of Board, Staff, and Membership* (New York, 1927). A recent analysis is Arnold J. Auerbach, "Aspirations of Power People and Agency Goals," *Social Work*, VI (1961), 66–73.

Supervision constitutes an important theme in Loüise C. Odencrantz, *The Social Worker in Family, Medical and Psychiatric Social Work* (New York, 1929). *The Family* contains many articles on supervision during the 1920's, and the subject is frequently examined in the *Newsletter* of the American Association for Organizing Family Social Work. An extreme interpretation of supervision as the "backbone of casework" appears in Grace F. Marcus, "The Casework of Supervision," *Survey*, LVIII (1927), 558–561. A recent discussion with some historical reference is Sidney S. Eisenberg, *Supervision in the Changing Field of Social Work* (Philadelphia, 1956).

Community organization as a quest for widespread citizen participation in all phases of civic life is explored in Mary P. Follett, *The New State: Group Organization the Solution of Popular Government* (New York, 1918); Eduard C. Lindeman, *The Community: An Introduction to the Study of Community Leadership and Organization* (New York, 1921); Joseph K. Hart, *Community Organization* (New York, 1920); Courtenay Dinwiddie, *Community Responsibility: A Review of the Cincinnati Social Unit Experiment* (New York, 1921). Community organization in the 1920's is discussed in B. A. McClenahan, *Organizing the Community: A Review of Practical Principles* (New York, 1922); Walter W. Pettit, *Case Studies in Community Organization* (New York, 1928); Jesse F. Steiner, *Community Organization: A Study of its Theory and Current Practice* (rev. ed., New York, 1930). A brief account with some historical perspective is Sidney Dillick, *Community Organization for Neighborhood Development, Past and Present* (New York, 1953).

Frank D. Watson, *The Charity Organization Movement in the United States: A Study of American Philanthropy* (New York, 1922), devotes some attention to the development of councils of social agencies. Francis H. McLean, the man most active in their formation, explains their function in "Central Councils and Community Planning," *Survey*, XXXVIII (1917), 216–219, and *the Central Council of Social Agencies: A Manual* (2nd rev. ed., American Association for Organizing Family Social Work, 1921). Frederick J. Ferris, "Letter to Editor," *Social Service Review*, XXXVI (1962), 86–87, discusses the origins of the pioneer Pittsburgh and Milwaukee councils. Charities endorsement is explained in the following articles, all of which appeared in the NCCC, *Proceedings:* Howard Strong, "The Relation of Commercial Bodies to Our Charitable and Social Standards" (1910),

Bibliographical Note

247–252; Henry Stewart, "Charities Endorsement in Retrospect and Prospect" (1913), 100–106; Henry Stewart, "Elementary Requirements of Standardization and Chief Obstacles to be Encountered" (1916), 329–334; Otto W. Davis, "Endorsement by Chambers of Commerce" (1916), 334–336.

FINANCIAL FEDERATION

A basic source of information on the pre-World War I federations is American Association for Organizing Charity, *Financial Federations: The Report of a Special Committee* (New York, 1917). William J. Norton, "Reminiscences," Columbia University Oral History Project, is the personal story of a leading federationist. The events leading to the formation of Cleveland's influential federation are related in the Cleveland Federation for Charity and Philanthropy, *The Social Year Book: The Human Problems and Resources of Cleveland* (1913). Henry M. Wriston, *Report on War Chest Practice* (n.p., n.d.), discusses the organization and activities of the local war chests. United War Work Campaign, *Bulletins I–XV* (1918), describe the organization of the last and greatest of the national war drives. On Jewish federation see Joseph Jacobs, "The Federation Movement in American Jewish Philanthropy," *American Jewish Yearbook, 1915–1916* (Philadelphia, 1915), 159–198; Barbara M. Solomon, *Pioneers in Service: The History of the Associated Jewish Philanthropies of Boston* (Boston, 1956); and Harry L. Lurie, *A Heritage Reaffirmed: The Jewish Federation Movement in America* (Philadelphia, 1961).

Many articles on federation in the 1920's appear in the NCSW, *Proceedings*, and *The Survey*. The *Bulletins* of the American Association for Community Organization constitute an important source. A great deal of factual data is contained in W. Frank Persons, *Central Financing of Social Agencies* (Columbus: Ohio Advisory Council, 1922), and Harvey Leebron, *The Financial Federation Movement: A Fact-Finding Investigation of Community Chest Developments, Methods and Results in 150 Cities* (Chicago, 1924). An over-all interpretation is William J. Norton, *The Cooperative Movement in Social Work* (New York, 1927). Joseph Lee is critical of federation in *Shall Boston Adopt the Community Chest?* (pamphlet, n.d.).

Reflecting the desire to formulate systematically the principles of fund-raising and giving are William H. Allen, *Modern Philanthropy: A Study of Efficient Appealing and Giving* (New York, 1912); Lilian Brandt, *How Much Shall I Give* (New York, 1921); Arthur W. Procter and Arthur A. Schuck, *The Financing of Social Work* (Chicago, 1926). On systematic publicity and interpretation see Charles C. Stillman, *Social Work Publicity: Its Message and Its Method* (New York, 1927), and Mary S. Routzahn and Evart G. Routzahn, *Publicity for Social Work* (New York, 1928).

Bibliographical Note

Pierce Williams and Frederick E. Croxton, *Corporation Contributions to Organized Community Welfare Services* (New York, 1930), is an indispensable source of information on corporate contributions up to 1930. F. Emerson Andrews, *Corporation Giving* (New York, 1952), provides a basis of comparison for later periods. Three articles by Aileen D. Ross deal with the relation between business and philanthropy: "Organized Philanthropy in an Urban Community," *Canadian Journal of Economics and Political Science*, XVIII (1952), 474–486; "The Social Control of Philanthropy," *American Journal of Sociology*, LVIII (1953), 451–460; "Philanthropic Activity and the Business Career," *Social Forces*, XXXII (1954), 274–280.

Harry P. Wareheim, "The Campaign," NCSW, *Proceedings* (1922), 410–415, is a chest executive's account of fund-raising technique. The professional fund-raiser's story is related in Tamblyn and Brown, *Raising Money: A New Business to Meet a New Need* (New York, 1925). See also, Arnaud C. Marts, *Philanthropy's Role in Civilization: Its Contribution to Human Freedom* (New York, 1953), and his *Man's Concern for His Fellow-Man* (Marts and Lundy, Inc., 1961). John Price Jones, *The Technique to Win in Fund Raising* (New York, 1934), contains detailed statistical analysis.

Useful factual data on chest campaigns is collected in Community Chests and Councils, Inc., *Yesterday and Today with Community Chests: A Record of Their History and Growth* (New York, 1937). Fund-raising is discussed in Robert H. Bremner, *American Philanthropy* (Chicago, 1960), and Edward Jenkins, *Philanthropy in America: An Introduction to the Practices and Prospects of Organizations Supported by Gifts and Endowments, 1924–1948* (New York, 1950). H. L. Lurie, "Private Philanthropy and Federated Fund-Raising," *Social Service Review*, XXIX (1955), 64–74, is a thoughtful analysis. John R. Seeley, et al., *Community Chest: A Case Study in Philanthropy* (Toronto, 1957), subjects Indianapolis to microscopic analysis. Critical of federation are Vaughn D. Bornet, *Welfare in America* (Norman, Okla., 1960); Richard Carter, *The Gentle Legions* (Garden City, N.Y., 1961); and Ad Hoc Citizens Committee, *Voluntary Health and Welfare Agencies in the United States: An Exploratory Study* (New York, 1961), a project sponsored by the Rockefeller Foundation. Public welfare expenditures since 1890 are surveyed in Mabel Newcomer, "Fifty Years of Public Support for Welfare Functions in the United States," *Social Service Review*, XV (1941), 651–660.

GENERAL

Helen L. Witmer, *Social Work: An Analysis of a Social Institution* (New York, 1942), is among the best general interpretations and benefits from historical perspective. A good index to current thinking in the field of social welfare is Alfred J. Kahn, ed., *Issues in American*

Bibliographical Note

Social Work (New York, 1959). Arthur E. Fink, *The Field of Social Work* (New York, 1942, 1955), surveys the various specialties and processes. Historical accounts include Nathan E. Cohen, *Social Work in the American Tradition* (New York, 1958), and Frank J. Bruno, *Trends in Social Work, 1874–1956: A History Based on The Proceedings of the National Conference of Social Work* (New York, 1957). Emma O. Lundberg, *Unto the Least of These: Social Services for Children* (New York, 1947), is a history of child welfare crammed with detail but wanting in synthesis. Ralph E. Pumphrey and Muriel W. Pumphrey, *The Heritage of American Social Work* (New York, 1961), is a collection of source readings from the seventeenth century to the present. The reform background of the years covered in this book is examined in Robert H. Bremner, *From the Depths: The Discovery of Poverty in the United States* (New York, 1956); Roy Lubove, *The Progressives and the Slums: Tenement House Reform in New York City, 1890–1917* (Pittsburgh, 1962); and Clarke A. Chambers, *Seedtime of Reform: Social Service and Social Action, 1918–1933* (Minneapolis, 1963).

Community organization is the subject of Bradley Buell and Associates, *Community Planning for Human Services* (New York, 1952). The influence of casework in shaping the group worker's assumptions concerning function and professional role is apparent in Harleigh B. Trecker, *Social Group Work: Principles and Practices* (rev. ed., New York, 1955). On the evolution of casework theory, see Gordon Hamilton, *Theory and Practice of Social Case Work* (rev. ed., New York, 1951); Kenneth L. M. Pray, *Social Work in a Revolutionary Age, and Other Papers* (Philadelphia, 1949); *Social Work as Human Relations: Anniversary Papers of the New York School of Social Work and the Community Service Society of New York* (New York, 1949); Cora Kasius, ed., *A Comparison of Diagnostic and Functional Casework Concepts: Report of the Family Service Association of America, Committee to Study Basic Concepts in Casework Practice* (Family Service Association of America, 1950). Helen H. Perlman, "Freud's Contribution to Social Welfare," *Social Service Review,* XXXI (1957), 192–202, is a social worker's evaluation of Freud's long-range significance.

Ernest Greenwood, "Socal Science and Social Work: A Theory of Their Relationship," *Social Service Review,* XXIX (1955), 20–33, deals with a subject of increasing significance. Arthur Hillman, *Sociology and Social Work* (Washington, 1956), is also pertinent. An elusive problem is explored in David G. French, *An Approach to Measuring Results in Social Work: A Report of the Michigan Reconnaissance Study of Evaluative Research in Social Work* (New York, 1952). The volunteer in an era of professional social work is considered in Family

Bibliographical Note

Welfare Association of America, *Volunteers for Family Service* (New York, 1942), and Nathan E. Cohen, ed., *The Citizen Volunteer: His Responsibility, Role, and Opportunity in Modern Society* (New York, 1960).

A. F. Young and E. T. Ashton, *British Social Work in the Nineteenth Century* (London, 1956), is useful for comparative purposes. Barbara Wootton, *Social Science and Social Pathology* (London, 1959), is a critical account of contemporary British social work.

Notes

Chapter I. Charity Organization and the New Gospel of Benevolence

1. Alexander Johnson, *Adventures in Social Welfare: Being Reminiscences of Things, Thoughts and Folks During Forty Years of Social Work* (Fort Wayne, Ind., 1923), 45.

2. Charles D. Kellogg, Report of the Committee of National Conference of Charities and Correction, *History of Charity Organization in the United States*, 1893 (Pub. No. 61, Charity Organization Society of the City of New York), 11–12.

3. For the early development of the AICP, see Roy Lubove, "The New York Association for Improving the Condition of the Poor: The Formative Years," *New-York Historical Society Quarterly*, XLIII (1959), 307–327.

4. Frank Dekker Watson, *The Charity Organization Movement in the United States: A Study in American Philanthropy* (New York, 1922), 58–59. Also Verl S. Lewis, "The Development of the Charity Organization Movement in the United States, 1875–1900: Its Principles and Methods" (unpub. diss., School of Applied Social Sciences, Western Reserve University, 1954), 21–24.

5. S. Humphreys Gurteen, *Provident Schemes* (Charity Organization Society of Buffalo, 1879), 16.

6. Charity Organization Society of New York, *Fifth Annual Report*, Jan. 1, 1887, 38.

7. J. J. McCook, "Charity Organization and Social Regeneration," *Lend-a-Hand*, XIII (1894), 469.

8. Robert Treat Paine, Jr., "The Work of Volunteer Visitors of the Associated Charities Among the Poor," *Journal of Social Science*, XII (1880), 113.

9. Charles D. Kellogg, "Statistics: Their Value in Charity Organization Work," National Conference of Charities and Correction, *Proceedings*, 1890, 32. "Every effectual reform," Kellogg explained, "must be founded on insight into the law of details which connects and explains them" (p. 32).

10. Hannah M. Todd, "Report of the Committee on the Organization of Charities," National Conference of Charities and Correction, *Proceedings*, 1891, 109.

11. Abram S. Hewitt, *Profits and Possibilities of the Proper Organization of Charity*, 1885 (Pub. No. 23, Charity Organization Society of the City of New York), 4.

12. John M. Glenn, "The Need of Organization in Charity Work," National Conference of Charities and Correction, *Proceedings*, 1899, 284.

13. Oscar C. McCulloch, "General and Special Methods of Operation in the Association of Charities," *Journal of Social Science*, XII (1880), 91. Richard L. Dugdale, a New York City merchant, first published his famous book, *The Jukes: A Study in Crime, Pauperism, and Heredity* in 1875 as part of the *Thirty-First Annual Report* of the Prison Association of New York. Although Dugdale did not attribute to heredity alone the pauperism and crime he traced in several generations of the Jukes family, hereditarians used his study to document their case for biological determinism and selective breeding. A Congregational clergyman and charity organization leader in Indianapolis, Oscar C. McCulloch published his account of a degenerate pedigree in, "The Tribe of Ishmael: A Study in Social Degradation," National Conference of Charities and Correction, *Proceedings*, 1888, 154–159.

14. Josephine Shaw Lowell, *Public Relief and Private Charity* (New York, 1884), 66, 76.

15. *Ibid.*, 66.

16. Associated Charities of Boston, *Third Annual Report*, November 1882, 39. The Associated Charities of Boston stressed the responsibilities of finding employment in its rules for visitors: "Make boys, or girls, over fourteen years old, work; and, if possible, in a trade where skill is well paid. Let them come to your house occasionally to report progress. Interest their employer. Teach in season and out of season that, if a man will be industrious, and will become a skilled workman in his trade, or a woman in hers, or boys and girls in theirs, steadier and paid employment can be procured." *Rules and Suggestions for Visitors of the Associated Charities*, Pub. No. 2 (1879; rev. 1882), 2.

17. S. Humphreys Gurteen, Address, Charity Organization Society of Buffalo, *Proceedings at Fourth Annual Meeting*, Feb. 23, 1882, 8.

18. C. R. Henderson, "The Scope and Influence of a Charity Organization Society," National Conference of Charities and Correction, *Proceedings*, 1896, 249.

19. Charity Organization Society of New York, *Fifth Annual Report*, 29.

20. Kellogg, "Statistics," 12; Charles M. Hubbard, "Relation of Charity-Organization Societies to Relief Societies and Relief-Giving," *American Journal of Sociology*, VI (1901), 783.

21. Amos G. Warner, "'Scientific Charity,'" *Popular Science Monthly*, XXXV (1889), 490.

22. Jane Addams, "The Subtle Problems of Charity," *Atlantic Monthly*, LXXXIII (1899), 165; Robert Hunter, "The Relation Between Social Settlements and Charity Organization," *Journal of Political Economy*, XI (1902), 81; James O. S. Huntington, "Philanthropy—Its Success and Failure," in Jane Addams et al., *Philanthropy and Social Progress* (Boston, 1893), 123, 127.

23. Mary E. Richmond, *Friendly Visiting Among the Poor: A Handbook for Charity Workers* (New York, 1899), 8–9.

24. Associated Charities of Boston, *Nineteenth Annual Report*, November 1898, 61–62.

25. A shortage of volunteers frequently forced the agent to undertake treatment, particularly in the summer when volunteers left the city for vacations. See Associated Charities of Boston, *First Annual Report*, November 1880, 22.

26. *Ibid.*, 9.

27. Associated Charities of Boston, *Seventh Annual Report*, November 1886, 9.

28. Charles D. Kellogg, "Report of the Committee on the Organization of Charities," National Conference of Charities and Correction, *Proceedings*, 1887, 132.

29. Lowell, *Public Relief*, 89.

30. Charles S. Fairchild, "Objects of Charity Organization," National Conference of Charities and Correction, *Proceedings*, 1884, 66.

31. Frederick J. Kingsbury, "Charity Organization a Necessity of Modern Conditions," *Lend-a-Hand*, XIV (1895), 7.

32. Associated Charities of Boston, *Nineteenth Annual Report*, 14–15. Romanticism in English charity organization and settlement work is explored in, Samuel Mencher, "The Influence of Romanticism on Nineteenth-Century British Social Work," *Social Service Review*, XXXVIII (1964), 174–190.

33. Jeffrey R. Brackett, "District Charity Organization," *Charities Review*, VII (1897), 598.

34. Kellogg, "Report of the Committee on the Organization of Charities," 135.

35. Charity Organization Society of New York, *Third Annual Report*, April 1, 1885, 12.

36. Associated Charities of Boston, *Thirteenth Annual Report*, November 1892, 24–25, 11–12.

37. Dorothy G. Becker, "Early Adventures in Social Casework: The Charity Agent, 1880–1910," *Social Casework*, XLIV (1963), 255–261.

38. Nathaniel S. Rosenau, "Farewell Address," Charity Organiza-

tion Society of Buffalo, *Sixteenth Annual Report*, Oct. 27, 1893, 26, 30.

39. Associated Charities of Boston, *Seventh Annual Report*, November 1886, 41.

Chapter II. From Friendly Visiting to Social Diagnosis

1. Boston Children's Aid Society, *Thirty-first Annual Report*, 1896, 8–11.

2. On the antecedents of medical social work see Garnet I. Pelton, "The History and Status of Hospital Social Work," National Conference of Charities and Correction, *Proceedings*, 1910, 332–341; and Ida M. Cannon, *Social Work in Hospitals: A Contribution to Progressive Medicine* (rev. ed., New York, 1923), 5–15; E. G. Stillman, "A Medical Point of View of Hospital Social Service," *Hospital Social Service Quarterly*, II (1920), 28–34.

3. Helen Bosanquet, *Social Work in London, 1869 to 1912. A History of the Charity Organisation Society* (London, 1914), 219–221.

4. Margaret S. Brogden, "Summary of Her Years of Service, Johns Hopkins Hospital, 1907–1931" (typed), 1939, Ida Cannon Papers, 1.

5. Richard C. Cabot, *Social Work: Essays on the Meeting-Ground of Doctor and Social Worker* (Boston and New York, 1919), xxi, xxii.

6. Richard C. Cabot, *Social Service and the Art of Healing* (New York, 1909), 33, vii.

7. Ida C. Cannon, "Medicine as a Social Instrument: Medical Social Service," *New England Journal of Medicine*, CCXLIV (1951), 718.

8. Charles P. Emerson, "Medical Social Service of the Future," *Hospital Social Service Quarterly*, I (1919), 269.

9. Cabot, *Social Work*, xxv.

10. Early Social Service referral slips, Ida Cannon Papers.

11. Letter from Richard C. Cabot to Frances R. Morse, Marion Jackson, and Joseph Lee, June 13, 1905, Ida Cannon Papers. As Cabot hoped, the Social Service Department did in coming years devote much attention to preventive medicine. In 1910, for example, it assisted Dr. Roger I. Lee in a study of the background of working girls who came to Massachusetts General as patients. Three years later it began "systematic work for the study and prevention of occupational disease" under the supervision of Dr. David L. Edsall.

12. "Editorial: The Future of the Hospital Social Service Movement," *Hospital Social Service*, V (1922), 46.

13. Ida M. Cannon, "Richard C. Cabot, A Tribute" (typed), January 1958, Ida M. Cannon Papers, 3.

14. These included Dr. T. S. Armstrong of Bellevue and Allied Hospitals in New York; Michael M. Davis, Jr., Director of the Boston Dispensary; John E. Ransom, Superintendent of the Michael

Reese Dispensary in Chicago; and Charles P. Emerson, who left Baltimore to become Dean of the Indiana School of Medicine.

15. Ida M. Cannon, *On the Social Frontier of Medicine: Pioneering in Medical Social Work* (Cambridge, Mass., 1952), 64.

16. Ida M. Cannon, "The Privileges and Responsibilities of a Profession" (Cannon-Thornton Lectures, Feb. 16, 1949) (typed), Ida Cannon Papers, 3.

17. "American Hospital Association Report of the Committee on the Survey of Hospital Social Service," *Hospital Social Service*, III (1921), 8.

18. Cannon, *Social Work in Hospitals*, 189; *Medical-Social Work at the Boston City Hospital, October 1914-January 1916*, pamphlet, 25.

19. Sidney E. Goldstein, "Hospital Social Service: Principles and Implications," National Conference of Charities and Correction, *Proceedings*, 1910, 346.

20. Cannon, *Social Work in Hospitals*, 98.

21. Ida M. Cannon, "Talk at Radcliffe College" (typed), February 1917, Ida Cannon Papers, 3.

22. Cannon, *Social Work in Hospitals*, 192.

23. Mary C. Jarrett, "Remarks," Conference on Function and Proper Training of Hospital Social Workers (called by officers of the Rockefeller Foundation, Feb. 21, 1920, New York City) (mimeographed), Ida Cannon Papers, 18.

24. Jessie L. Beard, "Efficiency in Hospital Social Service," *Hospital Social Service*, IV (1921), 191.

25. Letter from Jeffrey R. Brackett to Ida M. Cannon, March 22, 1912, Ida Cannon Papers; Brackett was Director of the Harvard-Simmons or Boston School of Social Work.

26. Social Service Department, Massachusetts General Hospital, Records of the Executive Committee, September 1914 to January 1917, Ida Cannon Papers (June 11, 1915).

27. "American Hospital Association Report of the Committee on the Survey of Hospital Social Service," 12; also Richard C. Cabot, "What of Medical Diagnosis Should the Social Case Worker Know and Apply?" National Conference of Social Work, *Proceedings*, 1917, 102–103.

28. "American Hospital Association Report of the Committee on the Survey of Hospital Social Service," 9.

29. Cabot, *Social Service and the Art of Healing*, 41, 47, 48.

30. Cannon, *Social Work in Hospitals*, 32, 44.

31. The early development of visiting teaching is discussed in Julius J. Oppenheimer, *The Visiting Teacher Movement, With Special Reference to Administrative Relationships* (New York, 1924).

32. The Public Education Association had been founded in 1895

by the women's auxiliary of Club E of the Federation of Good Government Clubs.

33. Harriet M. Johnson, *The Visiting Teacher in New York City* (New York, 1916), 1, 3.

34. Lydia H. Hodge, "Why a Visiting Teacher?" National Education Association, *Addresses and Proceedings*, 1917, 224. A similar view of the school was expressed by Jane F. Culbert: "With the development of the city school with its large classes, congestion, heterogeneous population and with a corps of teachers living in other parts of the city, frequently unacquainted with conditions under which the children live and study, and often unfamiliar with the customs, ideals and ambitions of the parents, there has arisen a situation in which the teacher fails to *know* the children whom she is trying to teach and develop." "Visiting Teachers and Their Activities," National Conference of Charities and Correction, *Proceedings*, 1916, 593.

35. A recent account of the progressive education movement is Lawrence A. Cremin, *The Transformation of the School: Progressivism in American Education, 1876–1957* (New York, 1961).

36. Hodge, "Why a Visiting Teacher?" 225.

37. Jessie L. Louderback, "The Function of the Visiting Teacher," *Survey*, XLII (1919), 253.

38. National Association of Visiting Teachers and Home and School Visitors, *The Visiting Teacher in the United States* (New York, 1921), 63.

39. *Ibid.*, 56.

40. Mabel B. Ellis, *The Visiting Teacher in Rochester: Report of a Study* (New York, 1925), 190.

41. The transition from charity organization to family social work was reflected in the change of title of the national federation: National Association of Societies for Organizing Charity, 1911; American Association of Societies for Organizing Charity, 1912; American Association for Organizing Charity, 1917; American Association for Organizing Family Social Work, 1919.

42. Edward T. Devine, *The Family and Social Work* (New York, 1912), 32.

43. Mary E. Richmond, "Some Next Steps in Social Treatment," National Conference of Social Work, *Proceedings*, 1920, 254.

44. Frederic Almy, "Constructive Relief," *Survey*, XXVII (1911), 1265.

45. Leo A. Frankel, "The Uses of Material Relief," National Conference of Charities and Correction, *Proceedings*, 1903, 320.

46. Almy, "Constructive Relief," 1265.

47. Edward T. Devine, *The Principles of Relief* (New York, 1904), 22.

48. Alice W. Solenberger, *One Thousand Homeless Men: A Study of Original Records* (New York, 1911), 6.

49. Zilpha D. Smith, *Deserted Wives and Deserting Husbands: A Study of 234 Families Based on the Experience of the District Committees and Agents of the Associated Charities of Boston* (Boston, 1901), 10.

50. Joanna C. Colcord, *Broken Homes: A Study of Family Desertion and Its Social Treatment* (New York, 1919), 21, 23, 50.

51. For additional background on developments in child welfare consult Henry W. Thurston, *The Dependent Child: A Story of Changing Aims and Methods in the Care of Dependent Children* (New York, 1930); and Emma O. Lundberg, *Unto the Least of These: Social Services for Children* (New York, 1947).

52. Boston Children's Aid Society, *Forty-Sixth Annual Report*, 1910, 11.

53. *Id., Forty-Eighth Annual Report*, 1912, 15–16.

54. *Id., Fiftieth Annual Report*, 1914, 8.

55. *Id., Fifty-Third Annual Report*, 1917, 11, 10. The Society noted that "no important personal work is ever assigned to an inexperienced visitor." *Ibid.*, 11.

56. *Ibid.*, 10.

57. Boston Children's Aid Society, *Fifty-Fourth Annual Report*, 1918, 10.

58. Mary E. Richmond, *Social Diagnosis* (New York, 1917), 25.

59. A detailed account of Mary Richmond's Baltimore experience is found in Muriel W. Pumphrey's "Mary Richmond and the Rise of Professional Social Work in Baltimore: The Foundations of a Creative Career," unpub. diss. Columbia School of Social Work, 1956.

60. Mary E. Richmond, "The Friendly Visitor," (address delivered at the annual meeting of the Baltimore Charity Organization Society, 1890), in Joanna C. Colcord and Ruth Z. S. Mann, eds., *Mary E. Richmond, The Long View: Papers and Addresses* (New York, 1930), 42.

61. Richmond, *Social Diagnosis*, 357.

62. *Ibid.*, 43, 62.

63. Mary E. Richmond, *What is Social Case Work? An Introductory Description* (New York, 1922), 98.

64. *Ibid.*, 101–102.

65. *Ibid.*, 9.

66. Erving Winslow, "Philanthropic Individualism," *Survey*, XXXIV (1915), 555.

67. Charles R. Henderson, "Foreword to the First Edition," in Amelia Sears, *The Charity Visitor: A Handbook for Beginners* (Chicago, 1917; 1st ed. 1913), iv; Mary E. Richmond, "The Case for the

Volunteer" in Colcord and Mann, *The Long View*, 345; see also Mary Conyngton, *How to Help: A Manual of Practical Charity* (New York, 1913), 24.

68. Edward T. Devine, "Social Forces: The Friendly Visitor," *Charities and the Commons*, XXI (1908), 321–322; and "The Essentials of a Relief Policy," American Academy of Political and Social Science, *Annals*, XXI (1903), 357.

69. Patten, a University of Pennsylvania economist, argued that "mere goodness must be replaced by efficiency and the trained agent must replace the volunteer who satisfies her curiosity at the expense of those she meets . . ." Simon N. Patten, "Who is the Good Neighbor?" *Charities and the Commons*, XIX (1908), 1645. Commenting on Patten's article in the same issue (p. 1636), Devine thought that charity organization societies should at least consider whether to encourage friendly visiting or whether to restrict volunteers to boards and committees.

70. Katharine D. Hardwick, "Good Things in Their Beginnings," unpub. manuscript, 11.

71. Miss Hardwick points out that the "workers of those days were commonly called agents, and by that title the volunteer board members meant exactly what the term implies," *ibid.*, 10. On the asssumption of responsibility by the agent see Dorothy G. Becker, "The Visitor to the New York City Poor, 1843–1920," unpub. diss., Columbia School of Social Work, 1960, 284 ff; and Muriel W. Pumphrey, "Mary Richmond and the Rise of Professional Social Work in Baltimore: The Foundations of a Creative Career," unpub. diss., Columbia School of Social Work, 1956, 306.

72. Elizabeth Case, "The Maligned Volunteer," *Survey*, XLII (1919), 819.

73. Cannon, *Social Work in Hospitals*, 198, 199.

74. Clare M. Tousley, "The Volunteer Professional," *The Family*, I (June 1, 1920), 2–6. See also Mary P. Wheeler, "New Methods of Approach to Volunteers," *The Family*, II (1921), 139–142.

75. Mabel Newcomer, "Fifty Years of Public Support of Welfare Functions in the United States," *Social Service Review*, XV (1941), 655, 656.

76. Gertrude Vaile, "Public Administration of Charity in Denver," National Conference of Charities and Correction, *Proceedings*, 1916, 417, 418; Sophie Irene Loeb, "Report of Investigations in Six Countries . . . ," State of New York, *Report of the New York State Commission on Relief for Widowed Mothers, transmitted to the Legislature March 27, 1914* (Albany, 1914), 190, 191; Hannah B. Einstein, "The Keeping Together of Families," Third New York City Conference of Charities and Correction, *Proceedings*, 1912, 61, 62; L. A.

Halbert, "The Organization of Municipal Charities and Corrections," National Conference of Charities and Correction, *Proceedings*, 1916, 394, 395. Rubinow's evaluation of the relative merits of social insurance and scientific charity was bluntly stated: "The progressive social worker must learn to understand that a sickness insurance law, even in one state, can do more to eradicate poverty, and is, therefore, a greater social gain, than a dozen organizations for scientific philanthropy with their investigations, their sermons on thrift, and their constant feverish hunt for liberal contributions." Isaac M. Rubinow, *Social Insurance: With Special Reference to American Conditions* (New York, 1913), 297.

Chapter III. Mind and Matter: Psychiatry in Social Work

1. Mary C. Jarrett, "Psychiatric Social Work," *Mental Hygiene*, II (1918), 290; and "Possibilities in Social Service for Psychopathic Patients," pamphlet, 1917, 10–11 (reprinted from the *Boston Medical and Surgical Journal*, Feb. 8, 1917).

2. Adolf Meyer, "The Birth and Development of the Mental Hygiene Movement," *Mental Hygiene*, XIX (1935), 29.

3. A. A. Brill, *Freud's Contribution to Psychiatry* (New York, 1962), 18–19. Care of the insane before the Civil War, including moral treatment and milieu therapy, are examined in J. Sanbourne Bockoven, *Moral Treatment in American Psychiatry* (New York, 1963), and Norman Dain, *Concepts of Insanity in the United States, 1789–1865* (New Brunswick, N. J., 1964).

4. Benjamin Rush, *Medical Inquiries and Observations Upon the Diseases of the Mind* (Philadelphia, 1812); Albert Deutsch, *The Mentally Ill in America: A History of Their Care and Treatment from Colonial Times* (2nd ed., rev., New York, 1949), 484. Richard Shryock points out that a comprehensive treatise on mental illness by Thomas C. Upham of Bowdoin College appeared in 1840. Upham, however, was not a physician and he "viewed mental illness in the older, philosophical manner rather than in the current, European terms of pathological anatomy." Richard C. Shryock, *Medicine and Society in America: 1660–1860* (Ithaca, N. Y., 1962), 130.

5. Adolf Meyer, "The Role of the Mental Factors in Psychiatry," in Alfred Lief, ed., *The Commonsense Psychiatry of Dr. Adolf Meyer* (New York, 1948), 172.

6. Adolf Meyer, "Address at the Celebration of the 100th Anniversary of Bloomingdale Hospital, May 26, 1921," in Lief, *ibid.*, 6–7.

7. On the social implications of clinical and therapeutic psychiatry see Adolf Meyer, "The Aims of a Psychiatric Clinic," Mental Hygiene Conference and Exhibit (at City College, New York, under the Joint Auspices of the National Committee for Mental Hygiene

and the Committee on Mental Hygiene of the State Charities Aid Association), *Proceedings*, 117–127.

8. Adolf Meyer, "Remarks at the Opening Exercises of the Henry Phipps Psychiatric Clinic, Baltimore, April 16, 1913," in Lief, *Commonsense Psychiatry*, 346–347.

9. William A. White, *Mechanisms of Character Formation: An Introduction to Psychoanalysis* (New York, 1916), 24, 51.

10. Meyer, "The Aims of a Psychiatric Clinic," 122.

11. Adolf Meyer, "Schedule for the Study of Mental Abnormalities in Children," in Lief, *Commonsense Psychiatry*, 71.

12. Abraham Myerson, "The Psychiatric Social Worker," pamphlet, 1918, 3 (reprinted from the *Journal of Abnormal Psychology*, October 1918).

13. Predecessors of the Boston Psychopathic Out-Patient Department include the free dispensary for persons with "incipient mental disease" opened in the Out-Patient Department of the Pennsylvania Hospital in Philadelphia in 1885, and the "nerve clinics" established in Philadelphia in 1867 and Boston in 1873. Deutsch, *Mentally Ill*, 296. Franklin G. Ebaugh and Charles A. Rymer, *Psychiatry in Medical Education* (New York, 1942), 5–6, discusses the establishment of outpatient departments in mental hospitals.

14. Before 1920 some form of psychiatric guidance for children also appeared at St. Elizabeth's Hospital in Washington; the Wayne County Juvenile Court, Michigan; Iowa Psychopathic Hospital, Iowa City; and the Philadelphia General Hospital.

15. Adolf Meyer, "Papers at the International Congress of Medicine, London, 1913," in Lief, *Commonsense Psychiatry*, 363.

16. Massachusetts General Hospital, Social Service Department, *Third Annual Report*, Oct. 1, 1907–Oct. 1, 1908, 57.

17. State Charities Aid Association, *Annual Report*, in State of New York, State Commission in Lunacy, *Twenty-First Annual Report*, Oct. 1, 1908–Sept. 30, 1909 (Albany, 1910), 322.

18. William Healy and Augusta F. Bronner, "The Child Guidance Clinic: Birth and Growth of an Idea," in Lawson G. Lowrey and Victoria Sloane, eds., *Orthopsychiatry, 1923–1948* (American Orthopsychiatric Association, 1948), 14.

19. The events leading to the establishment of the Juvenile Psychopathic Institute are described in the article cited above and Oral History Interviews of William Healy and Augusta Bronner (conducted with John C. Burnham, January, 1960; with supplements and corrections, June 1961), 50–53. Healy emphasizes the point that it was not physicians or psychiatrists who promoted the idea of careful diagnosis of delinquents before treatment and general research into the causes of delinquency, but such lay reformers as Julia Lathrop,

Ethel S. Dummer, and Allen Burns. They had originally taken the initiative and broached the subject to Healy.

20. Healy and Bronner, "Child Guidance Clinic," 19, 20–23, 28.

21. Mary E. Richmond, *Social Diagnosis* (New York, 1917), 34.

22. Healy and Bronner, "Child Guidance Clinic," 24. Healy recalled Dr. Walter Fernald's remark in 1908 that the "best he could do by way of classification of a child was to observe his motor coordinations, his posture and activities on alighting from the train or street car which brought him to the institution."

23. Itard, a student of Philippe Pinel, Physician-in-Chief of the Insane at the Bicêtre, was himself Chief Medical Officer of the National Institution for the Deaf and Dumb. He undertook around 1799 the task of educating the "Savage of Aveyron," a wild boy of about eleven or twelve who had been discovered by huntsmen in the woods of Caune. For an account of Itard's work see Stanley P. Davies, *Social Control of the Mentally Deficient* (New York, 1930), 17 ff. Davies' book is useful for the historical background on attitudes toward and treatment of the feeble-minded, and I have drawn liberally from it.

24. Henry H. Goddard, *The Kallikak Family: A Study in the Heredity of Feeble-Mindedness* (New York, 1912), 54; Henry H. Goddard, "Mental Deficiency from the Standpoint of Heredity," Massachusetts Society for Mental Hygiene, *Publications*, No. 15, 1916, 8 (reprinted from the *Boston Medical and Surgical Journal*, Aug. 24, 1916).

25. Quoted in Davies, *Social Control of the Mentally Deficient*, 92, 3–5.

26. Gregor Mendel, an Austrian Monk, had published a paper in 1865 describing his experiments in the crossbreeding of peas and the transmission of traits through several generations. Sir Francis Galton (1822–1911), had published *Hereditary Genius*, a study in the pedigrees of famous men, in 1865. After 1900 he became active in organizing the eugenics movement in England. His address on "The Possible Improvement of the Human Breed under Existing Conditions of Law and Sentiment" was delivered in 1901 before the Royal Anthropological Institute and stimulated interest in eugenics both in England and the United States.

27. Goddard, *Kallikak Family*, 12, 71.

28. Goddard, "Mental Deficiency from the Standpoint of Heredity," 4. With the possible exception of California, the sterilization measures were not vigorously enforced. One state's experience is discussed in Rudolph J. Vecoli, "Sterilization: A Progressive Measure?" *Wisconsin Magazine of History*, XLIII (Spring 1960), 190–202. A positive eugenics movement existed alongside the negative one, and

attempted to encourage breeding within the better American stock. Theodore Roosevelt was a leading spokesman for this group. Mark H. Haller, "Heredity in Progressive Thought," *Social Service Review*, XXXVII (1963), 173. For the best general treatment of the subject, also by Haller, see: *Eugenics: Hereditarian Attitudes in American Thought* (New Brunswick, N. J., 1963).

29. Massachusetts General Hospital, Social Service Department, *Fifth Annual Report*, Jan. 1, 1910–Jan. 1, 1911, 17, 20.

30. Boston Children's Aid Society, *Forty-Eighth Annual Report*, 1912, 11.

31. Edward T. Devine, *The Family and Social Work* (New York, 1912), 44, 45.

32. Richmond, *Social Diagnosis*, 229.

33. John C. Burnham, "Psychiatry, Psychology, and the Progressive Movement," *American Quarterly*, XII (1960), 461.

34. Myerson, "The Psychiatric Social Worker," 3.

35. H. Douglas Singer, "The Function of the Social Worker in Relation to the State Hospital Physician," *Mental Hygiene*, III (1919), 611.

36. Clifford W. Beers, *A Mind That Found Itself* (rev. ed., New York, 1925), 164.

37. *Ibid.*, 265.

38. *Ibid.*, 337.

39. William Healy, "The Bearings of Psychology on Social Case Work," National Conference of Social Work, *Proceedings*, 1917, 105.

40. George K. Pratt, "Twenty Years of the National Committee for Mental Hygiene," *Mental Hygiene*, XIV (1930), 405. On the early investigations and educational work of the Committee see also Lewellys F. Barker, "The First Ten Years of the National Committee for Mental Hygiene, with Some Comments on Its Future," *Mental Hygiene*, II (1918), 557–581.

41. Beers, *A Mind That Found Itself*, 344.

42. In 1917 Congress provided that servicemen who incurred disabilities were entitled to government medical care, monetary compensation, and vocational rehabilitation. The Bureau of War Risk Insurance, the Federal Board for Vocational Education, and the United States Public Health Service were designated to administer the acts. In 1921 these activities were centralized in a Veteran's Bureau, except for the hospitals and dispensaries operated by the Public Health Service.

43. On psychiatric social work and the Red Cross see Helen A. Young, "Psychiatric Social Work in the American Red Cross," *Hospital Social Service*, IV (1921), 216–218; Elizabeth C. Hayes, "Case Correspondence: A Method of Psychiatric Social Work,"

Mental Hygiene, VI (1922), 125–155; Margaret Worch, "Psychiatric Social Work in a Red Cross Chapter," *Mental Hygiene*, VI (1922), 312–331.

44. H. Douglas Singer, "The Function of the Social Worker in Relation to the State Hospital Physician," 610.

45. Adolf Meyer, "Report of the Pathological Institute, 1904–1905," in Lief, *Commonsense Psychiatry*, 153, 155.

46. William Healy, *The Individual Delinquent: A Text-Book of Diagnosis and Prognosis for all Concerned in Understanding Offenders* (Boston, 1915), 26.

47. White, Mechanisms of Character Formation, 318, 73; also, Healy, *Individual Delinquent*, 4.

48. Ada E. Sheffield, *The Social Case History, Its Construction and Content* (New York, 1920), 218.

49. Maida H. Solomon, "The Social Worker's Approach to the Family of the Syphilitic," *Hospital Social Service*, III (1921), 444.

50. On the association with physicians, Mildred C. Scoville later noted that "the close affiliation with the medical profession provided from the start a challenging stimulus and a continuous scrutiny which were powerful incentives to growth." "An Inquiry into the Status of Psychiatric Social Work," *American Journal of Orthopsychiatry*, I (1931), 146.

51. Jessie Taft, "Qualifications of the Psychiatric Social Worker," National Conference of Social Work, *Proceedings*, 1919, 595, 598.

52. Dorothy Q. Hale, "Inadequate Social Examinations in Psychopathic Clinics," *Mental Hygiene*, V (1921), 795.

53. Taft, "Qualifications of the Psychiatric Social Worker," 597; Margherita Ryther, "Place and Scope of Psychiatric Social Work in Mental Hygiene," National Conference of Social Work, *Proceedings*, 1919, 578.

54. Mary C. Jarrett, "An Emergency Course in a New Branch of Social Work," *Mental Hygiene*, II (1918), 594.

55. Mary C. Jarrett, "The Psychiatric Thread Running Through All Social Case Work," National Conference of Social Work, *Proceedings*, 1919, 587.

56. Harriet Gage, "The Place of Psychiatric Social Work in the Social Service Field," *Hospital Social Service*, IV (1921), 147.

57. Jarrett, "Psychiatric Social Work," 288.

58. Jarrett, "The Psychiatric Thread Running Through all Social Case Work," 589.

59. Jessie Taft, "The New Impulse in Mental Hygiene," *Mental Hygiene*, IV (1920), 210.

60. Bernard Glueck, "Special Preparation of the Psychiatric Social Worker," National Conference of Social Work, *Proceedings*, 1919, 600.

61. Mary E. Richmond, "The Interrelation of Social Movements," in Colcord and Mann, eds., *The Long View*, 290.

62. Mary E. Richmond, *The Good Neighbor in the Modern City* (New York, 1912; 1st ed. 1907), 103; *What is Social Case Work?*, 229.

63. Harriett M. Johnson, *The Visiting Teacher in New York City* (New York, 1916), 67.

64. Ida M. Cannon, *Social Work in Hospitals: A Contribution to Progressive Medicine* (New York, 1923; rev. ed.), 115; Massachusetts General Hospital, Social Service Department, *First Annual Report*, Oct. 1, 1905–Oct. 1, 1906, 22.

65. George M. Kline, "The Function of the Social Worker in Relation to a State Program," *Mental Hygiene*, III (1919), 624.

66. Hannah Curtis, "Social Service in Mental Cases," *Survey*, XLIV (1920), 442.

67. These included Paul Dubois, S. Weir Mitchell, Irwin H. Neff, and James J. Putnam.

68. Elmer E. Southard and Mary C. Jarrett, *The Kingdom of Evils* (New York, 1922), 547, 548, 549.

69. Josephine Shaw Lowell, "How to Adapt 'Charity Organization' Methods to Small Communities," National Conference of Charities and Correction, *Proceedings*, 1887, 137.

70. Simon N. Patten, "The Reorganization of Social Work," *Survey*, XXX (1913), 472. For works dealing with the role of the expert in Progressive America see Roy Lubove, "Twentieth Century City: The Progressive as Municipal Reformer," *Mid-America*, XLI (1959), 195–209; and *The Progressives and the Slums: Tenement House Reform in New York City, 1890–1917* (Pittsburgh, 1962). The subject enters into John Burnham's article on "Psychiatry, Psychology, and the Progressive Movement," cited earlier. Samuel P. Hays examines the conservation expert in *Conservation and the Gospel of Efficiency: The Progressive Conservation Movement, 1890–1920* (Cambridge, Mass., 1959). Although the theme of expertise is not central to Lawrence Cremin's account of progressivism in education, he deals with the rise of pedagogical "experts" anxious to convert Americans to their educational psychology and social concept of the school. *The Transformation of the School: Progressivism in American Education, 1876–1957* (New York, 1961). Relevant also is Dwight Waldo, *The Administrative State: A Study of the Political Theory of American Public Administration* (New York, 1948).

Chapter IV. Inner vs. Outer Need: Psychiatry and Fragmentation

1. For Lindeman's critique, see his articles, "The Social Worker and His Community," *Survey*, LII (1924), 83–85; "The Social

Worker as Statesman," *ibid.*, 222–224; and "The Social Worker as Prophet," *ibid.*, 346, 369, 371; also Abraham Epstein, "The Soullessness of Presentday Social Work," *Current History*, XXVIII (1928), 391, 392.

2. Clarke A. Chambers, "Creative Effort in an Age of Normalcy, 1918–33," *The Social Welfare Forum* (New York, 1961), 252–271. As evidence of continuity Chambers points to such figures as Florence Kelley, Margaret D. Robins, Owen R. Lovejoy, Mary Dewson, and Frances Perkins; and to such organizations as the National Consumers' League, Women's Trade Union League, National Child Labor Committee, American Association for Labor Legislation, and National Federation of Settlements. A fuller treatment of the subject by the same author is *Seedtime of Reform: American Social Service and Social Action, 1918–1933* (Minneapolis, 1963).

3. A. A. Brill, *Freud's Contribution to Psychiatry* (New York, 1962), 39. On the early years of Freudianism in America, see A. A. Brill, "The Introduction and Development of Freud's Work in the United States," *American Journal of Sociology*, XLV (1939), 318–325; Smith Ely Jelliffe, "Sigmund Freud and Psychiatry: A Partial Appraisal," *ibid.*, 326–340; Celia B. Stendler, "New Ideas for Old: How Freudianism was Received in the United States from 1900 to 1925," *Journal of Educational Psychology*, XXXVIII (1947), 193–206. Ernest W. Burgess found that Freud had virtually no impact upon American sociology before 1920. "The Influence of Sigmund Freud upon Sociology in the United States," *American Journal of Sociology*, XLV (1939), 356–374. Social workers discovered that they "had been fooled by appearances" and now possessed the "key to wisdom in human relations." Bertha C. Reynolds, *An Uncharted Journey: Fifty Years of Growth in Social Work* (New York, 1963), 59. Indispensable for the introduction of Freudianism into the United States is, John C. Burnham, *Psychoanalysis and American Medicine before 1918* (forthcoming).

4. Ida M. Cannon, "Medical Social Work" (typed) January 1947, Ida Cannon Papers.

5. Miriam Van Waters, "Philosophical Trends in Modern Social Work," in Fern Lowry, ed., *Readings in Social Case Work, 1920–1938: Selected Reprints for the Case Work Practitioner*, 43 (reprinted from National Conference of Social Work, *Proceedings*, 1930); also, Reynolds, *Uncharted Journey*, 58–59.

6. Ethel L. Ginsburg, "Freud's Contribution to the Philosophy and Practice of Social Work," *American Journal of Orthopsychiatry*, X (1940), 877.

7. Jessie Taft, "A Consideration of Character Training and Personality Development," *Mental Hygiene*, XIV (1930), 329.

8. Despite the early hopes of Meyer and other social psychiatrists, the psychiatric social workers found "less and less to challenge them in the state hospitals . . . , and gradually found their way into the early demonstration child guidance clinics and into subsequent clinical developments throughout the country. The development of the child guidance movement paralleled and gave rise to the practice of psychiatric social work as we know it today." Ethel L. Ginsburg, "Psychiatric Social Work," in Lawson G. Lowrey and Victoria Sloane, eds., *Orthopsychiatry, 1923–1948* (American Orthopsychiatric Association, 1948), 470.

9. The negotiations leading to the establishment of the Judge Baker Clinic and its early activities are described in, Oral History Interviews of William Healy and Augusta Bronner (conducted with John C. Burnham, January 1960; with supplements and correction, June 1961), 57, 84–86, 89–93, 157–169. Also influencing the decision of Healy and Bronner to leave Chicago was the fact that with transfer of the Juvenile Psychopathic Institute to county auspices in 1914 came increasing pressure to add more cases and even to drop Miss Bronner in favor of a psychologist with political connections.

10. The Commonwealth Fund, *Fifth Annual Report*, 1922–1923, 22.

11. The Lakewood Conference also included Dr. Max Farrand, general director of the Commonwealth Fund; H. C. Morrison, Professor of Education, University of Chicago; Judge Charles W. Hoffman, Court of Domestic Relations, Cincinnati; Mrs. Martha Falconer, director of the Department of Protective Measures, American Social Hygiene Association. Dr. Salmon had originally proposed that the best way to promote the child guidance work being done by Healy and Bronner was to subsidize an expanded program at the Judge Baker Clinic. Healy and Bronner, however, insisted that it was preferable to launch new clinics in other communities. Oral History Interviews of William Healy and Augusta Bronner, 94–95, 195.

12. The other proposals for study and action touched on the following subjects: child care and protection agencies, feeble-minded, sex education, recreation, broken families, child labor, juvenile courts, detention homes, institutions for delinquents, and training of probation officers.

13. Jessie Taft, "The Function of a Mental Hygienist in a Children's Agency," National Conference of Social Work, *Proceedings*, 1927, 393; and "A Consideration of Character Training and Personality Development," 329.

14. Two useful accounts of the activities and evolution of the child guidance clinics are George S. Stevenson and Geddes Smith, *Child Guidance Clinics: A Quarter Century of Development* (New York, 1934); and George S. Stevenson, "Child Guidance and the

National Committee for Mental Hygiene," an historical chapter in Lowrey and Sloan, *Orthopsychiatry*, 50–82.

15. Lawson G. Lowrey, "Some Trends in the Development of Relationships Between Psychiatry and General Social Case-Work," *Mental Hygiene*, X (1926), 281.

16. Quoted in Florence T. Waite, *A Warm Friend for the Spirit: A History of the Family Service Association of Cleveland and its Forebears, 1830–1952* (Cleveland, 1960), 178.

17. Edward D. Lynde, "Community Agencies and the Clinic," National Conference of Social Work, *Proceedings*, 1925, 418–421.

18. Stevenson and Smith, *Child Guidance Clinics*, 117–118.

19. Porter R. Lee and Marion E. Kenworthy, et al., *Mental Hygiene and Social Work* (New York, 1931; 1st printing 1929), 152.

20. *Ibid.*, 124, 133.

21. Lawson G. Lowrey and Geddes Smith, *The Institute for Child Guidance, 1927–1933* (New York, 1933), 7, 53.

22. Charlotte Towle, "Certain Changes in the Philosophy of Social Work," in Lawson G. Lowrey, ed., *Institute for Child Guidance Studies: Selected Reprints* (New York, 1931), 79, 72, 73; also, Elizabeth H. Dexter, "The Social Case Worker's Attitudes and Problems as They Affect Her Work," National Conference of Social Work, *Proceedings*, 1926, 436–442.

23. Division III also took over a grading experiment in New York City begun by the Public Education Association. This experiment started in Public School 64 and switched to Public School 61. It involved group and individual intelligence tests, and the organization of classes for gifted, normal, and dull-normal children in the first and second grades.

24. Howard W. Nudd, "The School and Social Work," National Conference of Social Work, *Proceedings*, 1927, 42, 43.

25. Bernard Glueck, "Some Extra-Curricular Problems of the Classroom," Joint Committee on Methods of Preventing Delinquency, Pub. No. 3 (1924), 3 (reprinted from *School and Society*, XIX, 1924).

26. Jessie Taft, "The Relation of the School to the Mental Health of the Average Child," *Mental Hygiene*, VII (1923), 678, 677.

27. Jane F. Culbert, *The Visiting Teacher at Work* (New York, 1929), 88.

28. William L. Connor, "The Child Guidance Clinic and the Public Schools," in Ralph P. Truitt et al., *The Child Guidance Clinic and the Community* (New York, 1928), 71.

29. The Lincoln School was one of the most famous experimental, ultraprogressive schools, and was attached to Teachers College, Columbia University.

30. Psychiatric work in the schools is described by Elma Olson, "Psychiatric Social Work in the Field of Education," *Mental Hygiene*, XIII (1929), 263–270. An additional innovation mentioned by Miss Olson was the employment of psychiatric social workers on the staffs of the Cannon Nursery School in New Haven, and the Tom-Tit Nursery School in Brooklyn.

31. White-Williams Foundation, June 1917–June 1927, *School Children as Social Workers See Them* (Philadelphia, 1927), 4, 5.

32. Culbert, *The Visiting Teacher at Work*, 12.

33. Ralph P. Truitt, "Mental Hygiene and the Public Schools," *Mental Hygiene*, XI (1927), 269.

34. Culbert, *The Visiting Teacher at Work*, 90. On the social worker's view of the classroom teacher's responsibilities see also Clara Bassett, *The School and Mental Health* (New York, 1931), 8–11.

35. Anna B. Pratt, "Should the Visiting Teacher be a New Official?" *Journal of Social Forces*, I (1923), 304.

36. Nudd, "The School and Social Work," 43.

37. Lawson G. Lowrey, "A Program for Meeting Mental Hygiene Needs in a City," in Truitt, *The Child Guidance Clinic and the Community*, 28, 29. Social work, as Charlotte Towle put it, had been "removed from a class or economic basis to an objective professional basis." "Certain Changes in the Philosophy of Social Work," in Lowrey, *Institute for Child Guidance Studies*, 98.

38. Jessie Taft, "The Social Worker's Opportunity," National Conference of Social Work, *Proceedings*, 1922, 375.

39. Helen L. Myrick, "Psychiatric Social Work, Its Nurture and Nature," *Mental Hygiene*, XIII (1929), 509.

40. Maurice J. Karpf, *The Scientific Basis of Social Work: A Study in Family Case Work* (New York, 1931), 352, 353.

41. Abraham Flexner, "Is Social Work a Profession?" National Conference of Charities and Correction, *Proceedings*, 1915, 585.

42. Ronald L. Warren, "Toward a Reformulation of Community Theory," *Human Organization* (Reprint No. 2), 9.

43. Reynolds, *Uncharted Journey*, 44.

44. *Ibid.*, 58.

45. Edith Baker, "The Contribution of Hospital Social Service to Health Conservation," National Conference of Social Work, *Proceedings*, 1923, 28; and "Fundamentals of Hospital Social Service and its Relation to Other Agencies," *Family*, VI (1925), 246.

46. "Committee on Functions, American Association of Hospital Social Workers, Report," *Hospital Social Service*, XVII (1928), 466, 474.

47. Ida M. Cannon, "The Functions of Medical Social Service in the United States," *Hospital Social Service*, XXVII (1933), 8. The

emerging psychiatric point of view in medical social work is apparent in Harriett M. Bartlett, *Medical Social Work: A Study of Current Aims and Methods in Medical Social Case Work* (Chicago, 1934). Miss Bartlett wrote that "All of the newer concepts of social case work—the philosophy which emphasizes the client's freedom to choose and the psychology which reveals the significance of emotion in behavior and relationship in treatment—are applicable here, though they need to be reformulated in terms of the medical social situation," 128.

48. "From Social Work to Social Science," *New Republic*, XLVII (1926), 49.

49. Laura J. Keiser, "Mental Hygiene in the Social Agency," *Family*, X (1929), 82; Miss Keiser added that mental hygiene led the social worker to consider "primarily the person" with his emotions, instincts, and ambitions, which she had "often lost sight of in the pressure of physical, economic problems, unemployment, and poor housing," 83.

50. Edward D. Lynde, "The Place of Psychiatric Social Work in a General Case Work Agency," National Conference of Social Work, *Proceedings*, 1924, 438.

51. Mildred P. Carpenter, "Forward Trends," *Family*, III (1923), 245.

52. Malcolm S. Nichols, "New Emphases in Family Social Work," *Family*, IX (1928), 190.

53. Beatrice Z. Levey, "New Trends in Psychiatric Social Treatment in the Family Agency," *Mental Hygiene*, XIII (1929), 130.

54. Homer E. Wichenden, "Examples of Case Treatment," National Conference of Social Work, *Proceedings*, 1920, 260.

55. Rebecca H. Boyle, "Psychiatric Social Work in a Family Agency," *Hospital Social Service* IV (1921), 209.

56. Grace F. Marcus, *Some Aspects of Relief in Family Casework: An Evaluation of Practice Based on a Study Made for the Charity Organization Society of New York* (New York, 1929), 63.

57. *Ibid.*, 42. On relief and casework see also Eleanor Neustaedter, "The Integration of Economic and Psychological Factors," National Conference of Social Work, *Proceedings*, 1930, 198–216.

58. Grace F. Marcus, "The Mental Hygiene of Economic Dependency," First International Congress on Mental Hygiene, *Proceedings* (1930), I, 728.

59. Charlotte Towle, "Review of *A Changing Psychology in Social Case Work*," *American Journal of Orthopsychiatry*, I (1931), 545.

60. Virginia P. Robinson, *A Changing Psychology in Social Case Work* (Philadelphia, 1930), 184.

61. Virginia P. Robinson, "Psychiatric Social Worker?" *Survey*, LII (1924), 233–234.

62. Robinson, *A Changing Psychology*, 36, 48.

63. An attempt to clarify the differences between the two groups is made in Cora Kasius, ed., *A Comparison of Diagnostic and Functional Case-Work Concepts. Report of the Family Service Association of America, Committee to Study Basic Concepts in Casework Practice* (Family Service Association of America, 1950).

64. Virginia P. Robinson, ed., *Jessie Taft: Therapist and Social Work Educator. A Professional Biography* (Philadelphia, 1962), 127, 215, 218.

65. *Ibid.*, 226. The association between Jessie Taft and Otto Rank which was instrumental in the development of functionalism is described in, Jessie Taft, *Otto Rank, A Biographical Study* (New York, 1958). The functionalist viewpoint is outlined in the *Journal of Social Work Process*, which began publication in November 1937. It is important to note that Rank was not directly responsible for the development of functional casework: "Rank was the last person to understand function as used by the social agency, for he himself had never been in the position of representing any agency. The only function he knew was a professional one, but in his case self-oriented and self-maintained. Its importance as a support for the social worker was hard for him to realize or to conceive of as allowing for a truly helpful relation to the client." Taft, *Otto Rank*, 228–229.

Chapter V. In-Group and Out-Group: The Molding of a
Professional Subculture

1. Everett C. Hughes, *Men and Their Work* (Glencoe, Ill., 1958), 36; also, Ernest Greenwood, "Attributes of a Profession," *Social Work*, II (July 1957), 45–55.

2. Harvey L. Smith, "Contingencies of Professional Differentiation," *American Journal of Sociology*, LXIII (1958), 414.

3. James H. S. Bossard, "The Functions and Limits of Social Work as Viewed by a Sociologist," in L. L. Bernard, ed., *The Fields and Methods of Sociology* (New York, 1934), 208–209.

4. Mary E. Richmond, *Social Diagnosis* (New York, 1917), 5.

5. M. Antoinette Cannon, "Underlying Principles and Common Practices in Social Work," National Conference of Social Work, *Proceedings*, 1928, 565.

6. American Association of Social Workers, *Social Case Work: Generic and Specific: An Outline. A Report of the Milford Conference*. Studies in the Practice of Social Work, No. 2 (New York, 1929), 3, 16.

7. Talcott Parsons, *Essays in Sociological Theory* (rev. ed., Glencoe, Ill., 1954), 34–49 ("The Professions and Social Structure").

8. Merton has pointed out, however, that in referring to the dis-

interestedness of science or the professions one implies a "basic institutional element": "Disinterestedness is not to be equated with altruism nor interested action with egoism. Such equivalences confuse institutional and motivational levels of analysis," Robert K. Merton, *Social Theory and Social Structure* (rev. ed., Glencoe, Ill., 1957), 558.

9. Edward T. Devine, "Introduction" to Joseph K. Hart, *Community Organization* (New York, 1920), v–vi.

10. Philip W. Ayres, "Training for Practical Philanthropy," *Review of Reviews* XIX (1899), 206; Ernest P. Bicknell, "The Preparedness of Organization Charity," Report of the Standing Committee on Needy Families in Their Homes, National Conference of Charities and Correction, *Proceedings,* 1904, 198; Kate H. Claghorn, *Social Work as a Profession for Men and Women* (pamphlet, Oct. 15, 1915), 1.

11. Edwin S. Burdell, "The Economic Value to the Community of Trained Social Workers," *Family,* X (1929), 105, 106.

12. William J. Goode, "Community Within a Community: The Professions," *American Sociological Review,* XXII (1957), 195.

13. Charles F. Weller, "Relief Work and Preventive Philanthropies as Related to Charity Organization," National Conference of Charities and Correction, *Proceedings,* 1902, 270–271.

14. A. M. Carr-Saunders and P. A. Wilson, *The Professions* (Oxford, 1933), 298.

15. On professional association in medical social work, see Mary A. Stites, *History of the American Association of Medical Social Workers* (Washington, 1955).

16. The origins of professional association in psychiatric social work are discussed in Lois M. French, *Psychiatric Social Work* (New York, 1940), appendix A, 295 ff.

17. The seventeen charter members included Mary C. Jarrett, Maida H. Solomon, and Jessie Taft.

18. Norman A. Polansky, "The Professional Identity in Social Work," in Alfred J. Kahn, ed., *Issues in American Social Work* (New York, 1959), 312.

19. J. B. Buell, "By Our Own Bootstraps," *Family,* II (1921), 65, 66; J. B. Buell, "The Challenge to Social Workers," *Survey,* XLV (1920), 164.

20. Paul L. Benjamin, "Social Workers," *Survey,* XLVI (1921), 181.

21. "A Call to Social Workers," *Survey,* XLV (1920), 169. Other signers included Howard S. Braucher, Baily B. Burritt, C. C. Carstens, Homer Folks, Lawson Purdy, Mary Van Kleeck, Nelle Swartz, and Philip P. Jacobs.

22. *The Compass,* I (December 1920), 1 and I (March 1921), 2.

23. Memorandum Concerning an Informal Meeting of Seven Social Case Workers at Kansas City, May 19, 1918, 1. Mary Richmond Papers.

24. On the Conference on Demobilization see Paul U. Kellogg, "The Conference on Demobilization," *Survey*, XLI (1918), 287–288; William T. Cross, "A National Council of Social Agencies," *ibid.*, 303–305; Arthur P. Kellogg, "Shall Social Agencies Unite for Reconstruction?" *ibid.*, 315–317; "Thrown Open to Discussion," *Survey*, XLI (1919), 560, 569.

25. "Square Pegs and Round Holes in Social Work," *Survey*, XXXI, (1914), 654.

26. See, for example, The National Social Workers' Exchange, *The Profession of Social Work* (pamphlet No. 1, n.d.).

27. Edith S. King, "Wanted—Social Workers," *Survey*, XL (1918), 126.

28. On the origins and early development of the AASW see also, Frances N. Harrison, *The Growth of a Professional Association* (New York, 1935); Walter B. Johnson, "History of the American Association of Social Workers," unpub. diss. Washington University, St. Louis, 1937; Frank J. Bruno, "The First Twenty-five Years of the AASW," *The Compass*, XXVII (June 1946), 9–12.

29. *The Compass*, III (March 1923), 3.

30. Edward T. Devine and Mary Van Kleeck, *Positions in Social Work* (pamphlet, New York School of Philanthropy, 1916), 6.

31. *Ibid., passim.*

32. Ralph G. Hurlin, *Social Work Salaries* (pamphlet, Russell Sage Foundation, New York, 1926), and Hurlin, "Measuring the Demand for Social Workers," National Conference of Social Work, *Proceedings*, 1926, 587–595.

33. Neva R. Deardorff, "The Objectives of Professional Organization," National Conference of Social Work, *Proceedings*, 1925, 637–638.

34. *Ibid.*, 638.

35. Veronica O. Wilder, "Our Salaries," *Family*, III (1922), 6–9.

36. Earle E. Eubank, "Toward Professional Social Work," *Survey*, LV (1925), 362–364.

37. Sydnor H. Walker, *Social Work and the Training of Social Workers* (Chapel Hill, N. C., 1928), 123.

38. All colleges, schools, courses, etc. had to be "approved" or accredited by the Association.

39. The Association originally accepted only field work done for credit under the auspices of a school of social work. For the benefit of those who had satisfied all the requirements save those of field work, it liberalized its interpretation of the requirement and accepted

field work done under supervision in an agency used by a school of social work for its field work.

40. Goode, "Community Within a Community," 194.

41. Ralph W. Tyler, "Distinctive Attributes of Education for the Professions," *Social Work Journal*, XXXIII (1952), 57.

42. Zilpha D. Smith, The Training of District Agents, 1890–1899 (Oct. 7, 1899) and Study Class, 1898–1900 (Feb. 9, 1900), Zilpha D. Smith Scrapbook.

43. Anna L. Dawes, "The Need of Training Schools for a New Profession," *Lend-A-Hand*, XI (1893), 90–97.

44. Mary E. Richmond, "The Need of a Training School in Applied Philanthropy," National Conference of Charities and Correction, *Proceedings*, 1897, 183.

45. On the origins of the early schools, see Edith Abbott, *Education for Social Work*, Department of the Interior, Bureau of Education, Report of the Commissioner of Education for the year ended June 30, 1915, I (Washington, 1915), 345–359.

46. Alice L. Higgins to Jeffrey R. Brackett, December 23, 1903. Archives, Simmons School of Social Work.

47. Virginia P. Robinson, "The University of Pennsylvania School of Social Work in Perspective: 1909–1959," *Journal of Social Work Process*, XI (1960), 11.

48. "A Social Science School At Western Reserve University," *School and Society*, III (1916), 383.

49. Jeffrey R. Brackett, *Supervision and Education in Charity* (New York, 1903), 212.

50. Chicago School of Civics and Philanthropy, "The New Profession and Preparation for It," *Bulletin*, I (1910), 173.

51. Edith Abbott, "Twenty-One Years of University Education for the Social Services, 1920–1941," *Social Service Review*, XV (1941), 670–671. On Edith Abbott's role see Elizabeth Wisner, "Edith Abbott's Contribution to Social Work Education," *Social Service Review*, XXXII (1958), 1–10. For Sophonisba Breckinridge, see Arlien Johnson, "Her Contribution to the Professional Schools of Social Work," *Social Service Review*, XXII (1948), 442–447; and Helen R. Wright, "The Debt of the School of Social Service Administration," *ibid.*, 448–450. Miss Breckinridge introduced the case method of instruction at Chicago and taught the first courses in casework.

52. Letter from Samuel M. Lindsay to the Committee on Philanthropic Education, March 27, 1912, quoted in Saul Bernstein et al., "The New York School of Social Work" (Institute of Welfare Research, Community Service Society of New York, 1942), mimeographed, 27; John M. Glenn to Samuel M. Lindsay, March 19, 1912,

Samuel M. Lindsay Papers (Columbia University), Folder, New York School of Social Work.

53. New York School of Philanthropy, *Bulletin*, V (1912), 9–10.

54. *School for Social Workers* (pamphlet, 1912–13), 3.

55. Useful in tracing the early development of the Boston School for Social Workers are the Minutes of the Administrative Board of the School for Social Workers. These were compiled by Frances R. Morse and can be found in the Archives of the Simmons School of Social Work.

56. For Woods's view of professional social work, see Robert A. Woods, "Social Work: A New Profession," *International Journal of Ethics*, XVI (1905), 25–39.

57. Mary Van Kleeck and Graham R. Taylor, "The Professional Organization of Social Work," American Academy of Political and Social Science, *Annals*, CI (1922), 166.

58. Katherine D. Hardwick, "The Boston School for Social Workers from 1904 to 1918," unpub. manuscript in Miss Hardwick's possession, 48.

59. F. Stuart Chapin to John B. Andrews, July 21, 1919; John B. Andrews to F. Stuart Chapin, July 25, 1919, American Association for Labor Legislation (John B. Andrews) Papers, Cornell University.

60. Jesse F. Steiner, *Education for Social Work* (Chicago, 1921), 21.

61. James H. Tufts, *Education and Training for Social Work* (New York, 1923), 182.

62. James E. Hagerty, *The Training of Social Workers* (New York, 1931), 99.

63. Edith Abbott, *Social Welfare and Professional Education* (2nd ed., Chicago, 1942), 12.

64. *Ibid.*, 30–31.

65. Maurice J. Karpf, *The Scientific Basis of Social Work: A Study in Family Case Work* (New York, 1931), 385. Karpf was another who criticized the schools' emphasis upon the "technical or trade aspects, instead of on the scientific or professional aspects" of social work, 368.

66. Milford Conference, *Report*, 77.

67. Neva R. Deardorff, "The Place of a Professional School in Training for Social Work," American Academy of Political and Social Science, *Annals*, CXXI (1925), 173.

68. On the Red Cross home service institutes in World War I and the university's role in social work education see Steiner, *Education for Social Work*, 26, and Hagerty, *Training of Social Workers*, 50–51. The development of the Association of Training Schools is discussed

in Frank J. Bruno, "Twenty-Five Years of Schools of Social Work," *Social Service Review*, XVIII (1944), 152–164.

69. Charlotte Towle, *The Learner in Education for the Professions, as Seen in Education for Social Work* (Chicago, 1954), 8; and, by the same author, "The Distinctive Attributes of Education for Social Work," *Social Work Journal* XXXIII (1952), 63–72, 94; see also Bertha C. Reynolds, *Learning and Teaching in the Practice of Social Work* (New York, 1942).

70. Rosa Wessel, "The Meaning of Professional Education for Social Work," *Social Service Review*, XXXV (1961), 158, 159.

71. Virginia P. Robinson, "Educational Problems in Preparation for Social Case-Work," *Mental Hygiene*, XIV (1930), 831.

72. *Ibid.*, 830.

73. Porter R. Lee, "Technical Training for Social Work," *Charity Organization Bulletin*, IV (new series, October 1913), 155.

74. Porter R. Lee, "The Future of Professional Social Work," in *Social Work as Cause and Function, and Other Papers* (New York, 1937), 138.

75. Porter R. Lee, "The Common Problems of the Family Case Work Agencies and the Schools," *Family*, II (1921), 133.

76. Jeffrey R. Brackett described the aim of the Boston School for Social Workers as professional quality training for both paid and volunteer workers. Minutes of the Administrative Board of the School for Social Workers, June 9, 1904.

77. Porter R. Lee, "Personality in Social Work," National Conference of Social Work, *Proceedings*, 1926, 29.

78. Porter R. Lee, and Marion E. Kenworthy, *Mental Hygiene and Social Work* (New York, 1929), 215.

79. *Ibid.*, 238.

80. Among the "focal points" of field-work supervision, according to Lee and Kenworthy, were "modification of certain typical attitudes which interfere with efficiency in the practice of psychiatric social work," and "development of certain personality traits in the student whose adaptation in certain ways makes for more effective social case work"; *ibid.*, 191. On the new objectives of social work education and the role of supervision see also Sarah H. Swift, *Training in Psychiatric Social Work at the Institute for Child Guidance, 1927–1933* (New York, 1934).

Chapter VI. Agency and Community: The Apotheosis of Efficiency

1. Porter R. Lee, *Social Work as Cause and Function, and Other Papers* (New York, 1937), 4, 9, 6.

2. Gertrude Vaile, "Some Significant Trends Since Cleveland, 1912," National Conference of Social Work, *Proceedings*, 1926, 7.

3. Elizabeth V. Trump, "What Does the Social Worker Do?," *Journal of Social Forces*, III (1925), 276.

4. Letter from Mornay Williams to Edward T. Devine, February 7, 1906. Archives, Community Service Society of New York.

5. Letter from R. S. Brewster to Edward T. Devine, July 20, 1908. Archives, Community Service Society of New York.

6. Peter M. Blau, *Bureaucracy in Modern Society* (New York, 1956), 60, 106.

7. See, e.g., David L. Sills, *The Volunteers: Means and Ends in a National Organization* (Glencoe, Ill., 1957).

8. Zilpha D. Smith, "Discussion: Needy Families in Their Homes," National Conference of Charities and Correction, *Proceedings*, 1901. 405, 406.

9. Lewis W. Hine, "Charity on a Business Basis: The Modern Method of Applying Business Principles to Social Service," *The World Today*, XIII (1907), 1254, 1259. Also Cromwell Childe, "First Aid for Lazarus: The New Science of Almsgiving and the Training Required of Those Who Direct Our Charities To-day," *Harper's Weekly*, LVII (Jan. 18, 1913), 9–10.

10. L. A. Halbert, "Developing Standards," National Conference of Charities and Correction, *Proceedings*, 1913, 109. Also by Halbert, see "Effective Charity Administration," American Academy of Political and Social Science, *Annals*, XLI (1912), 176–192.

11. Stockton Raymond, "The Executive and the Staff: Mutual Loyalty and Responsibility a Basis of Esprit de Corps," *Better Times*, V (June 9, 1924), 18s.

12. H. H. Gerth and C. Wright Mills, eds., *From Max Weber: Essays in Sociology* (New York, 1958), 216.

13. Helen P. Kempton, "Why the Volunteer?" *Family*, III (1922), 193. Also, Nadia Thomas, "Recruiting and Training Volunteers," *Family*, V (1925), 230.

14. Mrs. Elbert L. Carpenter, "Volunteers and the Community," *Family*, VII (1926), 23; "How to Make Volunteer Workers More Useful," *Better Times*, II (October 1921), 30.

15. Margaret E. Rich, "The Modern Spirit of Earlier Days," *Family*, IV (1924), 217.

16. Mary W. Glenn, "On Being a Board Member," *Family*, V (1924), 179.

17. Stockton Raymond, "The Executive and His Directors: Team Work and Definite Responsibilities are Necessary," *Better Times*, V (April 7, 1924), 12s.

18. Francis H. McLean, *The Family Society: Joint Responsibilities of Board, Staff, and Membership* (New York, 1927), 17, 18.

19. Robert W. Kelso, "Why is a Board of Directors?," *Survey*, LXVII (1931), 78.

20. Gladys E. H. Hosmer, "A Volunteer Takes a Look Around," *Survey* LXVII (1931), 195; Martin A. Meyer, "Social Service and the Rich," *Family*, V (1924), 57.

21. Mrs. Sidney Borg, "The Volunteer in the Present Field of Social Work," *Family*, VII (1927), 313.

22. Barbara Blackstock, "The Part Board Members Should Take in the Work of a Family Welfare Society," *Family*, V (1924), 169.

23. *Ibid.*, 171; cf. Elwood Street, *Social Work Administration* (New York, 1931), 97, 99, 262, 259.

24. Bernard Barber, " 'Mass Apathy' and Voluntary Social Participation in the United States," unpub. diss., Harvard University, 1948, 193, 194; Carpenter, "Volunteers and the Community," 23.

25. Edward L. Parker, "Unrealized Community Assets," *Family*, VII (1926), 44.

26. Ellen W. W. Geer, "The Place of the Volunteer," *Survey*, LVII (1926), 392. Also Maurice Taylor, "The Volunteer in Social Work," *Family*, VI (1925), 205–208; and Barbara Whitmore, "The Volunteer Speaks for Herself," *Family*, VIII (1928), 343–344.

27. John M. Glendenning, "Supervision Through Conferences on Specific Cases," *Family*, XII (1931), 8.

28. Grace Marcus, "How Case Work Training May be Adapted to Meet the Worker's Personal Problems," National Conference of Social Work, *Proceedings*, 1927, 386; Family Welfare Association of America, *Training in Family Social Work Agencies* (New York, 1933), 15.

29. Alfred W. Hobart, "What The Visitor Expects from Supervision," *Family*, XII (1931), 18; Glendenning, "Supervision Through Conferences on Specific Cases," 8.

30. Hobart, "What the Visitor Expects from Supervision," 17; also Mary A. Young, "Supervision—a Worm's Eye View," *Family*, XI (1930), 44.

31. John B. Dawson, "The Case Supervisor in a Family Agency without District Offices," *Family*, VI (1926), 293.

32. Sills, *Volunteers*, 1.

33. Caroline Bedford, "An Analysis of the Problem of Case Supervision," *Family*, X (1930), 310.

34. Hobart, "What the Visitor Expects from Supervision," 17.

35. Bedford, "An Analysis of the Problem of Case Supervision," 309.

36. Blau, *Bureaucracy in Modern Society*, 45 ff.

37. Gerth and Mills, *From Max Weber*, 216.

38. Eugene Litwak, "Models of Bureaucracy Which Permit Conflict," *American Journal of Sociology*, LXVII (1961), 180, 181.

39. For a defense of supervision which takes some account of the objections raised and the historical development of this form of agency control, see Sidney S. Eisenberg, *Supervision in the Changing Field of Social Work* (Philadelphia, 1956).

40. Robert D. Vinter, "The Social Structure of Service," in Alfred J. Kahn, ed., *Issues in American Social Work* (New York, 1959), 248-252.

41. Litwak's professional model bureaucracy, with its emphasis upon social skills, suggests one sequence of modifications necessary in Weber's rational model bureaucracy to account for the distinctive tensions and problems of formal organization in social work. The "natural system" model, identified with Talcott Parsons and Philip Selznick, and emphasizing irrational and goal-displacement features, points to other modifications. The "punishment-centered" and "representative" bureaucracy models devised by Alvin W. Gouldner are also relevant. For our purposes, however, the important consideration is not deviation in social work bureaucracy from Weber's rational model, but the distinctive components of rational administration, expertise, planning, and goal formulation incorporated in all modern bureaucratic structures, differentiating them from preurban-industrial modes of organization and affecting the status of a comparatively "nonrational" factor like the volunteer. A good critique of the natural system model because of its tendency to deflect attention from the uniquely rational components of modern formal organization is Alvin W. Gouldner, "Organizational Analysis," in Robert K. Merton et al., eds., *Sociology Today: Problems and Prospects* (New York, 1959), 400-428.

42. Letter from R. R. Bowker to Robert W. deForest, Jan. 14, 1916, Archives, Community Service Society of New York.

43. Letter from Frank J. Bruno to W. Frank Persons, April 15, 1912. Archives, Community Service Society of New York.

44. Joseph K. Hart, *Community Organization* (New York, 1920), 219.

45. Leroy E. Bowman, "Community Centers," *Social Work Year Book*, I, 1929 (New York, 1930), 93.

46. Courtenay Dinwiddie, *Community Responsibility: A Review of the Cincinnati Social Unit Experiment* (New York, 1921), 2. Much of the following discussion of the Social Unit is drawn from Dinwiddie's book.

47. Dwight Sanderson, "Democracy and Community Organization," American Sociological Society, *Publications*, XIV (1919), 89;

Arthur E. Wood, "The Philosophy of Community Organization," *American Sociological Society, Publications,* XVII (1922), 181.

48. Mary P. Follett, *The New State: Group Organization the Solution of Popular Government* (New York, 1918), 217.

49. *Ibid.,* 189.

50. Eduard C. Lindeman, *The Community: An Introduction to the Study of Community Leadership and Organization* (New York, 1921), 58, 173. Interest in community organization was not restricted to urban communities. Important rural developments which fed into the mainstream of community organization theory and practice included Theodore Roosevelt's Country Life Commission in 1909, the organization efforts of Kenyon Butterfield, E. L. Morgan, and the Extension Division of the Massachusetts State College of Agriculture, the Red Cross Home Service Program during and after World War I; and the progressive education experiments of Mrs. Marie T. Harvey in the Porter school district, located near Kirksville, Missouri. For an early general study of community organization with a focus on rural affairs see B. A. McClenahan, *Organizing the Community: A Review of Practical Principles* (New York, 1922). See also the chapters on rural community organization in Jesse F. Steiner, *Community Organization: A Study of its Theory and Current Practice* (rev. ed., New York, 1930).

51. Seba Eldridge, "Community Organization and Citizenship," *Social Forces,* VII (1928), 140, 133.

52. Henry Stewart, "Charities Endorsement in Retrospect and Prospect," National Conference of Charities and Correction, *Proceedings,* 1913, 101–102.

53. Howard Strong, "The Relation of Commercial Bodies to Our Charitable and Social Standards," National Conference of Charities and Correction, *Proceedings,* 1910, 247, 248.

54. J. J. O'Connor, "The Central Council," National Conference of Charities and Correction, *Proceedings,* 1913, 341, 344; C. M. Hubbard, "Formulation and Improvement of Standards by Central Councils of Social Agencies," National Conference of Charities and Correction, *Proceedings,* 1916, 328, 329.

55. Francis H. McLean, *The Central Council of Social Agencies: A Manual* (2nd ed., rev., New York, 1921), 25. Also Rev. Francis A. Gressle, "The Relation of Religious Organizations to a City-Wide Federation, "National Conference of Social Work, *Proceedings,* 1920, 451.

56. Francis H. McLean, "Central Councils and Community Planing," *Survey,* XXXVIII (June 2, 1917), 216. McLean referred also to councils in Pittsburgh, Seattle, and Cincinnati, pointing out, however, that the first two had become largely city conferences, while

the Cincinnati council had "fostered contractual relationships by arranging for joint money-raising . . ."

Chapter VII. Federation and the Bureaucratic Imperative

1. American Association for Organizing Charity, *Financial Federations, The Report of a Special Committee* (New York, 1917), 65. Hereafter referred to as AAOC, *Financial Federations.*

2. William J. Norton, "City Planning in Social Work," *Survey,* XXXVI (1916), 583.

3. Letter from Elwood Street to author, Nov. 15, 1961.

4. Harvey Leebron, *The Financial Federation Movement: A Fact-Finding Investigation of Community Chest Developments, Methods and Results in 150 Cities* (Chicago, 1924), 110; Edward Jenkins, *Philanthropy in America: An Introduction to the Practices and Prospects of Organizations Supported by Gifts and Endowments, 1924–1948* (New York, 1950), 105; William J. Norton, *The Cooperative Movement in Social Work* (New York, 1927), 50, 51; John Price Jones Corporation, United Hospital Fund (A Plan for Raising $1,500,000 for the United Hospital Fund, June 1920), 2, JPJC Papers, Harvard Business School Library; Guy T. Justis, *Twenty-Five Years of Social Welfare, 1917–1942* (Denver, 1943), 14–16; Joseph Jacobs, "The Federation Movement in American Jewish Philanthropy," *American Jewish Yearbook, 1915–1916* (Philadelphia, 1915), 159–198; Barbara M. Solomon, *Pioneers in Service: The History of the Associated Jewish Philanthropies of Boston* (Boston, 1956), ch. I.

5. Arnaud C. Marts, *Philanthropy's Role in Civilization: Its Contribution to Human Freedom* (New York, 1953), 108–111. Marts points out that the University of Pittsburgh was the first college to use the short-term, intensive campaign method of fund-raising. Ward directed the campaign (1914) and Pierce, general secretary of the Pittsburgh YMCA at the time, served as a volunteer. Arnaud C. Marts, *Man's Concern for His Fellow-Man* (Marts and Lundy, Inc., 1961), 30.

6. Letter from Elwood Street to Kenneth I. Wood, September 19, 1947. United Community Funds and Councils of America, Archives, Community Chest History, 1920 to 1949 Folder. Hereafter referred to as UCFC, Archives.

7. On the investigations of the Chamber of Commerce see: C. W. Williams, "Cleveland's Group Plan: A Large Scale Experiment in Good Will and Charitable Giving," *Survey,* XXIX (1913), 603–606, and also by Williams, "Cleveland's Federated Givers," *American Review of Reviews,* XLVIII (1913), 472–475; Cleveland Federation for Charity and Philanthropy, *The Social Year Book: The Human Problems and Resources of Cleveland* (1913), 14; Edward M. Wil-

liams, "The Essentials of the Cleveland Experiment in 'Cooperative Benevolence,'" National Conference of Charities and Correction, *Proceedings,* 1913, 112.

8. Guy T. Justis, "Values Resulting from the Federation of Private Charities in Erie, Pa." *American City,* XIV (1916), 468–469.

9. E. M. Williams, "Essentials of the Cleveland Experiment," 112.

10. Letter from Sherman Kingsley to Pierce Williams, July 7, 1928. UCFC, Archives, Cleveland, Ohio, Folder.

11. Cleveland Federation for Charity and Philanthropy, *Social Year Book,* 1913, 20; E. M. Williams, "Essentials of the Cleveland Experiment," 112, 114; *Cleveland Plain Dealer,* May 29, 1913 (typed clipping), UCFC, Archives, Cleveland, Ohio, Folder.

12. Fred R. Johnson, "The Ideals of Financial Federation," National Conference of Social Work, *Proceedings,* 1917, 510; AAOC, *Financial Federations,* 63.

13. William J. Norton, "The Progress of Financial Federation," "National Conference of Social Work, *Proceedings,* 1917, 507; Norton, "City Planning in Social Work," 581.

14. Elwood Street to author, Interview, Dec. 29, 1961.

15. William J. Norton, Reminiscences, Columbia Oral History Project, 24.

16. Henry M. Wriston, *Report on War Chest Practice* (presented to the Connecticut State Council of Defense, n.p., n.d., probably 1918), 14. Wriston claims that the first chests were organized in Syracuse, N. Y., and jointly in Ilion and Mohawk, N. Y., in the spring of 1917.

17. Sherman C. Kingsley, "Conserving War Time Spirit and Organization for Peace Time Needs," National Conference of Social Work, *Proceedings,* 1919, 697. The state councils were those of Michigan, New Mexico, New York, Washington, and Wisconsin.

18. Wriston, *War Chest Practice,* 95, 97, 115, 117, 128, 129.

19. William J. Norton, "The War Chest and the Federation Movement," National Conference of Social Work, *Proceedings,* 1918, 592, 593; Sherman C. Kingsley, "War Chests in Peace Times: The Contribution Which Financial Federations May Make to the Future of Social Work," *Survey,* XLII (1919), 345, 346.

20. *United War Work Campaign* (pamphlet, n.p., n.d.), 1; John R. Mott, *The Largest Voluntary Offering in History* (pamphlet, n.p., n.d.), 1.

21. United War Work Campaign for $170,500,000, November 11–18, 1918, *Bulletin I: Organization in the City, Large or Small,* 5; *Bulletin II: Organization in the County,* 3; *Bulletin IX: Meetings, How to Plan and Conduct,* 3.

22. Ralph J. Reed, "Relation of National Agencies to the Local

Community," National Conference of Social Work, *Proceedings,* 1922, 426.

23. William J. Norton, "The Growing Demand for Co-Ordination of National Social Work," National Conference of Social Work, *Proceedings,* 1920, 30.

24. National Information Bureau, *Report of a Study of the Interrelation of the Work of National Social Agencies in Fourteen American Communities* (New York, 1922), 35, 44, 104.

25. C. M. Bookman, "Functions of Public and Private Agencies in the Social Work of the Future," National Conference of Social Work, *Proceedings,* 1922, 92; William C. Procter, "A Chest Commander's Vision," *Survey,* LIX (1927), 138; Kingsley, "Conserving War Time Spirit and Organization for Peace Time Needs," 697–698; J. Lionberger Davis, "The Spirit of St. Louis," *Survey,* LIX (1927), 144.

26. John B. Dawson, "Community Responsibility," *Survey,* LXVI (1931), 222; Frank J. Bruno, "Co-operation in Social Work," *Family,* X (1929), 198–199.

27. Cecil Clare North, *The Community and Social Welfare: A Study in Community Organization* (New York, 1931), 334. Also, Bruno, "Co-operation in Social Work," 197.

28. Norton, "City Planning in Social Work," 581; William J. Norton, "Financial Federations—III. What Agencies Shall Be Admitted?" *Survey,* XLIX (1922), 368. Also, C. M. Bookman, "The Community Chest Movement—an Interpretation," National Conference of Social Work," *Proceedings,* 1924, 23.

29. Edward T. Devine, "Welfare Federations. IV. The National Agencies: General Considerations," *Survey,* XLVI (1921), 493.

30. William J. Norton, "Social Work Grows Up," *Survey,* LIX (1927), 135.

31. Raymond Clapp, "Who Shall Decide Personnel Policies?" *Survey,* LXV (1930), 103.

32. For Lee's criticisms of the chest see, *Shall Boston Adopt the Community Chest?* (pamphlet, n.p., n.d., probably 1925 or 1926); and "The Chest and Social Work," *Survey,* LIX (1928), 749–750.

33. Stockton Raymond, *Financial Federation and Social Work* (pamphlet, 1923), 4, 3.

34. According to Elwood Street, no federationist "equated efficiency in administration with reduction of paid staff and use of volunteers"; and, in the chests with which he was connected, the "whole pressure from the chest was improvement in quality of service and qualifications of agency personnel." One of the chief reasons for increase in budgets was the "endeavor to raise salaries of qualified workers and to make possible employment of other qualified ones."

Letter from Elwood Street to author, November 15, 1961. See, however, Clapp, "Who Shall Decide Personnel Policies?" for an expression of disagreement between federationists and the American Association of Social Workers concerning chest authority to "make recommendations to member agencies affecting relationships between staff and executive, and staff and client," 102.

35. The constructive programs of the prewar federations are described in detail in AAOC, *Financial Federations*.

36. William J. Shroder, "Relations Between Jewish Federations and Community Chests," National Conference of Jewish Social Service, *Proceedings*, 1925; James F. Jackson, "Community Organization of Social Forces: A. From the Standpoint of the Constituent Agency," National Conference of Social Work, *Proceedings*, 1921, 411; Norton, *Cooperative Movement in Social Work*, 348, 349.

37. William J. Norton, "Financial Federations—I. Fundamentals," *Survey*, XLIX (1922), 89.

38. W. Frank Persons, *Central Financing of Social Agencies* (Columbus, Ohio, 1922), chs. II, III.

39. Rowland Haynes, "The Contribution of the Community Chest to Community Welfare Planning," National Conference of Social Work, *Proceedings*, 1928, 405; Rev. C. H. Le Blond, "Increased Interest in Special Groups Through Central Financing," National Conference of Social Work, *Proceedings*, 1923, 516; Norton, *Cooperative Movement in Social Work*, 175. On budgeting and the general constructive goals of federation see also the following in the National Conference of Social Work, *Proceedings:* Roscoe C. Edlund, "The Social Service of a Federation" (1919), 717–723; Raymond Clapp, "Budget Making in a Federation" (1922), 398–402; Sherman C. Kingsley, "The Coordination of Agencies' Activities," (1922), 415–419; Charles C. Stillman, "Creation of New and Suppression of Unnecessary Activities," (1922), 419–422; Wilbur F. Maxwell, "What Types of Activities are Proving to be Best for a Co-ordinated Group of Social Agencies in Cities of Fifty Thousand to One Hundred and Fifty Thousand Population?" (1924), 480–485; Otto W. Davis, "Support and Interpretation of Professional Requirements in Social Work: By Councils of Social Agencies and Federations," (1925), 662–668. Also Edward N. Clopper, "Ten Years of Federation in Cincinnati," *Survey*, LIII (1925), 591–592; and Allen T. Burns, "Everyman's Chest," *Survey*, LIX (1927), 139–143.

40. This point is developed in connection with the present situation in *Voluntary Health and Welfare Agencies in the United States: An Exploratory Study by an Ad Hoc Citizens Committee* (New York, 1961), 30–32. The study director was Robert H. Hamlin of the Harvard School of Public Health.

41. Letter from Pierce Williams to Board of Directors, Association of Community Chests and Councils, April 30, 1928, UCFC, Archives, Washington, D. C., Folder.

42. Report of the Budget Committee of the Washington Community Chest, July 15, 1932. UCFC, Archives, Washington, D. C., Folders 1, 4, 5.

43. John A. Kingsbury, "Right Publicity and Public Health Work," National Conference of Charities and Correction, *Proceedings*, 1909, 337; Orlando F. Lewis, "Social Advertising," *National Conference of Charities and Correction, Proceedings*, 1910, 545; also, Karl de Schweinitz, "An Anatomy Most Melancholy," *Survey*, XXXV (1916), 509–510.

44. Elwood Street, "Where's the Money Coming From?" *Survey*, XXXIX (1917), 39.

45. Letter from Sherman Kingsley to Pierce Williams, July 7, 1928. UCFC, Archives, Cleveland, Ohio, Folder.

46. Norton, *Cooperative Movement in Social Work*, 279.

47. AAOC, *Financial Federations*, 63, 64.

48. *Ibid.*, 182, 183, 184, 185.

49. Clare M. Tousley, "Support and Interpretation of Professional Requirements in Social Work: Who are Our Interpreters" National Conference of Social Work, *Proceedings*, 1925, 669; Karl de Schweinitz, "A Federation Publicity Program," National Conference of Social Work, *Proceedings*, 1922, 406.

50. Dorothy E. Wysor, "How Can We Interpret Social Work to the Public?" *Family*, VII (1926), 248.

51. R. H. Wilder and K. L. Buell, *Publicity: A Manual for the Use of Business, Civic, or Social Service Organizations* (New York, 1923), 15, 16.

52. Elwood Street, "Current Methods of Social Service Publicity," National Conference of Social Work, *Proceedings*, 1919, 682; also, Tolman Lee, *Funds and Friends* (New York, 1925), 69; Elwood Street, *Sympathy and System in Giving* (Chicago, 1921), 112, 113.

53. William H. Allen, "The Importance of Publicity in Educational and Charitable Work," *North American Review*, CLXXXI (1905), 25. Also by Allen, "Enough Money to Uplift the World: The Results of Turning Benevolence in Scientific Channels," *World's Work*, XVIII (1909), 11,616–11,618.

54. William H. Allen, *Modern Philanthropy: A Study of Efficient Appealing and Giving* (New York, 1912), 3, vii, viii, 148, 170.

55. Street, *Sympathy and System in Giving*, 113. One sign of the times was the appearance of the social work publicity expert like Mary Swain Routzahn, who served with the National Committee on Publicity Methods in Social Work, and the Department of Ex-

hibits and Surveys of the Russell Sage Foundation. Her *Publicity for Social Work* (New York, 1928) (with Evart G. Routzahn) drew upon materials from community chests, national health agencies, and other welfare organizations to illustrate the defects and potentialities of social publicity.

56. Lilian Brandt, *How Much Shall I Give?* (New York, 1921), 113. For other expressions of interest in efficient giving see, Raymond Clapp, "Money Raising," *Better Times*, IV (April 1923), 28–29, 34; Mark M. Jones, *Responsible Giving* (pamphlet, 1927); Arthur W. Procter and Arthur A. Shuck, *The Financing of Social Work* (Chicago, 1926).

57. AAOC, *Financial Federations*, 63.

58. Community Chests and Councils, Inc., *Yesterday and Today with Community Chests: A Record of Their History and Growth* (New York, 1937), 16, 17.

59. Boston Chamber of Commerce, *Final Report of the Special Committee on Financing of Social Agencies* (Boston, 1925), 33, 34.

60. AACO, *Bulletin No. 72, June 15, 1924* (supplement), 2.

61. Harry P. Wareheim, "The Campaign," National Conference of Social Work, *Proceedings*, 1922, 410.

62. AACO, *Supplement to Bulletin No. 17* (n.d.), 7 ff. The following also illustrate chest techniques in reaching the salaried or wage-earning employee: J. L. Tuttle, "How Canton's Employes Take Part," *Survey*, LXII (1929), 616–617; Carter Taylor, "Harrisburg Breaks Loose," *Survey*, LXII (1929), 617; Thomas Devine, "Monthly Gifts and Fellowships," *Survey*, LXIII (1930), 481–482; S. Irving Rhys, "Suppose Nobody Cared," *New Republic*, XXXIV (1923), 317–318. Although New York City did not have a city-wide, nonsectarian federation, it possessed a number of specialized central fund-raising groups, such as the United Hospital Fund (successor to the Hospital Saturday and Sunday Association), the Federation for the Support of Jewish Philanthropic Societies, The Brooklyn Federation of Jewish Charities, the Catholic Charities of the Archdiocese of New York, and a unique "charity chest" organized by the fur industry. On the latter see, "Organized Generosity: The Fur Industry Measures the Results of Its First Effort at Unified Money Raising for Charity," *Better Times*, VI (Nov. 2, 1925), 8.

63. Aileen D. Ross, "Philanthropic Activity and the Business Career," *Social Forces*, XXXII (1954), 280. On the same theme by the same author see: "Organized Philanthropy in an Urban Community," *Canadian Journal of Economics and Political Science*, XVIII (1952), 474–486; and "The Social Control of Philanthropy," *American Journal of Sociology*, LVIII (1953), 451–460.

64. Pierce Williams and Frederick E. Croxton, *Corporation Con-*

tributions to Organized Community Welfare Services (New York: National Bureau of Economic Research, 1930), 50–56. Beginning in 1917, the Cambridge, Massachusetts, charities benefited from a "Manufacturers' Chest," which included thirty-four corporations in its general committee. The amount contributed rose from $8,855 in 1917 to $31,195 in 1928; *ibid.*, 216–217.

65. Wriston, *Report on War Chest Practice*, 47.

66. United War Work Campaign for $170,500,000, November 11–18, 1918, *Bulletin I: Organization in the City, Large or Small*, 8.

67. Williams and Croxton, *Corporation Contributions*, 11. Manufacturing accounted for 47.2 percent and trade concerns for 22.4 percent. Percentages for other categories went as follows: banks and trust companies, 10.7; insurance, 1.5; other financial corporations, 5.0; steam railroads, 0.3; water and other transportation, 1.4; public utilities other than transportation, 6.1; service corporations, 2.6; construction, 1.9; mining and quarrying, 1.0.

68. For later figures on corporation giving to chests consult F. Emerson Andrews, *Corporation Giving* (New York, 1952). By 1950, corporation gifts to chests aggregated about 40 percent of the total raised.

69. ACCC, *Bulletin No. 30, Jan. 8, 1927*, 1; Community Chests and Councils of America, Inc., Board of Directors, Minutes, I, 1918–28 (1927), 141; and "Big Business and Community Chests," 421. UCFC, Archives.

70. ACCC, *Bulletin No. 49, Nov. 15, 1929*.

71. Paul A. Schoellkopf, "The Corporation and Its Community," *Survey*, LX (1928), 540. Also, J. Herbert Case, *The Problems and the Opportunity of Community Chest Organizations in 1930* (pamphlet, 1930); A. V. Cannon, *The Relationship of Corporations to Community Welfare Services* (pamphlet, 1929).

72. Citizens Conference on Community Welfare, Washington, D.C., February 20 and 21, 1928, *Report of Group Conference No. 3: Relationship of Local and National Business Corporations to Community Welfare*, 11. UCFC, Archives, Confs. Washington, 1928 Folder.

73. Letter from Donaldson Brown to Allen Burns, July 29, 1936, with attached typed statement, "Corporation Community Chest Contributions," 4, 3. UCFC, Archives, *Corporation Giving*, Standards Folder.

74. R. J. Prendergast, "Raising the Big Wind," *American Mercury*, XIII (1928), 464.

75. John Price Jones Corporation, Unitarian Campaign, Inc. (1920–21), 13. JPJC Papers.

76. Memorandum from R. F. Duncan to J. P. Jones, Nov. 20, 1925. Box BX-4, JPJC Papers.

77. "The Plan—Its Purpose and Achievement in the Work of the John Price Jones Corporation," Dec. 20, 1929 (typed statement), 1, 8. Box BX-3, JPJC Papers.

78. John Price Jones, *Fundamental Factors in Fund-Raising* (pamphlet, 1930), 27. Box BX-2, JPJC Papers.

79. JPJC, United Hospital Fund (1920), 11, JPJC Papers. Also Tamblyn and Brown, *Raising Money: A New Business to Meet a New Need* (New York, 1925), 12, 13.

80. Harold J. Seymour, "Social Aspects of our Work," Semi-Annual Conference of the Staff on Clients' Problems and Standard Practices, June 4 and 5, 1928, 9, JPJC Papers (mimeographed).

81. Chester E. Tucker, "The Volunteer Worker," Annual Staff Conference on Clients' Problems and Standard Practices, June 17 and 18, 1929, 30, JPJC Papers. The indispensability of the larger giver in the professional fund-raising campaign is analyzed in John Price Jones, *The Technique to Win in Fund Raising* (New York, 1934).

82. Wareheim, "The Campaign," 415.

83. *Voluntary Health and Welfare Agencies in the United States*, 32.

Index

Abbott, Edith: social work education, criticism of, 148-149; mentioned, 86, 144
Abbott, Grace, 86
Addams, Jane, 10, 158
Akron, Ohio, 211
Albany, New York, 190
Albany Hospital, 61
Allen, William H., 206
Almy, Frederic, 41
American Association for Community Organization, 209, 213. See also Association of Community Chests and Councils, Inc.
American Association for Labor Legislation, 147
American Association for Organizing Charity, 183, 188, 204, 208. See also American Association for Organizing Family Social Work
American Association for Organizing Family Social Work, 134, 162, 182. See also American Association for Organizing Charity
American Association for the Study of the Feeble-minded, 68
American Association of Hospital Social Workers: organized, 125; activities of, 125–127; and Section on Psychiatric Social Work, 127; mentioned, 108
American Association of Psychiatric Social Workers, 127
American Association of Social Workers: organized, 131; membership requirements of, 135–136; mentioned, 127, 128, 133, 151
American Association of Visiting Teachers, 127

American Hospital Association, 31
American Journal of Insanity, 87
American Library Association, 191
American Mercury, 215
American Psychopathological Association, 88
American Unitarian Association, 216
Andrews, John B., 147
Angell, James R., 65
Associated Charities of Boston. See Boston Associated Charities
Association of Community Chests and Councils, Inc., 213, 214. See also American Association for Community Organization
Association of Junior Leagues of America, 166
Association of Massachusetts State Hospital Workers, 127
Association of Professional Schools of Social Work: accreditation requirements, 151–152. See also Association of Training Schools for Professional Social Work
Association of Training Schools for Professional Social Work, 150. See also Association of Professional Schools of Social Work

Bailly, Sylvain, 4
Baker, Harvey H., 66, 90
Baltimore, Maryland, 5, 46, 58, 61, 141, 163, 186, 198, 203
Baltimore Charity Organization Society: and medical social work, 25; mentioned, 45, 138
Bedford Hills, New York, 64
Beers, Clifford W.: mental breakdown, 72-73; and origins of Na-

tional Committee for Mental Hygiene, 73–74
Bellevue Hospital, 61
Biggs, Dr. Hermann M., 29
Birmingham, Alabama, 96, 186
Blackwell, Elizabeth, 24
Bleuler, Eugen, 87
Bookman, C. M., 184, 194, 218
Boston, Massachusetts: volunteers in, 50; Chamber of Commerce, 208; mentioned, 2, 5, 22, 66, 88, 90, 91, 125, 141, 178, 185, 196, 209
Boston Associated Charities: and immigrant, 17; training program of, 138–139; and volunteer, 160; mentioned, 8, 11, 13, 15, 20, 23, 30, 49, 141, 163, 188
Boston Association for Relief and Control of Tuberculosis, 29
Boston Children's Aid Society: casework standards of, 43–45; and feeble-minded, 71; mentioned, 26, 28, 90, 141
Boston Dispensary, 90
Boston Family Welfare Society, 163. *See also* Boston Associated Charities
Boston Home and School Association, 36
Boston Psychopathic Hospital, 62, 63, 79
Boston School for Social Workers: medical social work training, 34; field work training, 146; mentioned, 141, 144. *See also* Brackett, Jeffrey R.
Boston State Hospital, 61, 63
Bowditch, Dr. Vincent Y., 29
Brackett, Jeffrey R., 141, 146. *See also* Boston School for Social Workers
Breckinridge, Sophonisba, 141, 144
Brill, Dr. A. A.: and Freudian therapy, 86–88
Bronner, Dr. Augusta, 45, 90, 91. *See also* Healy, Dr. William; Juvenile Psychopathic Institute
Brooklyn, New York, 2
Bruno, Frank J., 128, 172
Bryn Mawr, Pennsylvania, 63

Buffalo, New York, 2, 5, 180
Buffalo Charity Organization Society, 2, 19, 41
Bureau of Children's Guidance, 92, 98, 99, 100, 153, 155. *See also* Commonwealth Fund
Bureau of Municipal Research (New York), 206
Bureaucracy: efficiency goal of, 159–160; Max Weber, defined by, 161–162; and social agency directors, 162–166; and financial federation, 172–173
Burleigh, Edith N., 62, 90
Burns, Allen T., 64, 184, 214
Burrage, Katherine, 63

Cabot, Frederick, 90
Cabot, Dr. Richard C.: and medical social work, origins of, 26, 28, 29–30; and expert in democracy, 35; and feeble-minded, 70; mentioned, 24, 25, 27, 34, 45, 56, 60, 62. *See also* Cannon, Ida M.; Massachusetts General Hospital; Medical social work
Campbell, Dr. C. Macfie, 56
Canada, 86
Cannon, Antoinette, 63
Cannon, Ida M.: and medical social work, challenge to, 30–31; medical social work, role of, 32–33; and casework relationship, 35; and volunteer, 51; mentioned, 34, 83, 109, 129. *See also* Cabot, Dr. Richard C.; Massachusetts General Hospital; Medical social work
Case, J. Herbert, 214
Casework: and professional relationship, 77–78; diagnostic, 114–115; functional, 114–116. *See also* Differential casework
Central Islip (Long Island) State Hospital, 63, 87
Chalmers, Thomas, 2, 3, 4
Chamber of Commerce: endorsement by, 180–181
Changing Psychology in Social Case Work, A, 113

Index

Chapin, F. Stuart, 147
Chapin, Dr. Henry Dwight, 24
Charcot, Jean Martin, 87
Charities and the Commons, Field Department, 46
Charities endorsement, 180–181
Charity organization: objectives of, 1–2, 158; origins of, 2–4; and relief policy, 7–10; and investigation, 10; and social reform, 11–12; and friendly visiting, 12–17; and neighborhood focus, 14–15, 81–82; and immigrant, 17; and status of volunteer, 18–20, 49–52; and public assistance, 52; training program of, 138-139; criticism of, 159; board of directors of, 162-163, mentioned, 171, 219. *See also* Friendly visitor
Charity Organization Institute, 46
Chicago, Illinois, 58, 61, 64, 76, 79, 90, 91, 141, 180
Chicago Bureau of Charities, 187
Chicago Commons, 140
Chicago Juvenile Court, 45, 64
Chicago Polyclinic, 64
Chicago Relief and Aid Society, 187
Chicago School of Civics and Philanthropy, 140, 142, 143
Chicago United Charities, 110
Chicago World's Fair, 139
Child guidance: and social work, 89, 95–96, 116–117; Commonwealth Fund clinics, 93–100; role of social worker in, 96–100. *See also* Commonwealth Fund
Children's Court (New York City), 75
Cincinnati: Social Unit experiment in, 175–178; mentioned, 2, 66, 76, 185, 186, 194, 199, 203
Cincinnati Anti-Tuberculosis League, 198
Cincinnati Associated Charities, 110
Cincinnati Community Chest and Council of Social Agencies, 200
Clapp, Raymond, 184
Clark University, 87, 88
Cleveland, Ohio, 76, 94, 96, 203
Cleveland Associated Charities:

Mental Hygiene Committee established, 94; mentioned, 95, 109, 199
Cleveland Chamber of Commerce: Committee on Benevolent Associations, 180, 186; mentioned, 181
Cleveland Federation for Charity and Philanthropy: objectives of, 187–188; mentioned, 186, 198
Cleveland Welfare Federation, 200
Cleveland Welfare Fund, 200
College Settlement (New York City), 36
Columbia University, 145
Committee on Professional Organization, 129
Commonwealth Fund: and visiting teaching, 37, 100–104; Program for the Prevention of Delinquency, origins of, 91–92; and social work, 92, 93; and child guidance, 93–100; mentioned, 90. *See also* Bureau of Children's Guidance
Community organization: and Social Unit plan, 175–178; and World War I, 178; and financial federation, 180; and charities endorsement, 180-181; and Council of Social Agencies, 181–182. *See also* Financial federation; Follett, Mary P.; Lindeman, Eduard C.
Compass, The, 129
Conference on Demobilization, 129, 130
Congress on Hygiene and Demography, 75
Connecticut Society for Mental Hygiene, 73
Cook County, Illinois, 66
Cornell Clinic of Psychopathology, 64
Council of Social Agencies, 181–182
Curtis, Frances G., 141

Dallas, Texas, 94, 186
Daniel, Dr. Annie S., 24
Danvers (Massachusetts) State Hospital, 63
Davis, Katherine Bement, 64

283

Index

Davison, Henry P., 191
Dawes, Anna L., 139
Day, Jane, 36
Dayton, Ohio, 186
Denison, Edward, 4
Denison House, 63
Denver, Colorado, 53, 54, 185, 211
De Schweinitz, Karl, 128
Detroit, Michigan, 76, 190
Devine, Edward T.: on relief policy, 42; on volunteer, 50; and feeble-minded, 71; mentioned, 29, 123, 132, 144, 159, 184
De Vries, Hugo, 69
Diagnostic casework. *See* Casework, diagnostic
Differential casework: and relief policy, 42; and vagrant, 42; and desertion, 43; and child welfare, 43–45; mentioned, 41. *See also* Casework; Richmond, Mary E.
Dugdale, Richard L., 7
Dummer, Ethel S., 65, 66

Education for Social Work, 148
Einstein, Hannah, 53
Elberfeld, Germany, 3, 4
Elmira, New York, 186
Emerson, Dr. Charles P., 17, 25
Epstein, Abraham: social work, criticized by, 85; mentioned, 104
Erie, Pennsylvania, 186, 187
Eugenics, 68–71. *See also* Feeble-minded
Extramural psychiatry, 60, 61, 62

Family social work: and functional specialization, consequences of, 40, 41
Fargo, North Dakota, 37
Feeble-minded: and social work, 67, 71, 72; and criminality, 68–71. *See also* Goddard, Dr. Henry H.
Financial federation: and democracy, 173, 180; and community organization, 180, 197–199; and bureaucracy, 182; and businessman, 183, 189, 211–212; opposition to, 183–184; significance of, 184, 188–189;

and volunteer, 185, 217–218; joint appeal by, 185; whirlwind campaign, 185; early examples of, 186; criticism of, 188, 196; and World War I, 189–192; and national agencies, relation to, 192–194; principles of, 194–196; budget committee, role of, 199–202; publicity work of, 202–206; and giving habits, 206–211; campaign organization of, 210–211; corporation contributions to, 212–213; and corporation, relation to, 213–214; mentioned, 172. *See also* Community organization; Fund-raising
Fitz, Margaret, 90
Flexner, Abraham: on social work as profession, 106; mentioned, 107
Follett, Mary P.: community organization, theory of, 178–179; mentioned, 173. *See also* Community organization
Fosdick, Harry E., 191
Foster care, 43, 44
Freud, Dr. Sigmund: therapy of, in U.S., 86–88; and social work, 88–89; mentioned, 55, 59, 98, 99, 113, 114
Friendly visitor, 1, 3, 4, 12–17, 23, 84. *See also* Volunteer
Friends' Quarterly Meeting (Philadelphia), 37
Functional casework. *See* Casework, functional
Functional specialization, 22, 40, 41, 48, 83, 97, 119
Fund-raising: professional organization for, 215–218. *See also* Financial federation; John Price Jones Corporation

Galton, Sir Francis, 69
General Motors Corporation, 214
Glasgow, Scotland, 2, 5
Glenn, John M.: and administration, centralization of, 6–7; mentioned 5, 145
Glenwood (Illinois) Manual Training School, 101

Index

Glueck, Dr. Bernard, 75, 91, 98, 100
Goddard, Dr. Henry H.: and mental testing, 68; *Kallikak Family*, author of, 69–70; mentioned, 65, 71. *See also* Feeble-minded
Goldmark, Josephine, 86
Goldmark, Pauline, 86
Grand Rapids, Michigan, 185, 186, 211
Greenwich House, 36
Greenwich Village, 86
Grohmann, Dr. J. C. A., 63
Gurteen, S. Humphreys, 2, 5, 8

Hagerty, James E., 148
Halbert, L. A., 53
Hall, G. Stanley, 87
Hall, Dr. Herbert J., 63
Hammond, William A., 57
Hanchette, Helen, 94
Harriman, Mrs. E. H., 206
Harrisburg, Pennsylvania, 211
Hart, Joseph K., 173
Hartford, Connecticut: psychological clinic in, 36
Hartley, Robert M., 3
Hartley House, 36
Harvard University, 64, 90, 141
Healy, Dr. William: and Juvenile Psychopathic Institute, origins of, 64–65; theories of delinquency, tested by, 65, 66; influence on social work, 66; and mental testing, 67, 68; and Judge Baker Foundation, 89–91; mentioned, 56, 74, 77, 83, 91, 103, 113. *See also* Judge Baker Foundation; Juvenile Psychopathic Institute
Henderson, Charles R.: and volunteer, 49
Henry Phipps Clinic, 61, 62
Hewitt, Abram S., 6
Higgins, Alice Louise. *See* Lothrop, Alice Louise Higgins
Hill, Octavia, 4
Hoch, Dr. August, 56, 64, 113
Hodder, Jessie, 90
Hoffman, Charles W., 66
Honesty, 66

Hospice de Bicêtre, 87
Hospital Saturday and Sunday Association, 185
Houston, Texas, 96, 186
Howe, Samuel G., 67
Hugo, Victor, 73
Hull House, 10, 64, 140
Hunter, Robert, 10
Huntington, James O. S., 10

Indiana, 70
Indianapolis, Indiana, 5, 96
Individual Delinquent, The, 66, 77
Institute for Child Guidance, 99
Institute of Social Science, 140
Intercollegiate Bureau of Occupations, 130, 132. *See also* National Social Workers' Exchange
Itard, Jean, 67

James, William, 65, 73
Jarrett, Mary, 63, 78, 79, 84, 125
Jelliffe, Dr. Smith Ely, 86, 88
Jewish Welfare Board, 191
John Price Jones Corporation: campaign techniques of, 216–217; mentioned, 215. *See also* Fund-raising
Johns Hopkins University: and medical social work, 25; mentioned, 61, 73, 198
Joint Committee on Methods of Preventing Deliquency, 92
Jones, Dr. Ernest, 86
Journal of Abnormal Psychology, 88
Judge Baker Foundation: established, 89–91; mentioned, 45, 62. *See also* Healey, Dr. William; Juvenile Psychopathic Institute
Jung, Dr. Carl G., 87
Juvenile Aid Society (Philadelphia), 37
Juvenile Protective Association (Philadelphia), 37
Juvenile Protective Association (Chicago), 64
Juvenile Psychopathic Institute (Chicago), 45, 61, 64, 66, 67, 89,

285

90, 103. *See also* Healy, Dr. William; Judge Baker Foundation

Kallikak, Martin, 70
Kallikak Family, The, 69-70
Kankakee, Illinois, 58
Kansas City, Missouri, 53
Karpf, Maurice J.: social work, criticized by, 105
Kelley, Florence, 86, 158
Kempton, Helen P., 162
Kenworthy, Marion E., 98, 155
Kingsley, Sherman, 184, 187
Kraepelin, Emil, 56, 57

Laboratory of Social Hygiene, 64
Lady almoner, 25
Lakewood, New Jersey, 91, 92. *See also* Commonwealth Fund
La Salle (Illinois) High School, 102
Lathrop, Julia C., 64, 65, 140, 141, 158
Laura Spelman Rockefeller Memorial Fund, 93
Lee, Joseph, 196
Lee, Porter R.: and social work education, theory of, 154-155; theory of cause and function, 157; mentioned, 98, 193
Leonard, Dr. Christine, 93
Les Misérables, 73
Levey, Beatrice Z., 110
Lincoln, Nebraska, 180
Lincoln School, 101
Lindeman, Eduard C.: social work, criticism of, 85; and mental hygiene, 109; community organization, theory of, 179; mentioned, 104, 173. *See also* Community organization
Lindsay, Samuel McCune: and social work education, 144-145
Liverpool, England, 185
Loch, Charles, 25
Loeb, Sophie Irene, 53
Lombroso, Cesare, 65
London, England, 5
London Society for Organizing Charitable Relief and Repressing Mendicancy, 2, 4, 25
London Society for the Relief of Distress, 4
Los Angeles, California, 94
Lothrop, Alice Louise Higgins, 29, 141
Louisville, Kentucky, 76
Louisville Associated Charities, 110
Louisville Welfare League, 200
Lowell, Josephine Shaw: relief policy, 7; mentioned 5, 14
Lowrey, Dr. Lawson, 95, 116
Lundy, George, 215
Lynde, Edward D.: on child guidance and social work, 95-96; mentioned, 109

McCulloch, Oscar, 5, 7
McLean, Francis H., 163, 182
Macon, Georgia, 96
Malthus, Thomas, 7
Manchesterian economics, 7
Manhattan State Hospital, 62, 63
Marblehead, Massachusetts, 63
Marcus, Grace: casework and relief, 110-112; mentioned, 116
Marie, Pierre, 87
Marks, Martin A., 186
Marot, Mary, 36
Marts, Arnaud C., 215
Marts and Lundy, 215
Mason City, Iowa, 37
Massachusetts, 63, 64
Massachusetts Conference of Charities and Correction, 141
Massachusetts General Hospital: social service referrals, 28; Social Service Supervisory Committee, 30; psychiatric social work at, 62, 63; and Freud, 88; mentioned, 24, 25, 26, 29, 30, 34, 80, 82, 125. *See also* Cabot, Dr. Richard C.; Cannon, Ida M.; Medical social work
Maxwell, William H., 36
Medical Inquiries, 57
Medical social work: origins of, 23-28; and nursing, 31-32; and professional education, 32-35; and vol-

unteer, 35; and neighborhood, 82; professional function of, 108–109; professional association in, 125–126; mentioned, 76. *See also* Cabot, Dr. Richard C.; Cannon, Ida M.; Massachusetts General Hospital

Memphis, Tennessee, 96

Mendel, Gregor, 67, 69

Mental hygiene: and social work, 109–110; mentioned, 56, 61, 92, 94, 97, 100, 101, 113, 153. *See also* Beers, Clifford W.; National Committee for Mental Hygiene

Mental Hygiene and Social Work, 155

Mesmer, F. A., 87

Meyer, Dr. Adolf: early career, 58; psychiatric theory of, 58–61; mentioned, 56, 57, 61, 62, 65, 73, 77, 83, 86, 113

Milford Conference, 120–121, 149

Milieu therapy, 56

Millet, Dr. Charles, 29

Milwaukee, Wisconsin, 96, 125, 176, 186

Milwaukee Child Welfare Commission, 175

Milwaukee Family Welfare Association, 109

Mind That Found Itself, A, 73

Minneapolis–St. Paul, Minnesota, 66, 94, 180

Missouri School of Social Economy, 142

Monmouth County, New Jersey, 93

Mott, John R., 192

Mount Vernon, New York, 37

Murphy, J. Prentice, 90, 91, 141

Myerson, Dr. Abraham, 72

Nassau County, Long Island, 75

National Association for the Study and Prevention of Tuberculosis, 29

National Catholic War Council, 191

National Committee for Mental Hygiene: Division on Mental Deficiency, 72; investigations by, 74–75; and World War I, 75–76; Division on the Prevention of Delinquency, 91, 92, 93; Division on Community Clinics, 96; mentioned, 79. *See also* Beers, Clifford W.

National Committee on Visiting Teachers, 37, 92, 100. *See also* Commonwealth Fund

National Committee on Volunteers in Social Work, 166

National Community Center Association, 174

National Conference of Charities and Correction, 9, 46, 106, 125

National Conference of Social Work, 95, 157

National Conference on Civic and Neighborhood Center Development, 174

National Information Bureau, 193

National Investigation Bureau. *See* National Information Bureau

National Social Unit Organization, 175. *See also* Social Unit

National Social Workers' Exchange, 129, 130, 131. *See also* American Association of Social Workers; Intercollegiate Bureau of Occupations

Newark (New Jersey) Board of Education, 101

New Bedford (Massachusetts) Welfare Society, 109

New Haven, Connecticut, 2

New Orleans, Louisiana, 96, 186

New State, The, 178

Newton, Massachusetts, 37

New York Association for Improving the Condition of the Poor: efficient administration of, 161; mentioned, 3, 4, 206

New York Charity Organization Society: on work as relief, 8; and friendly visiting, 16–17; establishes Summer School of Philanthropy, 19, 140; Committee on the Prevention of Tuberculosis, 29; and volunteer, 51, 52; Committee on Philanthropic Education, 141, 145; field work in, 145–146; criticized,

159; mentioned, 5, 50, 71, 110, 138, 145, 146, 171, 172

New York City, 2, 3, 5, 22, 29, 36, 61, 64, 79, 99, 101, 125, 129, 133, 175, 185

New York City Board of Education, 75

New York Infirmary for Women and Children, 24

New York Lying-In Hospital, 25

New York Post-Graduate Hospital, 24

New York Psychoanalytic Society, 88

New York School of Philanthropy: medical social work course, 34; conflict over educational goals, 144–145; mentioned, 132. *See also* New York School of Social Work

New York School of Social Work, 85, 92, 98, 99, 153, 154. *See also* New York School of Philanthropy

New York State, 63, 64, 125

New York State Charities Aid Association; psychiatric after-care, 25, 62, 63

New York State Hospitals: Pathological Institute, 58, 61, 86

Norfolk, Virginia, 94

Northampton State Hospital, 79

Norton, William J., 184, 199, 218

Nudd, Howard W., 100

Ohio, 134

Omaha, Nebraska, 185

Oshkosh, Wisconsin, 186

Otis, Dr. Edward O., 29

Ozanam, Frederick, 4

Paine, Robert Treat, 5

Paine, Robert Treat, Jr., 12

Paris, 4, 87

Parsons, Herbert, 90

Parsons, Talcott, 121

Pathological Lying, 66

Paton, Dr. Stewart, 73

Patten, Simon, 50, 84

Pennsylvania, 125

Pennsylvania Railroad, 6

Pennsylvania School for Social Service, 141

Pennsylvania School of Social Work, 34, 115, 154

Pennsylvania Training School for Social Workers. *See* Pennsylvania School of Social Work; Pennsylvania School for Social Service

Peterson, Dr. Frederick, 86, 87

Pettit, Walter, 193

Philadelphia, Pennsylvania, 2, 46, 79, 94, 115, 125, 134, 141, 200

Philadelphia Children's Bureau, 91

Philadelphia General Hospital, 61

Philadelphia Society for Organizing Charity, 46, 154

Phillips, Wilbur, 175

Phipps, Henry, 73

Phipps Psychiatric Clinic, 58, 64

Pierce, Lyman L., 185, 191

Pinchot, Gifford, 175

Pinel, Philippe, 57

Positions in Social Work, 132

Pratt, Anna Beach: and White-Williams Foundation, visiting teaching of, 102

Prince, Dr. Morton, 86, 88

Proctor, William C., 194

Professional association. *See* American Association of Hospital Social Workers; American Association of Psychiatric Social Workers; American Association of Social Workers; American Association of Visiting Teachers

Professional education: function of, 137. *See also* Abbott, Edith; Association of Professional Schools of Social Work; Association of Training Schools for Professional Social Work; Boston School for Social Workers; Brackett, Jeffrey R.; Breckinridge, Sophonisba; Chicago School of Civics and Philanthropy; New York School of Philanthropy; New York School of Social Work; Pennsylvania School of Social Work;

Smith, Zilpha D.; Social work education; Supervision
Professional subculture, 118-119, 121-123
Professionalization: and public welfare, 53-54
Progressive education: and visiting teaching, 38
Psychiatric social work: origins of, 62-64; function of, 78, training for, 78-79, 98, 99; and social work practice, changes in, 79, 80; and social environment, 82-83; professional organization, 127
Psychiatric Social Workers Club, 127
Psychiatry: and social work, 55-56; in nineteenth century, 56-57. *See also* Beers, Clifford W.; Child guidance; Commonwealth Fund; Freud, Dr. Sigmund; Healy, Dr. William; Judge Baker Foundation; Juvenile Psychopathic Institute; Mental hygiene; Meyer, Dr. Adolf; National Committee for Mental Hygiene; Psychiatric social work; Putnam, Dr. James J.; Rank, Dr. Otto; Robinson, Virginia; Smith College; Social psychiatry; Taft, Jessie
Psychoanalytic Review, 88
Psychobiology, 59
Public assistance, 52, 53
Public Education Association (New York), 36, 37, 92, 100
Putnam, Dr. James J.: and psychiatric social work, 62, 63; and feeble-minded, 71; and Freud, 88; mentioned, 56, 86

Rank, Dr. Otto, 113, 114, 115
Raymond, Stockton, 196
Red Cross: Home Service, 44, 151; psychiatric service, 76; mentioned, 191, 192, 193, 212, 215
Rice Institute, 142
Richman, Julia, 36
Richmond, Indiana, 186
Richmond, Mary E.: and social reform, 11, 81; early career, 45-46; casework theory of, 47-49; and volunteer, 49, 50; William Healy, influence of, 66; on feeble-minded, 71; and generic skill, 120; and social work training, 140; mentioned, 5, 41, 79, 82, 83, 88, 105, 107, 113, 117, 119, 120, 129, 138, 141, 154. *See also* Differential casework; *Social Diagnosis*
Richmond, Virginia, 96
Richmond Hill House, 36
Richmond School of Social Economy, 142
Richmond School of Social Work and Public Health, 142
Robinson, Virginia: casework theory of, 113-114; mentioned, 112
Rochester, New York, 39, 174, 200, 211
Rockefeller Foundation, 75
Romanticism, 7
Rosenau, Nathaniel S., 19
Royal Free Hospital, 25
Rubinow, Isaac M., 53
Rush, Dr. Benjamin, 57
Rush Medical College, 64
Russell Sage Foundation: Charity Organization Department, 46, 182; mentioned, 133, 140, 141, 146

St. Joseph, Missouri, 186
St. Louis, Missouri, 93, 125, 180, 194
St. Louis Provident Association, 142
St. Louis School of Philanthropy, 142
St. Vincent de Paul Society, 4
Salmon, Dr. Thomas W., 56, 74, 75, 76, 91, 92
Salt Lake City, Utah, 186
Salvation Army, 191
San Antonio, Texas, 186
San Francisco, California, 180
School of Handcraft, 63
Scranton, Pennsylvania, 211
Seattle, Washington, 180
Seguin, Edouard, 67
Seybert Foundation, 115
Simmons College, 141

Index

Simmons College School of Social Work, 91. *See also* Boston School for Social Workers

Simon-Binet test, 68

Sing Sing Prison, 75

Smith, Zilpha D.: and social work training, 138–139; mentioned, 5, 49, 141, 160, 163

Smith College: and psychiatric social work, training for, 78, 79; mentioned, 94

Smith College School of Social Work, 91, 99, 147

Social Darwinism, 7

Social Diagnosis, 20, 47, 48, 79, 83, 88, 113, 119, 120. *See also* Richmond, Mary E.

Social evidence, 47, 49, 83, 120

Social insurance, 53, 85

Social psychiatry: emergence of, 55–61; and psychiatric social work, 62–64; and social reform, 72; and social work, 76–78; mentioned, 71, 97. *See also* Healy, Dr. William; Meyer, Dr. Adolf; National Committee for Mental Hygiene

Social settlement: criticism of charity organization, 10; and neighborhood ethic, 15; and visiting teaching, 36; and professional education, 146, 147; and public school, 174

Social Unit, 175–178. *See also* Community organization

Social work education: apprenticeship training, 139; limited contribution of, 143, 147–149; challenges to, 149–150; as growth process, 152–156; supervisor, role of, 153. *See also* Professional education

Society for After Care of Poor Persons Discharged Recovered from Insane Asylums, 24

Solomon, Maida H., 78

Southard, Dr. Elmer E., 56, 79

South Bend, Indiana, 186, 211

Spitzka, E. L., 57

Springfield, Massachusetts, 186

Springfield (Illinois) Family Welfare Society, 109

State Industrial School for Girls (Massachusetts), 26

Steiner, Jesse F., 148

Stepney (London), 4

Sterilization, 70

Stern, Frances, 90

Stevenson, Dr. George S., 116

Stone, Galen, 90

Street, Elwood, 184, 218

Strong, Howard, 180

Supervision: in social work education, 155–156; in social agency, 167–170

Supervisors' Conference, 46

Switzerland, 58

Taft, Jessie, 79, 89, 92, 100, 104, 115. *See also* Casework, functional

Tamblyn, George O., 215

Tamblyn and Brown, 215

Taylor, Graham, 140

Texas School of Civics and Philanthropy, 142

Thayer, Mrs. Nathaniel, 30

Thom, Dr. Douglas, 76

Thurston, Henry W., 128

Towle, Charlotte, 99, 112

Training School for Jewish Social Work, 105

Training School for the Feebleminded (Vineland, New Jersey), 65, 68

Tuberculosis: preventive campaign against, 29

Tufts, James H., 148

United States Bureau of War Risk Insurance, 76

United States Children's Bureau, 198

United States Commission on Training Camp Activities, 191

United States Public Health Service, 74, 76

United Unitarian Fund Committee, 216

United War Work Campaign, 191–192, 212

Index

University of Chicago, 49, 140, 144
University of Michigan: psychopathic hospital, 61, 64
University of Missouri, 142
University of Pennsylvania, 65
University of Zurich, 58
Utica, New York, 37

Vaile, Gertrude: and public relief, 54; mentioned, 53, 129, 158
Van Kleeck, Mary, 132
Van Waters, Miriam, 94
Veiller, Lawrence, 86
Visiting teaching: origins of, 36–37; function of, 37–39; skills needed for, 39–40; and neighborhood, 82; and Commonwealth Fund, 100–104
Volunteer: status of, 49–52, 83, 218, 219, 220; and bureaucracy, consequences of, 160, 161, 166, 167, 170; selection of, 162, 167; and social agency, administration of, 162–166; and financial federation, 184; and professional fund-raising, 217–218; mentioned, 44. See also Friendly visitor

Waite, Edward F., 66
Walker, Sydnor, 135
War Camp Community Service, 191
Ward, Charles S., 185, 191, 215
Ward, Edward J., 174
Ward's Island, 58, 87
Washington, D.C.: financial federation in, 201–202; mentioned, 75, 185
Washington, D.C., Associated Charities, 124

Washington University: School of Social Economy, 142
Weber, Max: and bureaucracy, definition of, 161–162, 169–170
Weismann, August, 67
Westchester County, New York, 62
West End Neighborhood Association (Boston), 36
Western Reserve University: School of Applied Social Sciences, 95, 142
What is Social Case Work? 47, 48, 88. See also Richmond, Mary E.
White, Dr. William A., 56, 59, 60, 77, 86, 88
White-Williams Foundation: and visiting teaching, 102
Wilbur, Hervey B., 67
Williams, Charles W., 203
Williams, Morney, 159
Wilson, Woodrow, 191
Wisconsin State Hospital, 64
Witmer, Lightmer, 65
Woman's Education Association (Boston), 36
Woods, Robert A., 146, 158
Worcester, Massachusetts, 180
Worcester State Hospital, 58
World War I: and community organization, 178; and financial federation, 189–192; and professional fund-raising, 215

Yale University, 72, 102
Young Men's Christian Association: corporation contributions to, 212; mentioned, 185, 191, 193, 215
Young Women's Christian Association, 191
Youngstown, Ohio, 190

Zurich, Switzerland, 63, 87

291